AF601305

BREAKING INTO SONG

BREAKING INTO SONG

Television Musicals from Glee *to* Crazy Ex-Girlfriend

ERIN GIANNINI

BLOOMSBURY ACADEMIC
NEW YORK • LONDON • OXFORD • NEW DELHI • SYDNEY

BLOOMSBURY ACADEMIC
Bloomsbury Publishing Inc, 1359 Broadway, New York, NY 10018, USA
Bloomsbury Publishing Plc, 50 Bedford Square, London, WC1B 3DP, UK
Bloomsbury Publishing Ireland, 29 Earlsfort Terrace, Dublin 2, D02 AY28, Ireland

BLOOMSBURY, BLOOMSBURY ACADEMIC and the Diana logo are
trademarks of Bloomsbury Publishing Plc

First published in the United States of America 2026

Cover design by Diana Nuhn

Library of Congress Cataloging-in-Publication Data

Names: Giannini, Erin, 1974– author
Title: Breaking into song : television musicals from Glee to Crazy
Ex-Girlfriend / by Erin Giannini.
Identifiers: LCCN 2025051617 (print) | LCCN 2025051618 (ebook) | ISBN 9781538191910
hardback | ISBN 9781538191927 epub | ISBN 9798216444176 pdf
Subjects: LCSH: Television musicals | Television and music | Television programs–United
States–History | LCGFT: Television criticism and reviews
Classification: LCC ML2080 .G53 2026 (print) | LCC ML2080 (ebook)
LC record available at https://lccn.loc.gov/2025051617
LC ebook record available at https://lccn.loc.gov/2025051618

ISBN: HB: 978-1-538-19191-0
ePDF: 979-8-216-44417-6
eBook: 979-1-538-19192-7

Typeset by Integra Software Services Pvt. Ltd.
Printed and bound in the United States of America

For product safety related questions contact productsafety@bloomsbury.com.

To find out more about our authors and books visit www.bloomsbury.com
and sign up for our newsletters.

For Carol Giannini (Mom) and Pat Stephens (aunt), who loved watching musicals together.

CONTENTS

Introduction

All the World's a Stage . . . on TV

What is a musical? As commonly understood, a theatrical production in which music and dancing play an integral role. Yet, even broken down to its most basic components, "dancing, singing, acting, orchestration, design, production," it is nonetheless a complex form that can be interpreted in multiple ways; even just a focus on the performance elements could be an education in itself.[1] It is, in its original form, however, a communal experience, to be enjoyed in a theater surrounded by an audience. What happens when this communal art form transitions to that most domestic of mediums, the television? Considering that television itself was born out of both theater and radio, incorporating the musical genre into television should have worked. Like radio, television provides the sound, and as with theater, also provides the visuals, with the benefit of convenience (no long lines or crowded theaters). Yet the musical genre has a fraught history on US television, remembered too frequently for spectacular failures than stellar performances. As US television moved from the single-sponsor, anthology dramas of the 1950s into what was known as "magazine-style advertising"[2] (multiple ads throughout a program)—giving the power to the networks rather than the sponsors—it shifted focus to getting the widest possible audience for each program. This was known as least objectionable—or offensive—programming (LOP),[3] in that it would appeal to the greatest number of viewers without alienating them or making people not want to buy the advertised products. At the same time, the structure of US commercial television was such that executives and advertisers also wanted to draw viewers in with shows, or even episodes, that were "special"; this was clearest during what became known as the "sweeps" periods (November, February, and May), when the ratings for particular shows set the advertising prices. Consequently, the most dramatic, hilarious, or otherwise special episodes would air during these months, offering a window to take chances or switch things up. Or simply add a famous guest star, as when Brad Pitt appeared on *Friends* during the November sweeps.[4]

Musical programming, however, whether it's a variety show, a single episode of a series, or an airing of a Broadway show, already sets itself apart from the usual dramas, sitcoms, and news shows that comprised television for most of its history, regardless of whether it aired during sweeps, and yet it has been part of US TV from the beginning. The first written-for-TV musical aired on the DuMont Network in 1944 (*The Boys from Boise*), although this was a bit of a rarity at the time. Prime-time musical performance on US television were often airings of Broadway shows as part of broadcast "spectaculars" (later relegated to PBS series such as *Great Performances*), made-for-TV adaptations of musicals such as Rodgers and Hammerstein's *Cinderella*, and occasionally original pieces such as *Polly* (1989), a co-production between NBC and Disney based on the novel—and later film adaptation—of *Pollyanna* (1913). Shows in which musical numbers played an integral part tended to be limited to the variety shows of the 1950s (*The Ed Sullivan Show* [1948–1971], *Your Show of Shows* [1950–1954]) to the 1970s (*The Sonny and Cher Comedy Hour* [1971–1974], *Donny & Marie* [1976–1979]). Some non-variety series, such as *The Brady Bunch* (1969–1974) or *Moonlighting* (1985–1989), did incorporate musical numbers into some episodes, but this was rare. Generally, it was either part of the episode's storyline (Greg Brady [Barry Williams] needs money to cut a demo and ropes his siblings into singing with him)[5] or special episodes highlighting one of the actor's love of singing. *Moonlighting* did this more than once; Bruce Willis performed "Good Lovin'" at a wedding ceremony in *Moonlighting*'s "Atomic Shakespeare" episode; the episode right before it featured an original song by Billy Joel and an extended dance sequence, and "The Dream Sequence Always Rings Twice" featured two 1940s-era songs performed by Cybill Shepherd.[6] Aside from children's television, such as *Sesame Street*, which easily incorporated musical numbers into episodes, there were few series in the first few decades of US TV, like *Fame* (1982–1987, NBC/First-run syndication), set in the New York City High School for the Performing Arts, that made music and dancing integral parts of their narratives. While there were few musical series, music has been a part of television since it debuted.

Given this history, it was only a matter of time before someone attempted to create more musical series akin to their theatrical siblings, rather than one-off performances or variety shows. *Hull High*, debuting on NBC in 1990, was the first, created by Canadian country music singer Gil Grant and featuring original songs. One month later, Steven Bochco, creator of series such as *Hill Street Blues*, offered the appropriately named *Cop Rock*, airing on ABC. Both series featured several musical numbers per episode, primarily hip-hop/rap for *Hull High* and rock for *Cop Rock*, with the music in *Hull High* serving as a Greek chorus commenting on the action, and incorporated into courtroom scenes or interrogation rooms reminiscent of the grittiness of his other series in *Cop Rock*. The odd juxtaposition and lack of narrative justification for this, however, doomed both series to be short-lived curiosities. Keeping with a long tradition of adapting British series, in the mid-2000s, CBS finally tried its hand at a similar show, *Viva Laughlin*, an adaptation of a fairly successful UK series, *Viva Blackpool*. Unlike *Hull High* or *Cop Rock*, however, *Viva Laughlin* was a jukebox musical series, with the cast singing popular songs or known standards appropriate to the action. This too, however, failed, only to be repurposed far more successfully by Ryan Murphy two years later with *Glee* for Fox. Unlike its predecessors, the series did provide a justification for its music: the series is focused on the adventures and misadventures of a high school glee club. Its success likely paved the way for series such as *Zoey's Extraordinary Playlist* (jukebox) and the subversive *Crazy Ex-Girlfriend* (original).

While musical-focused series remain a small subset, the late 1990s to the present day saw prime-time series across genres incorporate at least a single musical episode into their run. Starting with the syndicated series *Xena: Warrior Princess*, shows from *Buffy the Vampire Slayer* to *Chicago Hope* aired such episodes, using either original music (*Buffy*, *Scrubs*, *Community*) or the jukebox format (*Chicago Hope*, *Lucifer*). These single episodes, like *Glee* would do in 2009, generally offer an external reason for the presence of singing, such as an altered mental state due to a medical issue (*Scrubs*, *Chicago Hope*) or the presence of a cosmic being forcing people to express themselves in song (*Buffy*, *Lucifer*). (And sometimes, merely to utilize the talents of actors with Broadway backgrounds such as Mandy Patinkin and Neil Patrick Harris; witness the random inclusion of "Nothing Suits Me Like a Suit" in the otherwise non-musical episode "Girls vs. Suits."[7]) More subtlety, *Zoey's Extraordinary Playlist* and *Crazy Ex-Girlfriend*, which featured several songs per episode, had protagonists who, for various reasons, filtered their environments or interactions through song as essential to the ongoing narrative.

This book seeks to trace the history of the musical on US television, from its variety show and adaptational beginnings to the rash of single-episode and full-on musical series of the 2000s. While the types can come and go—the old-school variety shows have been replaced with shows like *Saturday Night Live* (1975–present), which mixes sketch comedy and musical acts—music has been a vital part of US television decades before the debut of MTV in 1981. This can range from the "Broadway in your living room" types like PBS's *Great Performances* (1972–present) to the local and national music shows like *American Bandstand* (1952–1989) or *Soul Train* (1971–2006) capable of launching musical acts nationwide. The first part of this book offers a brief history of various ways music has been integral to US television programming since the beginning. I'll start with the variety shows that had their heydays in the 1950s—with a brief resurgence in the 1970s, before shifting over to the various musical specials that took their place, whether it was holiday airings of movie musicals like *The Sound of Music* (1965), the rarer original works, or the recent rash of live versions of Broadway hits. Chapter 3 shows the various ways that US television engaged with popular music, whether it was the television-created band *The Monkees* (1966–1968), whose fake "documentary" sitcom led to actual music careers for the four young men cast as the band, the early attempts to make teen actors/idols into pop stars, or the way the WB promoted its music arm through its television shows, and what happened to the shows that said no. Finally, I end this section with a look at what's commonly known as the "backstage musical"; that is, musicals about putting on a show. It was this type of show that was one of the earlier examples of "musical" series, with the television adaptation of *Fame* in 1982, but got a second life in the 2000s with shows like *Nashville* (2012–2018) and *Smash* (2012–2013).

In this second part, I do a deep dive into the various shows that either went full musical or spent an episode or two with a song in their hearts. I start with some of the early examples, including *Xena: Warrior Princess*'s (1995–2001) "The Bitter Suite" (3.12) before discussing two series whose musical episodes took different tacks while garnering critical acclaim: *Buffy The Vampire Slayer*'s (1997–2003) in-house created "Once More, With Feeling" and *Scrubs*' (2001–2010) "My Musical" (6.12), which brought in musical veterans to create its episode, as well as the ways in which this kicked off a flurry of series trying their hand at this particular sub-genre (some with more success than others). Following up on this is an examination of shows that went the jukebox musical route, using contemporary—or near contemporary—songs to advance both plot and character, such as the God-induced musical on *Lucifer*. Heading back to the 1990s, I examine the much-maligned *Cop Rock* (1990), created by 80s television fixture Steven Bochco, who hit the ratings and cultural jackpot with

Hill Street Blues and *LA Law* but stumbled when it came to creating a musical. Featuring music and lyrics by Greg Edmonson and Mike Post, both television composer veterans, as well as Randy Newman, the series nonetheless suffered from numerous challenges, including actors who couldn't sing, singers who couldn't act, and, most importantly, no narrative justification for its musical numbers. I'll also touch on a forgotten show from the same year—that met the same fate as *Cop Rock*—*Hull High* (1990), which offered a lighter touch and more contemporary sound. Both series end up as interesting failures that nonetheless set the groundwork for series that followed in their wake.

Of course, no analysis of musical television would be complete without the show that broke the *Cop Rock* curse: *Glee* (2009–2015). Created by Ryan Murphy, the show offered a mix of drama, music, and hijinks in a way that proved to be ratings—and zeitgeist—gold, despite a later dip in quality and reassessment of some of its stories and characters. I'll combine this with a look at *Zoey's Extraordinary Playlist* (2020–2021), which used the jukebox format less for in-narrative performance but rather as an indicator of the main character's state of mind, suggesting *Crazy Ex-Girlfriend* (2015–2019) more than *Glee*. Not surprisingly, the next chapter dives into *Crazy Ex-Girlfriend* itself, one of the few full-on musical series. Co-created by rom-com veteran Aline Brosh McKenna and Rachel Bloom, the series centers around Rebecca Bunch (Rachel Bloom), a high-powered New York-based attorney about to make partner when she runs into ex-boyfriend Josh Chan (Vincent Rodriguez III) and decides to quit her job and move to his hometown, West Covina, California; i.e., the plot of more than one rom-com (and at least one WB series in the early 2000s). Yet the series itself is dedicated to subverting not only its premise, but how the rom-com genre views women, men, and relationships, through both cringe comedy and song. I'll also examine the short-lived *Galavant* (2015–2016), which offered a lighter, if still somewhat subversive, take on heroes and the tropes of their stories, particularly through the lens of Disney's classic and contemporary animated films, with both series using original songs that simultaneously acted as parody and tribute to their source materials. I'll close out with a view on the future of television musicals, by looking at an early streaming success and a more recent offering: *Dr. Horrible's Sing-Along Blog* (2008) and Apple TV's *Schmigadoon!* (2021–2023). Created during the Writers' Guild strike in 2007, the goal of the limited series (three fifteen-minute episodes) was to offer tangible proof that online content was not simply promotional but could be a viable alternative to television programming; while the strike wasn't entirely successful, *Dr. Horrible* was, pointing, and in some ways paving, the way for streaming as an alternate medium. *Schmigadoon!*, released in 2021, is one of the outcomes, a self-aware musical series that nonetheless offered appropriately escapist fare during one of the many heights of the COVID-19 pandemic. Like many of the latter-day musical series of the mid-2000s, both *Dr. Horrible* and *Schmigadoon* take an ironic and self-reflexive stance toward the material, particularly highlighting elements such as the notion of media-driven personas and heroism (*Dr. Horrible*) or the more problematic elements or issues in the stories and characterizations in both classic and more recent Broadway hits (*Schmigadoon*) without dismissing them outright. I'll conclude this examination by arguing that the transition of the television musical series from terrestrial to streaming nevertheless retains the spirit of its television brethren.

PART ONE

MUSIC AND TELEVISION: SONGS ON TV BEFORE MTV

1

The Big Big Show: Variety Shows on TV

While television didn't take off as a medium until after World War II, there were a few channels that existed in the 1920s and 1930s, in large markets like Chicago, New York, Boston, and Los Angeles, based on a now obsolete technology called mechanical television, which could transmit long distances, but suffered from poor image quality. Even those stations, however, were mostly suspended from 1942 to 1945 for World War II, but this break in transmission offered an opportunity for manufacturers to improve the technology, readying them for mass production when the war ended. Economic prosperity, post-war, helped a larger group of people afford to buy televisions, but programming was still limited in a few ways. One was that recording programs on film or tape was not widespread, meaning that most aired live. (Recording programs on tape or film and airing them would not become the standard until the late 1950s.) It was also literally limited to half the day; television would "sign off" at night and start again the following morning, offering either what was called a test pattern or simply static. (For those too young to remember, the film *Poltergeist* [1982] offers a creepy example of what that looked like.[1]) In terms of television shows, however, early television adapted elements of theater, radio, and film when creating programming, including what became known as the "anthology dramas," which often combined the structure of a theater play and featured actors primarily known for their film work. (*Four Star Playhouse* was in fact produced by and starred Charles Boyer, Dick Powell, Rosalind Russell, and Ida Lupino, all of whom were primarily known for successful film careers.) News shows, children's programming, sports, and game shows were also early entries into television, but there was one other type, borrowed from vaudeville, that enjoyed significant success during the first few decades of US television: the variety show.

Taking its inspiration from vaudeville, variety shows tend to blend music and comedy skits, although some focus primarily on one or the other. In that respect, the term can cover everything from the *Texaco Star Theater* (1948–1956) to *Saturday Night Live* (1975–present), with many stops in between for shows like *The Brady Bunch Hour*, *Donny & Marie* (1976–1979), *American Bandstand*, or *The Ed Sullivan Show* (1948–1971). While many of these shows combined music and skits, there were a number of series, particularly before the debut of MTV in 1981, that focused only on music, providing a conduit for new (or new to viewers) songs, bands, or trends. Showing that music has been a part of US television since the beginning, this chapter focuses on examining the sketch/music shows as well as those that introduced new music to viewers. In particular, the way that television reinterpreted what was essentially a theatrical form (vaudeville) for a mass audience with variety shows from *The George Burns and Gracie Allen Show* (1950–1958) to *Sonny and Cher*, as well as supplementing—and perhaps outdoing—radio in combining the visual and aural by presenting acts from Elvis Presley to The Doors to a mass audience on series such as *The Ed Sullivan Show* and *American Bandstand*. On a cultural level, the latter were often the only series that showcased artists of color, providing greater exposure not only to the musicians but also to the audience.

Vaudeville Goes to Television: Variety Shows

From the late 19th century until the 1920s—and before radio and television became part of US homes—vaudeville was a significant form of entertainment.

While the word vaudeville can be traced back to mid-19th century French theater, in the United States, vaudeville was an outgrowth of older variety shows, traveling circuses, and even burlesque shows.[2] After the Civil War, performers-turned-impresarios such as Tony Pastor were some of the first in the United States to combine these into entertainment packages that featured singing, dancing, jokes, jugglers, and other acts familiar to audiences into more settled entertainments (that is, within theaters rather than only traveling troupes) and that would appeal to middle-class audiences (removing the more salacious elements) with good incomes—not unlike television would do half a century later.[3]

Over the next decades, regular theaters (usually in major cities) and the continuing vaudeville circuit would bring this entertainment around the country, with a continued emphasis on keeping it family-friendly. (One can see vaudeville's ancestry in, for instance, Branson, Missouri's numerous theaters, which at various points offered shows/theaters either primarily focused on music [i.e., Charley Pride] or went the more vaudeville route [Ray Stevens].) While vaudeville was lightly integrated, the demands of segregation and desire to move past the poor treatment and stereotypes that many Black performers were limited to led to the development of a separate Black vaudeville circuit, launching not only performers such as Ma Rainey and Bessie Smith, but bringing jazz and ragtime into the mainstream. While the advent of cinema spelled the beginning of the end for vaudeville, both in terms of serving as its competition and the (comparatively) easier working conditions of film versus vaudeville, vaudeville theaters not only often shared space with early cinema but provided it with its future stars.[4] Abbott and Costello, Don Ameche, Fatty Arbuckle, Fred Astaire, Pearl Bailey, most of the Barrymore family, Tod Browning, and Judy Garland (among many others) got their start in vaudeville; it also helped musicians like Duke Ellington, Ella Fitzgerald, and George Gershwin gain greater prominence.

Film may have signaled vaudeville's decline, with television offering the final blow, but its influence could still be felt, both in the screwball comedies of the 1930s[5] and later the variety shows that dominated 1950s television (and beyond). Many of the stars who got their start in vaudeville, like Morey Amsterdam and Red Skelton, transitioned to television with a format that was almost identical to its stage counterpart. Shows like *Texaco Star Theater* would have musical acts, famous guests, monologues, and sketches; former vaudevillian Milton Berle was so successful as host he became known as Mr. Television. Sid Caesar's *Your Show of Shows* not only employed adept vaudeville performers like Imogene Coca, but represented early opportunities for writers and directors such as Neil Simon, Mel Brooks, and Woody Allen; its ninety-minute run time and emphasis on sketch comedy were a clear influence on *Saturday Night Live*, as well.

The 1950s may have represented variety shows' high point on television, with performers of all types, from bandleader Lawrence Welk to Frank Sinatra serving as host, with dozens premiering throughout the decade. These included *The Colgate Comedy Hour* (1950–1955), *The Jack Benny Program* (1932–1955; transitioned from radio), *The Perry Como Show* (1955–1959), *The Red Skelton Show* (1951–1971), *and The Dinah Shore Show* (1951–1957), among many others. While performers like Sinatra remained popular, his variety show only lasted two seasons, with declining ratings based on competition from other shows. Betty White's early foray into television with the variety show *The Betty White Show* (1952–1954) was also canceled after two seasons, due to interference by the network (NBC) trying to avoid controversy with their southern affiliates, who objected to White's hiring and showcasing of African American dancer Arthur Duncan.[6] White not only refused to fire him, telling the network to "live with it"[7] but in fact gave Duncan more airtime.

Depending on the host, these variety shows would often emphasize one aspect of performance over another. Dinah Shore, who'd first come into prominence as a singer, focused primarily on musical acts, while Red Skelton, a comedian, had a variety show that focused more on sketches (although his show marked the first television appearance of the Beach Boys).[8] This would be the pattern moving forward, with a few tweaks. *The Andy Williams Show* (1962–1971) featured a number of singers from a variety of genres (although generally not rock until the late 1960s), guests, and a few sketches (he would later open a popular theater in Branson); *The Carol Burnett Show* (1967–1978) focused primarily on comedy, with a regular cast that included Harvey Korman, Vicky Lawrence, and Tim Conway, although each episode ended with a song. By the 1970s, shows like *The Sonny & Cher Comedy Hour* (1971–1974) and *Donny & Marie* (1976–1979) mixed both musical performances and sketch comedy more evenly, and the format was still lively enough to encourage shows like *The Brady Bunch* to spin-off into the short-lived *The Brady Bunch Hour* (1976–1977), which moves the blended family to a beachfront location when they are given the opportunity to star in a variety show, extending the original series stories as the "backstage" part of the variety show. (Episodes of the original show did have a couple of stories centered around music: "Dough Re Mi" has Greg team up with his siblings to cut a record, and "Adios, Johnny Bravo" features a predatory talent scout who promises to make Greg a star.[9] They also released four studio albums between 1970 and 1973.) Like all of the *Brady Bunch* spin-offs (three in the 1970s, as well as an attempted reboot in 1990), *The Brady Bunch Hour* was not a critical or ratings success, and was canceled after nine episodes.

The 1970s, however, would be the last gasp of the old school variety show. With the exception of *The Muppet Show* (1976–1981), which ran in first-run syndication after appearing on *Saturday Night Live* during *SNL*'s first season, it was in many respects the last of its kind in near prime time. Although ostensibly geared toward younger audiences, *The Muppet Show*'s employment of song, dance, backstage shenanigans, and special guests, from Rita Moreno to Vincent Price, is straight from the variety show playbook. The show was well-aware of its origins, as the format itself was the basis for much of the humor, from Fozzie Bear's (Frank Oz) silly jokes to the elderly Statler (Richard Hunt) and Waldorf (Jim Henson) up in a box seat and offering sarcastic commentary on the performances. Instead, the defining elements of the variety show, including musical acts and sketch comedy, would be maintained by shows like *Saturday Night Live* (1975–present), *MadTV* (1995–2016), *In Living Color* (1990–1994), and *A Black Lady Sketch Show* (2019–2023), with some of the combination of special guests, sketch comedy, and musical acts continuing to be a part of the late night talk shows on broadcast. The original *Muppet Show*, however, would prove to be the last successful take on the vaudeville-inspired variety show.

Bandstands and Soul Trains: Music on TV before MTV

An Emmy category for variety show has existed since 1951, but what it means—and its title—has changed more than once over the past seventy years. During the 1950s, the nominees were easily classed as variety shows, but by the late 1960s, the award started being given for "outstanding musical or variety series," suggesting that there was an appreciable difference, and the nominees included talk shows (like Dick Cavett) alongside *Rowan & Martin's Laugh-In* (1968–1973). There was another category, however, that primarily aired outside of prime time and yet became a conduit for music on television, and a way to introduce various acts to a broad audience: the music and dance shows. That is, shows that featured both live and recorded musical acts, with a group of young people dancing to the music, such as *American Bandstand*, *Soul Train*, and a variety of local series that used the same format. *American Bandstand*, which started out by showing short music videos (a precursor to MTV) mixed with guests, premiered in Philadelphia in 1952, before shifting to a dance program. When its original host and radio personality Bob Horn was arrested for drunk driving and solicitation,[10] he was replaced by Dick Clark, who ended up pitching it to ABC as an afternoon program that would air around the time that kids would be finished with school for the day. By the early 1960s, it was shifted to Saturdays, where it would air after a block of cartoons, a position it stayed in until the late 1980s before airing its final original broadcast on October 7, 1989. The dancers featured on the show (and others like it) were not professionals, but regulars could gain a bit of celebrity and a following among viewers. Clark would also pick out a couple of audience members for the "Rate a Record" segment; they would listen to new music and offer their opinions (e.g., "it's got a good beat and you can dance to it"). Live acts would also appear; musicians that appeared on the show over its decades-long history included acts as divergent as ABBA, The Beastie Boys, Adam Ant, Tony Bennett, and Creedence Clearwater Revival.

While *American Bandstand* did feature live performances by Black artists, from Chubby Checker in 1960 to Prince in 1980, the dancers and studio audience remained primarily white, particularly when it was filmed in Philadelphia (less so after its mid-60s move to Los Angeles). The neighborhood in which it was originally filmed was racially mixed, but Black teens who wanted to get on the show were accused of starting fights or not adhering to dress code requirements and were denied tickets. There was also a desire not to alienate Southern affiliates by showing Black and White teens dancing together as it moved from local to national.[11] This was not uncommon; Baltimore's *The Buddy Deane Show* (1957–1964), which served as the inspiration for *The Corny Collins Show* in John Waters' *Hairspray* (1988) and aired daily on Baltimore's ABC affiliate, would not allow racially integrated dancing, and allowed Black teens their own episode only every other Friday. A brief period of integration, requested by the network, sparked complaints from segregationists, and ended quickly. This fight over integration was a significant part of the plot of Waters' *Hairspray*, which, despite being a fictional depiction, emphasized the reality of Baltimore as a majority Black population, as well as its particular challenges as neither a northern city nor 100 percent southern.[12] While there were other local programs, *The Buddy Deane Show* is of particular interest because of the way it was in competition with the local-gone-national *American Bandstand*; both were on ABC, and *American Bandstand* was not aired at all in Baltimore. *Buddy Deane* featured "The Committee," a group of local teens who were essentially the stars of the show, setting dance and fashion trends for other teens.[13] A version of The Committee (known as The Council) was a significant part of the narrative of *Hairspray*, as was the question of integration, and despite Waters' love for the original show, he doesn't downplay the role of certain council members—and parents—in both social gatekeeping and fighting integration.[14]

Waters wasn't the only one to use these shows as inspiration; *American Dreams* (2002–2005), which ran on NBC for three seasons (and was co-produced by Dick Clark) was another. While featuring an ensemble cast attempting to navigate the cultural shifts of the 1960s, a significant focus was placed on teen Meg Pryor (Brittany Snow) and her desire to become one of the featured dancers on *American Bandstand*.[15] Set in Philadelphia, music was integral to the series, particularly bands performing on *American Bandstand* (which in the series did not move to Los Angeles in 1964); *American Dreams* hired contemporary musicians to perform as these earlier artists, including Usher as Marvin Gaye, the band Third Eye Blind as The Kinks, Brad Paisley as Ricky Nelson, and John Legend as Stevie Wonder, among dozens of others.[16] Of course, the amount of music featured on the show, both as performances and as part of the soundtrack, has seemingly kept the series from a full release on DVD or streaming.

Seeking to address the particular limitations of shows like *American Bandstand* with regard to both artists and dancers, *Soul Train* debuted in 1971 with a focus on genres dominated by Black artists: hip-hop, R & B, and soul. Don Cornelius, who, like Buddy Deane, got his start on the radio (in Chicago), created a series of concerts of local artists to play at Chicago area high schools, calling his traveling shows The Soul Train. It was picked up by public access channel WCIU-TV in Chicago and sponsored by Sears. It did well enough in

Chicago to be picked up for national syndication the next year, and Cornelius moved the show to Los Angeles.[17] While a few white artists appeared on *Soul Train* (David Bowie, Elton John, who'd specifically asked to perform),[18] it was a showcase—and an answer—to the exclusion of dancers and artists of color on other shows. As author Ericka Blount Danois says, "*Soul Train* was one of the first national shows to showcase Black joy and our everyday lives on television,"[19] an element that is still a work-in-progress in the twenty-first century. Creating the show itself was a political act on Cornelius's part, and when it cut into *American Bandstand*'s ratings, Dick Clark created a competing program in 1973 called *Soul Unlimited*, prompting angry letters to ABC from fans and community leaders like Jesse Jackson, which apparently led Clark to suggest that an all-Black show was nothing but another form of "segregation."[20] Besides making Clark look, at best, out of touch for going after the only Black-run program on television at the time, *Soul Unlimited* couldn't compete in ratings, was not worth the backlash it caused, and disappeared after a few episodes.

FIGURE 1.1 ***The Jackson Five perform on Soul Train. Tribune Entertainment / Photofest © Tribune Entertainment.***

Like *Bandstand*, *Soul Train* left enough of a cultural impact—the Soul Train Line has been referenced numerous times across various media[21]—to also inspire a dramatic series. While *American Dreams* focused primarily on an audience member who wants to be part of the *Bandstand* dancers, *American Soul* (2019–2020) was a dramatized biographical series focused on Cornelius himself. It ran for two seasons on BET, covering the time from the debut of the show in 1971 to 1975, with his son Tony serving as one of the executive producers; like *American Dreams*, it also incorporated contemporary musicians into episodes to play Soul Train's famous performers, including Rufus Thomas (Bobby Brown), Diana Ross (Michelle Williams), and George Clinton (Big Boi), among others.[22] Given the roadblocks and challenges to even bringing the show to air—sponsorship was a continual challenge—both Cornelius' and the series' stories certainly had dramatic potential. While *American Bandstand* technically ran three years longer than *Soul Train*'s total run, *Soul Train* managed to last in continual production until 2006, long after Cornelius stepped down from hosting, suggesting its cultural relevance remained intact longer than its predecessor.

Variety shows and music shows like *Soul Train* and *Bandstand* were vital in disseminating new music to wide audiences, reaching both large urban centers and small towns. Long before MTV, and alongside aired musicals, they kept music as an integral part of television from nearly its earliest days. There was one final program that was culturally significant in this regard: *The Ed Sullivan Show* (1948–1971). While it was considered a variety show, featuring recurring characters such as Senor Wences (a ventriloquist) and interviews, its most lasting imprint on American culture came from the musical guests featured on the program—Elvis Presley, The Beatles, The Rolling Stones, The Doors, and Itzhak Perlman—all of whom either debuted on the show (stateside) or whose appearance launched them to greater heights. And, unlike the tentative moves of shows like *American Bandstand* in featuring artists of color, Sullivan's roster of African American singers, actors, and comedians was extensive across the two-plus decades it ran in prime time. While Sullivan was culturally and politically conservative—bands like the Stones, the Doors, Bob Dylan, and Bo Diddley were pressured to change lyrics or song choices to avoid backlash from audiences or Standards and Practices and he worked with anti-communists in the early years of his show to avoid controversial guests[23]—his show nonetheless provided a venue for an extensive catalog of music that dominated prime time while it aired.

What binds many of these variety and music shows is a shared collective memory, even for those too young to have watched *Sullivan*, *Bandstand*, or *Soul Train* (or the dozens of variety shows) when they aired. *The Simpsons* have referenced either Ed Sullivan or his show on at least six different episodes. Nirvana's video for "In Bloom," filmed with the same Kinescope cameras used in early television and airing in black and white, did a take-off on *The Ed Sullivan Show* (Doug Llewelyn played a Sullivan knock-off), with the band dressed in suits and smiling as they sang, interspliced with the band in drag tearing up the set. This, despite no member of the band being old enough to have any significant memories of the show when it aired lived and debuting more than twenty years after the show went off the air. More importantly, however, was the ways in which both the vaudeville-inspired variety shows and the music programs pre-MTV kept music as a part of television throughout its history, paving the way for the films and series on television in which music was an integral part of the narrative and production.

2

Broadway in Your Living Room: Musical Specials

One of television's early selling points—and an area of concern for other mediums like film and live theater—was the availability of home-based entertainment. Unlike England, for instance, US television went the commercial rather than public route. That meant that rather than charging a yearly license fee for use, US viewers only needed the initial outlay to purchase a TV, and potential future repairs, with no additional costs to use it. It's easy to trace the concern this elicited in the film industry in the 1950s, with innovations such as Technicolor created to compete with US television's black-and-white screens and inferior picture quality. (Indeed, the standard for analog television was NTSC, which stood for National Television Systems Committee, unlike the UK, which used what was known as a Phase Alternating Line [PAL]. The NTSC color system was considered significantly inferior, with many joking it stood for Never Twice the Same Color.[1]) However, as television became more entrenched in American homes, both the variety and quality of programming expanded, including the anthology dramas of the 1950s, groundbreaking genre series like *The Twilight Zone* (1959–1964), and exposure, as discussed in the previous chapter, to musical acts from around the country and abroad viewers might not have otherwise had a chance to see.

As time went on, film and theater seemed to make enough peace with the upstart medium to allow their work to appear on it, more so as the technology improved. In the days before VHS—and long before DVD—the only way to rewatch a film was either at a second-run or revival theater, or when it was finally licensed to television. (And that excluded any movies that weren't considered appropriate for TV's standards and practices without editing or dubbing; ask any Gen X-er who saw *The Breakfast Club* [1985] on broadcast TV and the questionable dubbing choices it used to cover swearing.) Further, with the formation of PBS in 1970, theater found its way back to television, offering dramas and musicals from Broadway and the West End. Yet this was just one of the ways that music remained a part of television, even after the variety shows fell out of fashion after a brief explosion in the 1970s. The 1980s through to the 2000s featured a significant amount of musical specials, whether it was holiday airings of standards like *The Sound of Music* (1967), adaptations such as *Annie* (1999, 2014), or originals that made use of popular television stars, including *Polly* (1989), featuring both Keisha Knight Pulliam and Phylicia Rashad from *The Cosby Show* (1984–1992) as the main leads. Starting in the 2010s with *The Sound of Music* (2013), television also began incorporating live versions of older, contemporary, and even jukebox (Tyler Perry's *The Passion: New Orleans* [2016]) musicals across most of the broadcast networks.

All the World's a Stage: Bringing Theater to Television

By making television a commercial enterprise first, the United States differed from the UK and many countries in Europe, which used the public television model first, with commercially supported networks developing later. A public television channel was established a little under a decade after nationwide broadcast started in 1941 (although most ceased broadcasting during World War II); it was known as National Education Television (NET). In its earliest days, NET focused on educational programming almost exclusively, usually produced by local stations as part of adult education programs, and it came to be known as the University of the Air. By the early 1960s, however, they started importing programs from abroad, and, by the middle of that decade, attempted to create original programming that would air on NET. One of these programs was *NET Playhouse* (1966–1970), which offered plays and musical performances both developed by NET and imported from England. It included both plays written for the stage (Henrik Ibsen's *An Enemy of the People*) and those created for the program itself (Paul Zindel's *Let Me Hear You Whisper*). These aired during prime-time slots and were likely positioned to help elevate NET to be the "fourth network" after the demise of DuMont.[2] These would often include musical performances, including a tribute to composer Kurt Weill, a sketch show with "musical themes," and *Jesus, A Passion Play for Americans*, which was essentially a jukebox musical created by and featuring songs from Peter Ivers' album *Knight of the Blue Communion*.[3]

With the creation of PBS in 1969, which absorbed and replaced NET, this trend continued. The program *Great Performances*, which started in 1971, featured—and continues to air—plays, musicals, and concerts from the United States and abroad. Because PBS is part of the broadcast spectrum, and is funded by both donations and entities like the Corporation for Public Broadcasting (at least until August 2025, when it shut down following defunding and other actions by the Trump administration),[4] these performances are basically free to viewers, who do not even have to sit through ads to enjoy them. (Although, during certain times of year, they might be interrupted for fundraising drives.) While these can feature well-known musicals such as *Oklahoma*, or more recently, parts of contemporary ones like *Hamilton* (clips from the play interspersed with interviews with writers, actors, politicians, and pundits), they also featured music from *Einstein on the Beach*, an opera co-created by avant-garde composer Philip Glass, and *Jammin': Jelly's Last Jam*, a documentary about the making of the show that had debuted on Broadway the year before it aired on PBS.[5] While not the full performances that other plays and musicals got, due to how close in time they were to their debuts, these programs nonetheless exposed audiences to works they might not have had access to otherwise.

This, however, wasn't limited to PBS. The broadcast networks also began airing musicals, particularly movie musicals. The film version of *The Sound of Music* (1965) was first broadcast on ABC in 1976 and scored in the top 20 in the Nielsens. In fact, it did well enough for NBC to buy the broadcast rights the next year, with the option to show it 20 times over the next 22 years, which they did,[6] most frequently right before the Easter holiday. Unlike most programs, these airings tended to be shown with limited commercial interruption, making them closer to the theater experience. When that option expired and NBC quit showing it regularly in 2001, it was picked up by and aired on Fox, ABC again, and the cable channel Freeform (owned by Disney). (It also aired on the BBC in 1978 and was repeated around Christmas time up until 2016.) The musical *Gypsy* was adapted for television in 1993, directed by Emile Ardolino, who had directed *Dirty Dancing* in 1987, and starring Bette Midler; it did well enough to be released in theaters abroad, a rare feat for a television production, and was a critical smash.[7] (Sadly, Ardolino didn't live to see this; he died of complications from AIDS a few weeks before it aired.[8]) Rodgers and Hammerstein's version of *Cinderella* was adapted for television three times. The first was in 1957, with Julie Andrews as the titular character and Edie Adams as the Fairy Godmother.[9] Yet because it was filmed in black and white, the transition to color made it hard to repeat. Because of that, CBS elected to remake it in 1965, with Lesley Ann Warren as Cinderella and Celeste Holm as the Fairy Godmother, and did well enough to be rebroadcast multiple times over the next nine years.[10] Finally, it was revived as part of the newly relaunched *Wonderful World of Disney* series, with Brandy Norwood as Cinderella and Whitney Houston as the Fairy Godmother, with ratings that outstripped the previous two adaptations—no easy feat in the 1990s, when viewership was starting to fragment amongst more channels and increased competition from cable.[11] The trend seemed to trail off again with 2001's adaptation of *South Pacific*, which debuted to mixed reviews.

The latest turn, however, started again with *The Sound of Music*. Bob Greenblatt, who'd been named NBC Chairman in 2011, had a background in theater, including developing a stage adaptation of the film *9 to 5* (1981) for Broadway. (It should be noted that NBC had an earlier success with the live format in 1982, when they aired a live version of *Ain't Misbehavin'* filmed at their Burbank studios and starring Nell Carter, who'd appeared in the Broadway version and at the time was starring in NBC's *Gimme a Break* [1981–1987].) Greenblatt's musical background was apparent in his programming choices; while *The Voice* (2011–present), a singing competition, had been brought in earlier, it debuted early in his tenure, he subsequently developed *Smash*, a backstage musical series, which debuted in early 2012. He also embraced the idea of a live musical for television. Given how well the film version continued to perform from the 1970s to the 2000s, it perhaps wasn't surprising that *The Sound of Music* was the first live musical to be produced, with a holiday debut (December 2013).[12] The broadcast did so well (22 million viewers) that it elevated NBC, which had struggled in the Nielsen ratings since *Friends* and *Frasier* ended in 2004, to the number one spot for the night.[13]

It was also successful enough for NBC—as well as other networks—to keep going with this concept. In 2014, they aired *Peter Pan Live!* followed by *The Wiz Live!* in 2015, and *Grease Live!* and *Hairspray Live!* in 2016. As Maureen Lee Lenker points out, both *Grease* and *Hairspray*, which itself is partly set within an *American Bandstand*-type music show, adapted particularly well to the television format.[14] Not all of these, including *The Sound of Music Live!* were as critically successful as their viewing numbers might imply, but they drew large audiences. Both Fox and ABC also tried their hand at the format, with ABC (owned by Disney), airing a combination of the original film and live action in 2019, and Fox going forward with *Rent: Live* the same year, despite an actor injury that required mixing live and pre-recorded footage, as well as elements of the musical being toned down or censored for broadcast. These productions would primarily use singers (Carrie Underwood in *The Sound of Music*; Ariana Grande in *Hairspray*) or actors (Matthew Morrison from *Glee* in *How the Grinch Stole Christmas*), with some crossover artists, such as Queen Latifah (*The Little Mermaid Live!*). It is surprising that only a few of these specials cast stars with Broadway experience, with *Hairspray* featuring Kristin Chenoweth and Harvey Fierstein, and 2018's *Jesus Christ Superstar Live in Concert* (which offered a stripped-down production-appropriate set) casting Brandon Victor Dixon, who'd created the role of Harpo in the musical adaptation of *The Color Purple* as well as taking over as Aaron Burr on Leslie Odom Jr.'s recommendation in *Hamilton* in 2016, as Judas Iscariot to John Legend's Jesus, as well as Norm Lewis, who'd appeared in numerous productions on both Broadway and in the West End, as Caiaphas.

It should be noted that all of these live specials focus on the broadly familiar across multiple generations: *The Sound of Music*, *Grease*, and even *Hairspray*, which started as a film and transitioned to a musical, are all rooted in the past (the 1930s, 1950s, and 1960s, respectively). One of the last of these, *Annie Live!*, which aired in 2021, started as a comic strip and has been adapted for the stage in 1977 and for film five times, although the first two, in 1932 and 1938, were not musicals. The three later films, in 1982, 1999 (for television), and 2014 (co-produced by Will Smith and Jay-Z, among others, and casting Jamie Foxx as Daddy Warbucks and Quvenzhané Wallis as Annie and set in the present day) were all adapted from the musical. The live version offers a mix of both the 1982 film (featuring songs written specifically for the film) and the stage version, but maintains the ending of the stage musical rather than the kidnapping and helicopter chase of the film.[15] *Annie*, however, would be the last of these live adaptations; no new adaptations have aired in the past four years.

Writing for the Box: TV-Only Musicals

While nowhere near as common as either the live musicals of the 2010s or filmed stage productions aired on PBS, musicals written exclusively for television stretch back to the earliest days of television. Indeed, the first musical written exclusively for television was *The Boys from Boise*, written and composed by Samuel Medoff (later known as Dick Manning), who came to prominence due to his radio show Sam Medoff and His Yiddish Swing Orchestra on WHN in New York. Set—and airing—during World War II, it tells the story of a group of showgirls who get stranded in Idaho, who turn to tending cattle in order to earn enough to get home, as well as dealing with cattle rustlers. While hampered by limited space—and the fact that few people owned a set—it was still a pioneering broadcast in that it suggested how to mount such a production within television's confines.[16] (Sadly, no version currently exists; most of DuMont's filmed programming was destroyed or junked by the 1970s.[17]) The head of NBC at the time, Sylvester Weaver, subsequently added a number of musical programs to the schedule, from variety shows to the *NBC Opera Theater* (1949–1964), which aired operas created specifically for television. The first, a Nativity play called "Amahl and the Night Visitors," by Gian Carlo Menotti, aired on Christmas Eve, 1951, to critical and ratings success.[18] (Menotti would also compose one of the last ones, called *Labyrinth* [1963].) *NBC Opera Theater* would subsequently mix known operas, such as Mozart's *Abduction From the Seraglio* (1954)[19] with originals, some of which would go on to theatrical runs. These were part of both Weaver and NBC founder David Sarnoff's desire to mix the educational with entertainment, as well as an early appeal to the "upscale" viewer.[20] ABC got in on the trend with *The Thirteen Clocks*, adapted from James Thurber's novel of the same name, for *The Motorola Television Hour* (1953–1954). Unlike "Amahl and the Night Visitors," this production featured recognizable actors, including Basil Rathbone and John Raitt (a major Broadway star of the time).[21] *Satins and*

Spurs, produced by Max Liebman (*Your Show of Shows* [1950–1954], among others) and starring Betty Hutton as a rodeo star who falls in love with a reporter,[22] was the first NBC show in color, although the reviews were harsh enough to convince Hutton to retire. Steve Allen, a comedian, actor, composer, and writer, penned several musicals for television, including the music and lyrics for *The Bachelor*, a musical comedy for NBC about an advertising executive juggling three women. It was also an early role for Jayne Mansfield.[23]

Suggesting the rural-based programming CBS would adopt in the 1960s, they debuted *Tom Sawyer*, based on Mark Twain's novel, with music and lyrics by Frank Luther, who worked as a singer (primarily country music) and playwright, among other things.[24] This was followed up almost immediately

FIGURE 2.1 ***"Amahl and the Night Visitors" was an early made-for-TV musical. NBC / Photofest © NBC.***

with an adaptation of *The Adventures of Huckleberry Finn*, featuring a pre-*Brady Bunch* Florence Henderson.[25] Both aired as part of the *United States Steel Hour* (1953–1963). Indeed, the 1950s were the heyday for original TV musicals, not all of which survived, some that were transitioned to theater, and in the case of *The Stingiest Man in Town* (1956), a musical adaptation of *A Christmas Carol*, reworked as a Rankin-Bass animated special in 1978.[26] Sydney Lumet, who'd already been nominated for an Oscar for *12 Angry Men*, briefly transitioned to TV the following year to direct a live musical adaptation of the novel *Hans Brinker and the Silver Skates* with Tab Hunter for NBC as part of the *Hallmark Hall of Fame* anthology series.[27] While NBC seemed to air most of both original and adapted musicals, ABC debuted *The Dangerous Christmas of Red Riding Hood* (1965), a kind of revisionist/fractured fairy tale that tells the story from the wolf's point of view, with music and lyrics by Jule Styne and Bob Merrill, who would go on to work on film score projects, and starring a young Liza Minelli as Red Riding Hood.[28] This was a choice that suited ABC, which was frequently the third-place network and often took more programming risks than either NBC or CBS.

By the 1970s, however, these TV-created musicals tapered off and changed form, with many of them turning to animation or puppetry for specials like *Santa Claus Is Coming to Town* (Rankin and Bass) or *The Great Santa Claus Switch* (an early venue for Henson's Muppets), *The Emperor's New Clothes* (ABC), *Really Rosie* (CBS), and *Oliver and the Artful Dodger* (CBS) (Hanna-Barbera). NBC continued to air new original musicals, including *The Great Man's Whiskers*, a musical about Abraham Lincoln, and a musical version of Robert Louis Stevenson's *The Strange Case of Dr. Jekyll and Mr. Hyde* called *Dr. Jekyll and Mr. Hyde*,[29] starring Kirk Douglas, with music by Lionel Bart, best known for the musical *Oliver!*. Over at CBS, and in keeping with their more grounded programming in the 1970s, they offered *Three for the Girls*, a series of one-act plays (both comedic and dramatic) starring *All in the Family*'s Carroll O'Connor, with the second, "Clothes Make the Girl," the musical segment.[30] More poignant, *Queen of the Stardust Ballroom*, with Charles Durning and Maureen Stapleton, focused on a later-life romance between the newly widowed Bea and postal carrier Al, who meet and fall in love over dancing.[31] In keeping with their remit for more socially relevant programming, CBS also aired *Minstrel Man*, a musical drama about two brothers who grew up performing in their father's minstrel act; after his death, they are initially at odds as to whether to stay with it. Harry wants to continue, while his brother Rennie finds it degrading to their culture and their position as Black men in the early 1900s. While they eventually come together, with Rennie adding a more contemporary Ragtime sound to their work, a confrontation with locals in a small Illinois town, in which Rennie appears in whiteface, leads to his death by lynching.[32] (And one can see at least some progress in television content; twenty years earlier, Rod Serling faced censorship and pushback from networks and advertisers in his attempts to bring Emmett Till's story to television.)

The 1980s, however, brought fewer original musicals to television, even as shows like *Happy Days* (1974–1984) or *The Love Boat* (1977–1986) tried their hands at musical episodes: *Happy Days* offered an "educational" musical about US history as Chachi (Scott Baio) studies for a test, while *The Love Boat*, in keeping with its cruise ship setting, offered a musical revue with an impressive roster of musically inclined guest stars, including Ethel Merman, Della Reese, Carol Channing, Ann Miller, and Cab Calloway.[33] Cable networks like Showtime offered airings of both new and revived productions, such as *Camelot*. *Alice at the Palace* was a musical adaptation of Lewis Carroll's *Alice's Adventures in Wonderland* (1865) and *Through the Looking Glass* (1971), starring Meryl Streep (as Alice) and Debbie Allen (as the Red Queen), and was an early directing credit for Ardolino.[34] "Polly" (1989) was a musical adaptation of the novel *Pollyanna* (1913), with an all-Black cast and set in the 1950s South, a co-production of NBC and Disney, who'd done the original film version. It aired on NBC and starred Phylicia Rashad and Keisha Knight Pulliam, who played mother and daughter on NBC's *The Cosby Show* (1984–

1992). The songs were written by several people, including Alan Menken (*The Little Mermaid*), Debbie Allen (*Fame*), and Steve Nelson, who'd composed music for several *Winnie the Pooh* cartoons as well as the theme song for the series *Webster* (1983–1989).[35] It did well enough for NBC to commission and air a sequel that aired in 1990, "Polly: Comin' Home."[36] Yet the only original musical of the decade was *Copacabana* (CBS), based on Barry Manilow's hit song. Produced by Dick Clark, it dramatized the story in the song, about the doomed love of Lola (Annette O'Toole) and Tony (Barry Manilow) at the titular nightclub. In addition to starring, Manilow wrote the songs, which were released as a soundtrack album the same year.[37] Reviews seemed mixed,[38] but the ratings were good, and it garnered an Emmy win for director Waris Hussein (who directed the first-ever episode of *Doctor Who* [1963–present]). (Fun fact: the script was written by James Lipton, best known now for his *Inside the Actor's Studio* [1994–2019] series). It later became a stage show in Atlantic City before being adapted as a full-length musical in both London and the United States.

In the 1990s, despite the aforementioned "Polly" sequel, television largely turned away from the one-off made-for-TV musicals. In its place were one-off musical episodes (*Xena: Warrior Princess*'s "The Bitter Suite"; MTV's *Daria*'s "Daria!" musical), or full-blown TV series (*Cop Rock*, *Hull High*).[39] One of the only exceptions was *Mrs. Santa Claus* (1996), a Christmas musical starring Angela Lansbury as the titular Mrs. Claus, who gets stuck in turn-of-the-century New York City, where she gets involved in the woman's suffrage movement and unionization of a toy factory before returning home. The production itself was well-pedigreed, with Jerry Herman, who composed *Hello, Dolly!* (1964) and *La Cage Aux Folles* (1983), among others, as the composer, and costume design by Bob Mackie.[40] The 2000s continued this trend, with both broadcast and cable channels, from PBS to A & E, primarily offering new takes on older musicals, like *Joseph and the Amazing Technicolor Dreamcoat* (PBS) or *South Pacific* (ABC), with only a couple of new entries, one of which would become a significant franchise. The first, and far less successful, was a new version of *Pinocchio* told from toymaker Geppetto's perspective, called, of course, *Geppetto* (2000), airing on ABC. Likely because of Disney owning ABC, it was able to use some songs from the original film, including "I've Got No Strings"; the remainder of the music was original, primarily composed and written by Stephen Schwartz, who'd written the music for Disney's *Pocahantas* in 1995 and Dreamwork's *Prince of Egypt* in 1998.[41] Reviews of the musical tended toward mixed or negative, and both it and Drew Carey's performance, who played both Geppetto and starred in ABC's *The Drew Carey Show* (1995–2004), became a running joke during his time hosting the US version of the improv show *Whose Line Is It Anyway?* (1998–present).

Far more successful was another Disney product: *High School Musical* (2006). With music by Lynn Ahrens, who had written the music for *Schoolhouse Rock!*, and lyrics by Stephen Flaherty, who had written the lyrics for Don Bluth's animated film *Anastasia* (1997), directed and choreographed by Kenny Ortega, and starring Zac Efron and Vanessa Hudgens, *High School Musical* was a huge win for the Disney Channel. And for both Efron and Hudgens, whose acting and music careers, respectively, took off with the films' successes. While the critical response was, at best, mixed (one reviewer called it "schmaltzy" and "horrendous"), its viewing numbers were significant for a cable channel (7.7 million viewers), it was Emmy-nominated for its costuming and choreography, and its soundtrack album was certified quadruple platinum, suggesting a significant audience with disposable income.[42] It should come as no surprise that it spawned two sequels (*High School Musical 2* [2007] and *High School Musical 3* [2008]), a spin-off film [*Sharpay's Fabulous Adventure* [2011]), numerous international versions, a reality show, and a mockumentary-style TV series with a new cast: *High School Musical: The Musical: The Series* (2019–2023). The series actually takes a more metatextual approach with its mockumentary format, with the cast preparing for the aforementioned films. This, however, would prove to be the last hurrah for original made-for-TV musical films, as broadcast networks focused on the aforementioned live musicals. The only exception was a one-off production that existed in the middle ground between the live musicals and original content: *The Passion: New Orleans*. Bringing in Peter Barsocchini, who wrote the scripts for the *High School Musical* films, to adapt that portion of the New Testament, and Adam Anders, who served as musical producer for *Glee*, *The Passion* was a jukebox musical adapted from a Dutch production that had aired since 2011. A contemporary retelling set in a post-Katrina New Orleans, it featured music that ranged from classic Broadway ("You'll Never Walk Alone" from *Carousel*, sung by Mary [Trisha Yearwood]), to 1980s ("We Don't Need Another Hero" by Tina Turner, re-conceived as a duet between Jesus [Jencarlos] and Pontius Pilate [Seal] to near-contemporary ("Bring Me to Life" by Evanescence, sung by Judas Iscariot [Chris Daughtry], who'd been a contestant on *American Idol*).[43] It aired on Sunday, March 20, 2016, which was Palm Sunday in that year's liturgical calendar, and garnered mixed reviews from critics. The soundtrack album that followed, however, charted in the top 10 of the Billboard chart, with Daughtry's cover of "Bring Me to Life" reaching number two. The rest of the 2010s, however, would prove to be the era of the musical series over one-off specials or episodes.

Television has long dealt with an image problem, of airing only mediocre or "least offensive programming," in no small part because it is funded by advertising; successfully selling products largely means both appealing to a broad audience and avoiding controversy. This, however, did not prevent networks from wanting to expand their offerings into what would be considered more high culture or educational areas, even before PBS debuted. Musicals, plays, and concerts have been an essential part of television's offerings since the 1940s, and often served as a way to expose viewers to performances and works they wouldn't otherwise have access to, whether due to location or cost.

While not all the productions, whether airings of staged performances, musical films like *The Sound of Music* around holidays, or the occasional made-for-TV originals, could match the song or performance quality of their stage counterparts—stage, film, and television acting have particular differences—they always offered the opportunity for something different than the usual television fare. While early originals and recorded performances were hampered by television's screen size, as well as visual and aural capabilities, watching these musicals, from "Amahl and the Night Visitors" to *High School Musical*, offers an excellent historical tour of television itself.

3

The Mix Tapes: Synergy and Soundtracks

Television targeting teens didn't start with Fox and the WB in the 1990s. Long before either network even existed, there was a robust industry geared toward teens, picking out actors or musicians that seemed to be popular with teens and, at the very least, featuring them in magazines as early as 1957, when arguably the first fan magazine aimed at teens debuted, *16*, featuring Elvis Presley as its cover model. These magazines were, in some ways, an offshoot of magazines such as *Photoplay*, which initially focused on film stars and offered glimpses into their "private" lives. Others soon followed, such as *Tiger Beat* (1965) and *Teen Beat* (1967), encompassing musicians and TV and movie stars throughout their runs. The combination of good looks and popularity, in some instances, suggested that some of these stars could expand their reach, whether transitioning to another medium (i.e., TV to film) or expanding into other areas, such as music.

The television-to-pop star pipeline existed long before *American Idol* (or its offshoots), dating back at least to the debut of *The Monkees* in 1966, a sitcom featuring four musicians that essentially created a band that went on to moderate chart success. The 1970s in particular saw the launch of television actors Leif Garrett, John Travolta, and David Cassidy into music careers as part of their teen idol images. While this became less common in the 1980s and 1990s, the debut of networks such as the WB, which produced music as well as films and television series, provided the network the opportunity to incorporate WB artists into their teen series, both through scene soundtracks and in-person performances to boost the profiles of both the series and the music: synergy in action through dual product branding even as said music was used to characterize or drive scenes between its teen characters. I'll also touch on two series that resisted these placements in favor of unsigned artists and classic rock, respectively: *Buffy the Vampire Slayer* and *Supernatural.*

The Next Big Thing: Music and Television before MTV

If there's a single figure who popularized the trend of music/media crossover, it would be Elvis Presley. He wasn't the first musician to shift between music and movies (Frank Sinatra got there first), but there were a few differences. While Sinatra as musician did appeal to younger audiences, his films generally skewed in favor of adults, with several movie musicals (e.g., *On the Town* [1949]) that showcased his singing talent. Three years before Elvis's debut album, Sinatra had already won an Academy Award for *From Here to Eternity* (1953). There was one element that made Sinatra's rise different from Elvis's: television. Like the variety shows discussed in Chapter 1, series like *The Ed Sullivan Show* or *American Bandstand* introduced music and musicians to a wider audience, adding the visual component absent in radio. While not his first time on TV, when Elvis appeared on *Ed Sullivan*, more than 80 percent of the total viewing audience (about 60 million people) watched.[1] With that level of crossover appeal, and the start of a more intense focus on teen audiences in the 1950s, making Presley a film star, many of which featured his music, would be a no-brainer; suburban teens in particular had disposable income their parents hadn't, with a significant proportion spent on entertainment like film and music.[2] Other musicians took notice, with Sinatra reviving his variety series *The Frank Sinatra Show* in 1957 on ABC, although it only lasted a single season. *The Andy Williams Show*, a half-hour syndicated series, aired on NBC from 1962 to 1971, also using the variety format, as did Johnny Cash, from 1969 to 1971.

As discussed in the previous chapters, these shows, plus others like *American Bandstand* and *Soul Train*, were a conduit for music on television and a way for musicians to promote themselves and broaden their exposure. What was not as common, however, were fictional TV series that either centered on music and musicians, or provided a conduit for their actors to launch a side gig as a singer. The first is not as common and is exemplified by *The Monkees.* The Monkees, both as a series and a band, remains a bit of an oddity in the annals of television and music. It was a musical sitcom that aired on NBC from 1966 to 1968, and focused on the adventures of four young men—Davy Jones, Micky Dolenz, Michael Nesmith, and Peter Tork—trying to make it as a band. Further, it was a single-camera sitcom long before that became the norm, and often used more avant-garde filming techniques, including jump cuts, fourth-wall breaks, and improvisation, and the laugh track was eliminated for the second season. Despite the *Scooby-Doo*-ish nature of many of their adventures (e.g., kidnapped to create a musical Frankenstein-like creature),[3] all four were actual musicians, with a premise that suggested a sort of "making the band" type of documentary. (Indeed, the first season finale was a mockumentary of a stop on their tour.[4]) Each episode featured the band playing songs, set apart from the main story in what ended up being a kind of early version of the music video. Of course, the Monkees as a band were not real, but viewers at the time were nonetheless surprised to find out that the songs they performed in the first seasons had not been written by any of them. The backlash to this revelation led to the show's creator and the network allowing them to write music in the second season.[5]

While Davy, Mickey, Michael, and Peter were all musicians in their own rights, the Monkees as a band didn't exist as an actual band until after the

FIGURE 3.1 ***The Monkees: the made-by-TV band. NBC / Photofest © NBC.***

television series debuted. Despite the producers' objections, the band actually played live concerts following the first season, and clocked several number one hits (e.g., "Last Train to Clarksville," "Daydream Believer"). Essentially, the TV series created the band, making the fictional (somewhat) real. This was kind of underscored by the fact that the Monkees' cast used their actual names, suggesting they were playing exaggerated versions of themselves. This is in contrast to shows like *The Partridge Family* (1970–1974), in which actors played the fictional family band The Partridges, and only David Cassidy, who played Keith Partridge, and Shirley Jones as Shirley Partridge, actually sang on the show or on subsequent albums. While not primarily a musical series, *The Brady Bunch* got in on the trend by featuring the Brady kids singing on more than one episode, with the most famous likely "Dough Re Mi," in which Greg (Barry Williams), who needs $150 to record an album, ends up roping his siblings into singing with him (to share the expenses), only for the whole project to be endangered by Peter's (Chris Knight) changing voice.[6] Not only did the network attempt a spin-off based on the cast's singing (*The Brady*

Bunch Variety Hour [1976]), but several albums featuring various members of the cast were released between 1970 and 1973.

There was a subset that featured albums from television stars in which singing really didn't feature in the narrative at all. Leif Garrett's appearance on a miniseries in 1975 garnered enough reaction from younger fans to catapult him to teen idol status, with spreads in magazines like *Tiger Beat* and later a recording contract with Atlantic Records. John Travolta ended up being the breakout star in *Welcome Back, Kotter* (1975–1979); his singing ability not only led to roles that showcased it, like *Grease* (1978), but also to a recording contract. One of the singles, "Let Her In," charted in Billboard's Top 10 in July of 1976, the only one of his singles to do so that wasn't part of a soundtrack album ("You're the One That I Want" and "Summer Nights" from *Grease* made it into the Billboard Top 5 in 1978). This trend continued, to a limited extent, in the 1980s. Michael Damien, who started in music as part of his family's band and appeared solo on *American Bandstand* in 1981, was cast on the soap opera *The Young and the Restless* (1973–present) as a struggling singer, a role he remained in until 1998, although he made subsequent guest appearances. His biggest hit, however, was a cover of David Essex's "Rock On," which was featured in the teen film *Dream a Little Dream* (with Corey Haim and Corey Feldman), in which Feldman's character lip syncs and dances to it to woo the girl he likes.[7] Jack Wagner's role as Frisco Jones on *General Hospital* (1963–present) as part of what was known in soap opera parlance as a "supercouple" proved popular enough to launch a limited singing career, with his single "All I Need" reaching number 2 on Billboard in 1984. At this point, however, both Wagner and Damien were aided by the debut of MTV, extending their (musical) reach beyond radio, and neither fit the "teen idol" mold of Travolta or Garrett. ("All I Need," in fact, was classified as adult contemporary rather than rock or pop.) Actors continue to launch singing careers aided by their established profile. Bruce Willis parlayed his breakout role on *Moonlighting* into a record deal, although it was not particularly critically well-regarded;

James Marsters from *Buffy* (1997–2003), Christian Kane from *Angel* (1999–2004) and *Leverage* (2008–2012), and Jensen Ackles from *Supernatural* (200–2020) have all released albums, mostly self-produced or with independent labels. (All three also showed off their singing skills on their respective series: Marsters in *Buffy*'s musical episode, Kane performing an original song on *Angel*, while Kane and Ackles also performed together on the final season of *Supernatural*.[8]) While not as common, contestants and winners from shows like *American Idol* have managed, to a limited extent, to parlay their musical success on these television competitions beyond recording contracts; Clay Aiken appeared as a guest star on *Scrubs*,[9] while Carrie Underwood not only became probably the most successful American Idol contestant in terms of record sales, but has appeared in both film and numerous television series or specials (i.e., *The Sound of Music Live!*). In both instances, either the networks or the performers were able to synergistically parlay their fame in one medium into another to a lesser or greater extent.

"Cibo Matto can clog dance?" Drama, Music, and Synergy in Teen Television

Given the limited space on the broadcast spectrum, it was always a challenge to introduce a new network beyond what was known as The Big Three: CBS, ABC, and NBC. Fox succeeded not only by buying up local stations not already affiliated with a network, with its biggest acquisition, Metromedia (created in the wake of the DuMont Network's demise), giving it affiliate stations in the major media markets, but also by branding itself as a viable alternative to the other networks. One way they managed this is by appealing to demographics overlooked by the Big Three, including (at the time) teens and viewers of color, as well as green-lighting series that would have been considered too odd or untested for the other networks. This included a series about a thirty-year-old paperboy, played by Chris Elliot, who lived with his parents, as well as a sketch show from British comedian Tracey Ullman, which featured end-of-episode cartoons about a family called the Simpsons. On the teen side, Fox gave its own spin to the police drama with *21 Jump Street* (1987–1991), about a group of young detectives tasked to go undercover at high schools to ferret out crime, *Parker Lewis Can't Lose* (1990–1993), which took (light) inspiration from *Ferris Bueller's Day Off* (1986) to tell the story of the misadventures and shenanigans of its eponymous hero and his friends, and hit the jackpot with a fish-out-of-water drama about a brother and sister who relocate from Minnesota to Beverly Hills and navigate a whole different culture—and income bracket—called *Beverly Hills, 90210* (1990–2000).

These three shows ended up setting up how subsequent teen dramas would unfold, particularly around music. Musicians had appeared on television series before; Davy Jones appeared on the third season of *The Brady Bunch*, in an episode unsurprisingly titled "Getting Davy Jones."[10] *WKRP in Cincinnati*, set in a radio station that had recently changed its format from easy listening to rock, featured a huge variety of music, including Blondie, the Rolling Stones, Ray Charles, Bob Dylan, Chicago, and the Beatles, among many others. (As might be imagined, the process to get permission for even some of the music meant the complete series didn't appear on DVD until 2018.) Between these three Fox shows, however, they incorporated contemporary music into their soundtracks that often spoke to the mood or theme of the plot (i.e., an episode of *21 Jump Street* about a young man who goes absent without leave from a military academy featured "Orange Crush" by R.E.M., a song about the horrors inflicted by the US military in Vietnam).[11] Ozzy Osbourne, Weird Al, and Taime Down (from Faster Pussycat) all cameoed on *Parker Lewis Can't Lose*, either as themselves (Ozzy) or as extras.[12] *Beverly Hills, 90210*, however, not only included contemporary songs on their soundtrack, but starting with the fifth season, added a music venue (Peach Pit After Dark) that featured bands such as The Flaming Lips, The Barenaked Ladies, Collective Soul, Luther

Vandross, and The Cramps, among dozens of others. In a bit of a throwback to earlier shows, Jamie Walters, who played a musician boyfriend of Donna's (Tori Spelling), headed up an Aaron Spelling series, *The Heights* (1992), a teen drama about a band trying to break into the business. When it was canceled after one season, Spelling moved him over to *90210*; his first album debuted around the same time.

Given the success of Fox, Warner Brothers, Paramount, and Viacom elected to make a move into television, forming the WB and UPN networks in 1995. The WB in particular focused on teen/young adult programming, starting with *Buffy the Vampire Slayer* in 1997, followed by *Charmed* (1998–2006) and *Dawson's Creek* in 1998, *Roswell* and *Angel* in 1999, *Smallville* in 2001, and after a string of one-season wonders, *Supernatural* in 2005. (*Everwood* [2002–2006] did have a teen protagonist, Ephram [Gregory Smith], but the narrative revolved around both Ephram and his father, Andy [Treat Williams], and it is thus harder to classify as a teen drama.) All of them, however, incorporated contemporary rock and pop music into their soundtracks. Like *90210*, three of them also incorporated a space in which bands could perform: The Talon on *Smallville*, P3 on *Charmed*, and The Bronze on *Buffy*. (*Angel* also featured a music venue, but it was a karaoke bar called Caritas, and did not generally feature bands.)

This, plus the soundtracks, became an excellent venue for synergy between Warner Brothers' television and music divisions. On the soundtrack side, series were given access to music by Warner Brothers' artists in exchange for a mention at the end of episodes; i.e., "Tonight's episode of *Dawson's Creek* featured music by . . . " and letting viewers know they could buy the artist's album on the Warner Brothers website. In this instance, the network didn't need to license music from outside of their own company for use on these programs. It should be noted that this was only for initial airings and broadcast reruns; for *Charmed*, *Dawson's Creek*, and *Felicity* (among a few others), music from individual episodes, and, in the case of both *Charmed* and *Dawson's*

Creek, the theme songs, were changed for streaming and DVD releases. This was for one very simple reason: the shows themselves were created by different production companies and were themselves licensed to the WB. *Charmed* was created by Spelling Television, *Dawson's Creek* by Sony Pictures Television, and *Felicity* by Touchstone Television, meaning they would have to pay Warner Brothers to continue to use the music on DVD and streaming. *Smallville*, on the other hand, was produced by Warner Brothers; its WB music was not replaced.

With one exception, neither *Buffy the Vampire Slayer* nor *Supernatural*—the last original genre show to debut on the WB—faced the licensing problems of their cohorts. *Buffy*, which launched the WB's rebranding into a teen network, rarely used Warner Brothers' music on either the soundtrack or as performers in the in-universe all-ages club The Bronze. While some better-known artists appeared on the show, including Cibo Matto, Aimee Mann, and the Breeders, the show often relied on indie or unsigned bands, which would be more realistic for a small club in a mid-sized California town.[13] *Supernatural*, however, took a different approach. A series about two brothers, Dean and Sam Winchester, from Kansas who were raised to fight demons and other supernatural creatures—known as "hunters"—series creator Eric Kripke had particular ideas of the kind of music that the brothers would listen to, as well as would appear within episodes: classic rock. That is, Led Zeppelin, Bob Segar, the Rolling Stones, Bon Jovi (who rock "on occasion" according to Dean),[14] and others. Indeed, he threatened to "walk" if the network did not accede to his demands to include these artists in the show, as they represented both the taste of the brothers as well as served to deepen narrative and characterization.[15] He won the fight, with music from Seger, Bon Jovi, Triumph, and Kansas appearing across all seasons of the show. (Kansas's "Carry On Wayward Son," which was used at the start of every season finale starting with season two of the show, became the unofficial theme song of the series.) While Led Zeppelin's songs appeared only as episode titles—Zeppelin's music was too expensive to license—even the Rolling Stones made an appearance in the episode "Family Feud"; "Play with Fire" is played during a tense confrontation between witch Rowena (Ruth Connell) and her son Crowley (Mark Sheppard).[16] The same music appeared on the DVDs, setting them apart from both other WB shows and series such as *WKRP in Cincinnati* (1978–1982), for whom gaining the rights to the music played in the episodes would make a DVD release cost-prohibitive. Obviously, there was no way a show like *WKRP* could have anticipated TV on DVD in the late 1970s; later shows like *Moonlighting*, *Murphy Brown* (1988–1998), and *Homicide: Life on the Street* (1993–1999) also fell foul of this, making them challenging to release on either DVD or streaming. Even *Supernatural*'s first season, when it was licensed to Netflix, was forced to replace its music with more generic offerings; because the music was so often tied to plot or character, season one on streaming offers a somewhat different viewing experience of certain episodes than those who watched it on DVD or terrestrial television. The ability of both *Buffy* and *Supernatural* to essentially curate their series' music without relying on the Warner Brothers catalog sets them apart from their contemporaries, at least in the ability to choose beyond a particular set of music and genre.

The use of Warner Brothers' music, however, did not carry over in the same way when the WB merged with rival network UPN in 2006 to form the CW. Aside from some holdovers from the original networks, most of the successful series on the then-new network took a cue from the last new WB show, *Supernatural*, and aged up its protagonists to at least college-aged, if not older. Moreover, while *Supernatural* would hold its own for fifteen seasons, it was not the series that defined the network as much as what came to be called the *Arrow*verse. That is, the show based on the DC Comics hero Green Arrow debuted in 2012 and was quickly spun off into several other series based on heroes like the Flash, Black Lightning, Batwoman, Supergirl, and several others; by the mid-2010s, they constituted six series on the CW. (Two other comics-based series, *Riverdale* [2017–2023], based on the Archie comics, and *iZombie*

[2015–2019], from the DC Vertigo line, were unrelated to the *Arrowverse*.) None of these series necessarily lent themselves to the use of contemporary music in the same ways as their predecessors. They did attempt to revive both *Roswell* and *Charmed* from the WB era, with one aging up the characters from high school to post-college (*Roswell, New Mexico* [2019–2022]), and one aging them down (*Charmed* [2018–2022]). The new *Charmed* did not feature live or soundtrack music to the same extent as the original; *Roswell, New Mexico*, however, blended contemporary and 90s-era music into each episode, with each episode's title corresponding to a 90s hit song. *Crazy Ex-Girlfriend*, as I will discuss in Chapter 9, featured original music and performances in every episode.

Long before "synergy" was an advertising buzzword, television found ways to either create or enhance its performers on both their original medium and a new one. Shows like *The Partridge Family* and *The Monkees* latched onto youth culture not only by building series focused on making music, but ones that ended up creating careers for the musicians/actors, leading to the idea that it could work the other way around (the actor/musician), as witnessed by the brief—if popular—releases and subsequent music careers of John Travolta, Leif Garrett, and Jack Wagner. While this sort of cross-career promotion tapered off after the 1980s (aside from aforementioned *The Heights*, which blended the *90210* style drama into a story about a band trying to make the big time), it instead morphed into either reality series about or used to launch singing careers, or a more subtle branching out of TV stars into the music space, with occasional in-universe performances.

The WB, on the other hand, employed a different kind of synergy by incorporating the music arm of their business into the television side, which worked as promotion for both series and artists, whether through an end card mention or full-on soundtrack albums featuring said bands, not unlike John Hughes and others did with the teen films of the 1980s; the shows got a boost from association with contemporary music, as did the musicians with programs popular with teens. While these later series would not be considered musicals by any definition, music was nonetheless integral in many of them in terms of mood, plot, and characterization, and reflecting the ways in which teens and young adults often define themselves by the music they listen to, and frequently used in the same way as regular musicals in deepening or advancing stories and characters.

4

How the Sausage Is Made: *Fame*, *Smash*, and the Backstage Musical

Media studies scholar Richard Dyer defined three general categories of musicals: (1) those in which the narrative and the musical numbers are separated (e.g., backstage musicals); (2) those structured with the narrative representing the various problems of the character, while the musical numbers function as an escape; the numbers are integrated through "cueing" for the song; or (3) those that dissolve the walls between narrative and number.[1] While not as common as the other forms discussed, the "backstage" musical, in which the narrative revolves around rehearsal and production of songs or performances, enjoyed an early prominence in films like Busby Berkeley's *42nd Street* (1933) or *Gold Diggers of 1933* (1933). Plays such as *Noises Off* (1983) use a similar structure, in which the bulk of the action takes place backstage, with only occasional views of the play in question. These types of stories have a whiff of the metafictional about them, in that they are primarily focused on the creation of a story or performance, rather than the performance itself. *Kiss Me, Kate* (1948), a musical about the backstage drama between the two stars of a production of Shakespeare's *The Taming of the Shrew*, embraces this idea, particularly since it was apparently based on producer Arnold Saint-Subber's interactions with famous acting couple Alfred Lunt and Lynn Fontaine, who apparently argued both on- (as Petruchio and Katherine) and off-stage,[2] adding additional self-reflective layers to the story. British writer Noel Streatfeild built a career on writing for children about the process of the performing arts in what are known (in the United States) as the Shoe Books: *Ballet Shoes* (1936), *Theater Shoes* (UK title: *Curtain Up*) (1944), *Movie Shoes* (UK: *The Painted Garden*) (1949), and *Dancing Shoes* (UK: *Wintle's Wonders*) (1957), all of which focus more on learning the craft, auditions, and performing challenges than the performances themselves.

While early television shows like *The Dick Van Dyke Show* (1961–1966) focused equally on Rob Petrie's (Dick Van Dyke) home life and job as a television writer, the sort of backstage stories mentioned above tended to remain in film, theater, and novels. This changed with the television adaptation of the film *Fame* in 1982. Set at the New York School for the Performing Arts, it mixed teen- and school-based drama with the challenges of breaking into the performing arts (dance, music, theater). (It was also an early showcase for future stars such as Janet Jackson.) Yet it didn't produce spin-offs or copycats until the 2000s, with the debut of shows such as *Nashville* and *Smash*, whose narratives similarly turned on the challenges of not only breaking into these industries, but the work that goes into performance itself.

"Fame costs, and right here is where you start paying": *Fame* and the Challenges of Training

In 1982, *Fame*, the series, was merely the latest television series based on a movie, with the most successful being *M*A*S*H* (1972–1983), which was still airing at the time *Fame* debuted. These adaptations tend to work best when the premise of the original easily lends itself to multiple stories that couldn't fit in the shorter film running time. The challenges of a mobile army hospital in a war zone, filled with doctors, nurses, administrators, soldiers, and enemy combatants, could supply numerous permutations that could be dramatic, comedic, or both. The series *Buffy the Vampire Slayer*, based on the 1992 film of the same name, was in part driven by its screenwriter's disappointment in the final product, but the positioning of his heroine on a "hellmouth" that attracts any number of monsters provided a wealth of potential plots.[3] Conversely, a show like CBS's *Uncle Buck* (1990), based on John Hughes comedy of the year before about the ne'er-do-well slob of an uncle who has to take (temporary) responsibility for his nieces and nephew during a family crisis, might be enough to sustain a 90-minute film, but harder to stretch into 22 episodes per season. (It probably didn't help that the TV show started by killing off the parents.[4])

Fame's source material and premise fall into the former category. The 1980 film follows the lives of a group of students focused on dance, drama, and music throughout their four years of high school.[5] Given the film's running time (just over two hours), the series allowed the existing stories to be deepened and new ones to be told. It was also one of the rare instances in which multiple actors reprised their roles from the film in the series, including Debbie Allen as dance teacher Lydia Grant, Lee Curreri as Bruno, a musician, Albert Hague as music teacher Professor Shorofsky, and Gene Anthony Ray as Leroy, a dance major. Characters such as Coco Hernandez, played by Irene Cara in the film, and Montgomery McNeil (Paul McCrane) were also transitioned to the series, with Erica Gimpel playing Coco and P. R. Paul as Montgomery. (Unfortunately, Montgomery was straight-washed in the series, erasing his character development in the film; the character ended up appearing only in the first season and the series finale.)

What sets *Fame* apart from later series like *Glee* and *Smash*, which similarly focus on performance preparation, is the lack of a single performance goal that unites them. For *Glee*, it is preparing for various competitions, and *Smash*, putting together a musical (or two); only *Nashville* comes closest, as its main singers and songwriters are frequently in competition for gigs and contracts.

It is set at the real-life High School of Performing Arts in Manhattan, which offers both academic and studio programs in dance, drama, fine arts, and music, three of which are the focus of both the film and the series. There is no single performance or venue for which the students are preparing, but a career. It also weaves in high-school drama, including a conflict between the football team and dancers over the use of the gym or the challenges of a school election and particular tropes of teen drama (especially in the 1980s), such as pregnancy scares or drunk driving.[6] These events, however, occur within the context of preparing for (and attending) auditions, attempting to launch a stand-up career, or getting work.[7] It also suggests that success isn't guaranteed even for those who make it through the program.

Like *Smash* and *Nashville*, music was an integral part of the show, although it didn't play as large a role as in other shows. It mixed original compositions, like "I Still Believe in Me," with known songs, including "Sing Sing Sing (with a Swing)," particularly in its first season.[8] Yet it also integrated concert

FIGURE 4.1 ***The kids from* Fame *take to the streets. NBC / Photofest © NBC.***

episodes, in which the cast of the series would perform as themselves, rather than in character. "The Kids from *Fame* in Concert"[9] aired near the end of the second season, although it was basically a recording of a concert the cast performed in England. Both seasons three and four offered two: "The Kids From 'Fame' in Israel" combined performance with a bit of a travelogue, and "Fame Looks at Music '83" featured cast performing covers of that year's most popular songs, including two covers of Prince ("Little Red Corvette" and "1999"), Bonnie Tyler's "Total Eclipse of the Heart," and Pat Benatar's "Love Is a Battlefield" among many others.[10] Season four, the last season to feature these concert episodes, also aired two, "The Heart of Rock 'N' Roll Part 1" and "The Heart of Rock 'N' Roll Part 2," the first of which focused on the music of the 1950s and 1960s, and the second of which offered more contemporary covers.[11] All of these were filmed performances in different venues, both in the United States and abroad. (They also might be the reason why only the first two seasons were released on DVD, and the original series isn't available on streaming.) Yet this hadn't been common, nor was it adopted by other musical series, with only 2015's *Crazy Ex-Girlfriend* doing something similar for its final episode.[12] Original songs became less frequent as the series moved from prime time into first-run syndication following its second season, but performance preparation remained centered within the series' narrative. Moreover, the series had a significant bench of guest stars from the world of entertainment, from the well-known (Milton Berle in "Coco Returns"; Joan Baez in "Tomorrow's Children"; Gwen Verden in "Come One, Come All") to the up-and-coming (Malcolm Jamal-Warner in "Ending on a High Note"; Fran Drescher in "Metamorphosis"; and Don Cheadle in "Choices").[13] For actors like Jamal-Warner, Drescher, and Cheadle, as well as Janet Jackson, who was in the main cast for the series' fourth season, *Fame* was an early break, serving as an audition in and of itself.

Bombshell? *Smash, Nashville,* and the Year of the Backstage Musical

In 1990, both NBC and Fox aired new series that were directly or indirectly based on/inspired by John Hughes' 1986 love letter to Chicago, *Ferris Bueller's Day Off*. It's unclear why, considering more than four years had passed since the movie had been released, and there was little indication that the viewing audience was clamoring for a weekly foray into Ferris's world. Nonetheless, both *Ferris Bueller* (NBC) and *Parker Lewis Can't Lose* (Fox) debuted in the 1990 season. Hughes himself refused to be involved with the *Ferris Bueller* television series; the pilot episode responded by suggesting that the film was an in-name-only version of his life and chain-sawing a cutout of Matthew Broderick as Ferris.[14] It was canceled after thirteen episodes. *Parker Lewis*, however, seemed to capture more of the "anything can happen" spirit of the source material; it was likely that, and airing on the then more teen-oriented Fox, that helped it run for three. (They also took a jab at the canceled *Ferris Bueller* series in their first season finale.[15])

This wasn't the first time—or the last—that similarly themed series would debut and air around the same time, without any real explanation as to why these shows aired at this time. *The Addams Family* (ABC) and *The Munsters* (CBS), both of which used a Gothic aesthetic (to varying degrees) and were known as the "spooky" sitcoms,[16] both debuted in 1964 and both ran for exactly two seasons. Like *Parker* and *Ferris*, however, both series took a slightly different approach: *The Munsters* was more about the Munster family, the majority of whom corresponded to Universal-era monsters (Frankenstein, Wolf Boy, vampires) trying to fit into suburbia, while *The Addams Family* focused on how suburbia responds to the Addams, who embraced their Gothic-ness enthusiastically. Based on the popularity of *Star Wars* in 1977, *Battlestar Galactica* debuted on ABC in 1978 and *Buck Rogers in the 25th*

Century on NBC in 1979, the latter of which was based on existing material (a radio serial from 1932 to 1947) but also hoping to cash in on the science fiction craze generated by *Star Wars*. In 1994, *Chicago Hope* (CBS) and *ER* (NBC), both set in Chicago hospitals, debuted within a day of each other before going head-to-head on Thursday nights. (*ER* won the ratings battle and ran nine seasons longer than *Chicago Hope*.)

In 2012, both NBC and ABC debuted shows that fit into the backstage musical genre, the first ones since *Fame* went off the air in 1987. In some respects, *Glee* could fit into this category, as preparing and enacting performances is its overarching plot, but it also branches out into other, non-Glee Club related stories, while series such as *Fame* are almost entirely focused on the minutiae of performance and preparation and how that affects their personal and professional lives. These two series were *Smash* (NBC), which focused on the producers, directors, and actors preparing to launch a Broadway musical (*Bombshell*) based on the life of Marilyn Monroe, and *Nashville* (ABC), which initially revolved around the rivalry between Rayna (Connie Britton), a more old-school country music star, and the younger Juliette (Hayden Panettiere), who fits more into the country pop genre, giving it a bit of an *All About Eve* vibe. Both featured original songs; both also incorporated some covers. One of these series was canceled after two seasons; the other lasted for four on broadcast and was picked up for an additional two seasons on cable. While there were slight differences, both fit comfortably into the same genre, and yet only one succeeded.

Smash had a significant pedigree in terms of both production and casting. Steven Spielberg served as co-executive producer, and Anjelica Huston was cast as one of the leads. Theresa Rebeck, whose play *Mauritius* debuted on Broadway in 2007, and had numerous film and television writing credits before *Smash* debuted, served as showrunner. Marc Shaiman and Scott Wittman wrote most of the original music featured on the show; Shaiman is an EGOT (Emmy, Grammy, Oscar, Tony) winner with an extensive resume across theater, film, and television, and Wittman had directed several concerts for singers like Bette Midler and Patti LuPone and worked with Shaiman on *Hairspray*. The network went all in, with the pilot costing approximately $7.5 million to produce and with an additional $25 million for promotion.[17] The premise itself—the development and performance of a Broadway show—has drama naturally baked into it. Indeed, its pilot episode debuted to a significant amount of critical acclaim,[18] with particular praise for the original song "Let Me Be Your Star," sung as a duet in the pilot by Karen (Katherine McPhee) and Ivy (Megan Hilty) at their audition for the role of Marilyn Monroe (and reprised numerous times throughout the series' two seasons). And yet the critical consensus darkened and the viewing numbers trailed off as the first season went on, faulting the writing as messy and the characterizations as "one-dimensional caricatures."[19] There were complaints that the series focused less on the backstage and musical elements to zero in on the characters' personal lives.[20] Like *Cop Rock*, it also got dinged for bizarre tonal shifts and musical numbers that made little sense in the context of the story.[21]

Perhaps the biggest element working against *Smash* was, ironically, the amount of actual backstage drama during the making of the show. There were significant conflicts between Rebeck, the showrunner for the first season, Spielberg, and the network, all of whom had different ideas about story arcs and characterization. Robert Greenblatt, who had brought the show's concept with him when he started at NBC, had particular ideas as to how it should go, and Rebeck based the songwriter characters of Julia (Debra Messing) and Tom (Christian Borle) on herself and her husband, which complicated things in terms of how close to "real life" their portrayals were. (More writing guides than anyone can count have cautioned about the dangers of basing characters on oneself, particularly because one's instinct is to shield that character from harm and the subsequent growth it can engender.) While Rebeck had writing experience, she did not have showrunning experience and was thus paired with David Marshall Grant, who'd worked on the series *Brothers and Sisters*

(2006–2011). This was common practice; in the final four seasons of *Supernatural*, for instance, Robert Singer, who'd served as showrunner on previous projects and had a lengthy history with the show, was paired with the newest, and last, showrunner of the long-running series, Andrew Dabb. Some characters, whom Spielberg apparently liked, rose to greater prominence, and it was reported that Rebeck and Spielberg apparently clashed over certain casting and writing decisions.[22] Rebeck was let go at the end of the first season, to be replaced by Josh Safran, who worked on the CW's *Gossip Girl* (2007–2012).

The series got more self-referential following Rebeck's departure, with the second season premiere taking shots at Rebeck's self-insert, Julia, when the premiere of *Bombshell* bombs,[23] and adding a second, rival musical coming out of an off-Broadway production, called *The Hit List*. This was not uncommon; shows like *Rent* came to Broadway through Off-Broadway, a connection the show underscores by casting Jesse L. Martin, who originated the role of Tom Collins in its Off-Broadway debut, transitioning to playing Tom in the Broadway and West End productions as well as in the 2005 film adaptation. It also offers a neat stand-in for the shifting showrunners and their different visions for *Smash* itself. None of this, however, was enough to save it from the indignity of being moved to Saturdays (when few are expected to watch) before finally being canceled.

Nashville, on ABC, garnered much better reviews and less bad press than its competition on NBC. Created by Callie Khouri, who'd written the screenplay for *Thelma and Louise* (1991) as well as others (including directing *Divine Secrets of the Ya-Ya Sisterhood* [2002]), it also provided an opportunity to work with her husband, musician and composer T Bone Burnett, during the first season. The series focuses on the lives of various country music artists in Nashville, with a particular focus on the conflict between Rayna's more classic country style (à la Faith Hill or Reba McEntire) and Juliette's pop-country style, like *American Idol* winner Carrie Underwood. (Later episodes would add stories for upcoming singer-songwriter Scarlett [Clare Bowen], who works at a local cafe.) Like *Smash*, it blended the stories of its singers' and songwriters' professional and personal lives and offered a mix of original songs and country standards. Like the real Nashville, however, the series not only used Burnett and others for songwriting but also "scouted" around Nashville for unsigned and up-and-coming musicians, whose songs would go on to be incorporated in the series (and appear on the soundtracks released later).[24] Characters within the series, such as Gunnar (Sam Palladio) and Avery (Jonathan Jackson), are the in-show equivalent to these artists.[25] Places like the Bluebird Cafe, a haven and launching pad for musicians from Kathy Mattea to Garth Brooks, are a regular part of the series' storylines.

While *Nashville* is arguably just as soapy as *Smash*, with stories that involve car crashes and comas, assassinations, and emotional spirals that end in accidental death, it lasted for six seasons (the final two on cable channel Country Music Television, appropriately) while *Smash* only managed two.[26] There was backstage drama on *Nashville* as well; T Bone Burnett left after the first season, not only due to his commitment to the show being completed but, in his own words, because he didn't like how the ABC network executives treated Khouri.[27] Yet, unlike *Smash*, these backstage issues did not become the dominant story told about the series. Despite its status as a prime-time soap opera, Khouri indicated that she did strive for realism in terms of the dynamics of the country music scene in *Nashville*: "*Nashville* does an impressive job of weaving in real artists, events, ABC news programs and venues to help lend to the show's authenticity."[28] Indeed, by the later seasons, after Rayna's death in a car accident,[29] it is Juliette who becomes the aging star looking for a comeback, and Rayna's daughter Maddie (Lennon Stella) who is the young ingenue, suggesting the relentless forward momentum of the entertainment industry.

So why did *Nashville* succeed where *Smash* failed? The aforementioned authenticity, including incorporating the Bluebird Cafe into the narrative, was a likely factor. The city of Nashville also benefited from the series; apparently, 1 out of 5 visitors to the city were there as fans of the series, prompting its tourism board to add *Nashville*-themed tours and events to significant financial benefit.[30] (Albuquerque, New Mexico, did the same when *Breaking Bad* became a cultural phenomenon, with themed tours and merchandise.[31]) Despite the millions spent on publicity, and scheduling it to follow the highly rated reality singing competition *The Voice*, NBC in 2012 was in a weaker position than ABC in terms of ratings. *Nashville* had the benefit of airing between *Castle* (2009–2016) and *Glee*, the latter of which was also a musical series. Putting aside the backstage drama, network issues, and scheduling, it might be, however, that *Nashville*'s subject matter, country music, appealed to a larger audience segment than Broadway musicals.

Musicals on their own aren't the easiest sell on television. Shows like *Fame* and *Nashville* had multi-season runs; *Smash* only lasted two. *Cop Rock* managed to eke out eleven episodes, but *Viva Laughlin*, adapted from the critically acclaimed BBC series *Blackpool* (*Viva Blackpool* abroad) only aired two of its five filmed episodes before it was pulled from CBS's schedule, with reviews referring to it as a "train wreck" or "worst new show of the season," despite star Hugh Jackman's acknowledged singing talent.[32] (Further, what works for UK viewers doesn't always resonate for US ones; see the US version of *Coupling*.) All three of the series discussed previously do address one of the issues that can plague musical series: there is a compelling reason for characters to sing, whether in rehearsals, Broadway shows, or Nashville cafes.

The thing that sets these three series apart from their other musical brethren, however, is their focus on the process of performance. As a series, *Fame* set the standard, focusing on a variety of performing arts to show viewers exactly how much work goes into its creation. While it did not do well enough in the ratings to stay in prime time in the United States, it was enormously popular in the United Kingdom, with at least three concerts performed there during the run of the series. In 2008, Channel 4 aired a reunion special, "Bring Back . . . *Fame*," that brought together several members of the cast, and in 2022, there was a fan-organized *Fame* convention ("Fame UK Reunion 2022") to celebrate the fortieth anniversary of the series debut, featuring selected cast members and a performance to raise money for Claire House Children's Hospice. It's conceivable that the series resonated in the UK, which continues to have a lively theater culture, as well as being the setting for Noel Streatfeild's "Shoe" books, themselves "backstage" stories praised for the accuracy of the depiction of the process in the first half of the twentieth century. While all three series blended these backstage elements with dramatic stories, what perhaps set *Fame* and *Nashville* apart from the less successful *Smash* was both of the former finding a balance between the drama of performance and interpersonal drama. As dance teacher Linda Grant (Debbie Allen) says in the first episode, anyone who pursues the performing arts will "pay in sweat";[33] these series offered a glimpse at what exactly that would entail.

PART TWO

WITH A SONG IN THEIR HEARTS: WHEN TELEVISION GOES MUSICAL

5

"And You Can Sing Along": *Buffy*, *Scrubs*, and Beyond

Possibly the easiest genre to incorporate a musical episode would be the sci-fi/fantasy genre. Unlike, for example, the police procedural, it takes less of a suspension of disbelief that television shows that feature demons, gods, or time/space travel to come up with a scenario that makes everyone burst into song. That didn't keep numerous shows from trying, from the *Beavis and Butthead* (1993–1997) spin-off *Daria* (1997–2002) and its "Daria!" musical episode to the Randy Newman–fest *Ally McBeal* (1997–2002) season finale.[1] In all fairness, one was animated and the other embraced a heightened reality—e.g., the "dancing baby" in "Cro-Magnon"[2]—from early on, so it's not entirely surprising they'd go musical. The same goes for *Northern Exposure* (1990–1995), and "Old Tree";[3] a character temporarily able only to sing rather than speak fits in with the series quirky narrative and aesthetic. Yet with the successful debut of "Once More, With Feeling" during the sixth season of *Buffy the Vampire Slayer* (2001), shows across the genre spectrum seemed interested in trying their hand at the one-off musical episode, with varying degrees of success.

While *Buffy*'s position as a critically acclaimed prime-time series meant that it got more attention, the single-episode musical episode spree that kicked off in the early 2000s actually started with first-run syndication series *Xena: Warrior Princess*

("The Bitter Suite"),[4] a show that boasted a fair degree of viewer/fan crossover with *Buffy*. While musical episodes in the 2000s, showing up in everything from medical dramas to sitcoms, were a mix of originals and jukebox, this chapter will examine musicals written by either the series' writers (e.g., *Supernatural*'s "Fan Fiction" high school musical) or those that imported pedigreed composers and lyricists to work alongside the series' staff, allowing both actors and writers to showcase performance elements outside of the usual fare.

"Get your kumbaya-yas out": *Buffy* and the In-House Musical

As suggested above, some series more naturally lend themselves to taking a musical detour for an episode (or more than one). Teen dramas in particular, in which the soundtrack can be as much a part of the narrative as the dialogue, can be a perfect venue for having its cast burst into song; for example, while never doing a full musical episode, *Dawson's Creek* first season featured a performance of "On My Own" from *Les Misérables* performed by Katie Holmes' Joey Potter at a beauty pageant and *Roswell* featured a character, Maria DeLuca (Majandra Delfino), who explores becoming a professional singer and performs several songs.[5] The former worked well on a narrative level; "On My Own" is a song about unreciprocated love, which was a big part of Joey's arc in the first season of the show, and Majandra Delfino has mixed singing and acting for most of her career. More recently, *Riverdale* (2017–2023) dedicated more than one episode to its high school's musical performances of shows like *Heathers: The Musical* and *Hedwig and the Angry Inch*.[6] The heightened emotion of adolescence and young adulthood works well with the heightened emotions created by music.

The combination of heightened emotions and repressed feelings forms the basis of "Once More, With Feeling," the musical episode of *Buffy the Vampire*

Slayer. The basic premise of the show itself is that the town of Sunnydale, California, is situated on top of a hellmouth, which attracts vampires and demons from around the world. Buffy Summers (Sarah Michelle Gellar) is the Slayer, a young woman invested with super-strength and thus the ability to fight monsters. She is joined in this fight by her friends Willow (Alyson Hannigan), a powerful witch, and Xander (Nicholas Brendan), as well as Rupert Giles (Anthony Stewart Head), who acts as trainer and guide (known as a Watcher). By the sixth season of the show, when this episode aired, her circle of friends had grown to include a mystically created sister Dawn (Michelle Trachtenberg), Willow's girlfriend Tara (Amber Benson), Xander's fiancée Anya (Emma Caulfield), and Spike (James Marsters), a vampire foe turned reluctant ally when his ability to feed on or otherwise physically harm humans was taken away; he eventually develops an (unrequited) crush on Buffy.[7] By this point in the series, Buffy has died (twice, although the first death was only a few minutes long) and has recently been resurrected by her friends, particularly Willow, invoking dark magic to bring her back to life out of worry that her death at the end of the previous season might have sent her to a hell dimension.[8] Willow, who discovered her magical abilities in the second season of the show,[9] has grown increasingly powerful and willing to use magic for almost any reason, something that scares Tara, who is also a witch. On a less mystical level, Xander and Anya are experiencing fairly normal fears about their impending marriage that they struggle to share with each other. It is Buffy, however, who is hiding the biggest secret: the spell that resurrected her pulled her out of a heaven-like existence, and she has struggled to adjust to being alive in a world she feels is its own hell: "everything here is hard and bright and violent."[10]

It is into this mess that Sweet (Hinton Battle), a musical demon, appears. His presence makes everyone in town sing about their deepest secrets or desires or fears; however, as becomes clear, if left unchecked "some customers just start combusting."[11] While he doesn't actually appear in the episode until the first act break, his influence is felt by all of the Sunnydale residents, who sing about a variety of issues, from a stained shirt ("They Got the Mustard Out!") to the opening number, in which Buffy laments her inability to reconnect to life ("Going Through the Motions"). Unsurprisingly, the episode is highly self-aware, which would become a feature, not a bug, for musical episodes going forward. Everyone is aware they are singing; they even sing about trying to figure out why they're singing, in a number that lists several of the threats they'd faced before ("I've Got a Theory"). As the episode progresses, however, the songs get deeper into the issues plaguing all of them, whether it's Xander and Anya's fears over their relationship and upcoming marriage ("I'll Never Tell"), Tara's love song to Willow ("Under Your Spell") taking on a darker tone in its reprise when she realizes Willow used magic on her to forget a fight, or Giles' worries that his presence is holding Buffy back from dealing with adulthood ("Standing in the Way"). This culminates in a big ensemble number ("Walk Through the Fire"), as Buffy goes to face down Sweet (who kidnapped Dawn; "Dawn's in trouble? Must be Tuesday" is Buffy's initial response). It is during this confrontation that Buffy reveals her big secret: her friends pulled her out of heaven, not hell, and attempts to dance herself to death to escape ("Life's a Show"). She is saved by Spike, who reminds her that living is hard, but worth it. Sweet, not entirely defeated, nonetheless leaves, with a final song sung by the ensemble trying to figure out their next moves, literally and figuratively ("Where Do We Go From Here?").[12]

Written and primarily composed by creator Joss Whedon, the episode relies heavily on both the series' mythology and the musical genre across multiple iterations. On an episode level, "Once More, With Feeling" can be watched by itself, but takes on additional dimensions to those familiar with the series (e.g., "I Have a Theory" makes more than one reference to previous episodes, stretching back to the first season of the show). Further, while the songs are original, they nonetheless pay tribute to particular source material. Whedon himself points out that Buffy's opening number, "Going

Through the Motions," was inspired by Disney musicals and their use of the "I want" songs, like Ariel's "Part of Your World" in *The Little Mermaid* (1989) or "Belle" from *Beauty and the Beast* (1991). Anya and Xander's duet recalls the movie musicals of Ginger Rogers and Fred Astaire, down to their syncopated dance moves.[13] Spike's plea to Buffy to leave him alone if she can't reciprocate his feelings ("Rest in Peace") recalls the rock operas of the 1970s, while Giles' song to Buffy suggests the power ballads of the same era. Yet these choices (Disney song, rock opera, old-fashioned movie musical) are also character-appropriate. Buffy is the heroine of the series; Spike dresses like Billy Idol and embraces a 70s punk aesthetic that hides a softer and more artistic side, and Anya and Xander are following a more traditional life and relationship path than their friends, hence their more old-fashioned performance. These songs—and performances—come from a place of significant familiarity with the characters on the part of both the writer (Whedon) and the actors.

The episode also shows a significant amount of self-awareness, an element that hardens into a trope for subsequent musical episodes. Not only is everyone aware they are singing, but some are well-versed enough to know the intricacies of the genre. When Xander and Anya discuss their musical number with Giles, Anya not only points out that it felt like a performance ("there were three walls but no fourth wall") but laments that their duet is a "retro pastiche that's never gonna be a breakaway pop hit."[14] (It was not uncommon in the 1970s and 1980s for songs from musicals to hit the pop charts; "I Don't Know How to Love Him" from *Jesus Christ Superstar* [1971] was in Billboard's top 40 in 1971 and charted internationally, and "One Night in Bangkok," from the musical *Chess* [1984], topped charts in multiple countries, including the United States. Fun fact: "One Night in Bangkok" was sung by Murray Head, brother of Anthony Head, who plays Giles.) Spike, mere moments after claiming to Buffy he was "immune" to the musical curse, rolls his eyes as he bursts into song. This self-awareness is tied together in one of the final numbers of the episode, when Buffy sings about the inherent falsity of the life she's living, claiming "Life's a Show" put on for others.

The concept of lives as a performance is literalized in *Supernatural*'s "Fan Fiction," although unlike *Buffy*, none of the main cast sings in this one. The series, about two brothers who fight demons across the United States, shares more than a few elements with the earlier *Buffy*, including some storylines and cast members,[15] but unlike the more gender-balanced cast of *Buffy*, *Supernatural*'s main cast—Sam Winchester (Jared Padalecki), Dean Winchester (Jensen Ackles), and Castiel (Misha Collins)—are all men. Which makes the musical in the episode all the more interesting; it is the story of their lives written by a young woman named Marie (Katie Sarife) and featuring an all-female cast at a girls' school in Michigan. Within the world of *Supernatural*, this element was set up in the fourth season, when Sam and Dean discover that their lives had been chronicled in a series of books called *Supernatural*, written by an author named Chuck Shurley.[16] They later find themselves briefly flung into an alternate reality where *Supernatural* has been made into a television show, and they are simply actors named Jared Padalecki and Jensen Ackles.[17] That is, by this point, the metatextual element of the show had been well-established, so an all-female musical about the show was not a huge stretch by its tenth season. In this instance, they discover the production because both the drama teacher and some cast members have gone missing. (It is later revealed to be the muse of epic poetry/goddess Calliope, who in *Supernatural* protects the author and their work until their vision is realized, and then consumes them.[18])

While the episode did not go full musical—it featured only two full original songs, one short song ("I'll Just Wait Here"), and a choral version of Kansas's "Carry On Wayward Son"—the songs it did feature spoke directly to the character and episode history, particularly as seen through the series' fandom. The episode's title, "Fan Fiction," is no accident: *Supernatural: The Musical* would be considered a transformative work created by a fan, although in reality, it was written and composed by staff writer Robbie Thompson and composer Jay Gruska, both who had been with the series for several seasons. The elements that Marie chose to highlight are those that resonate with the fans: "The Road So Far," the opening song that sets the stage for the play's narrative, is the exact term used at the start of significant episodes of the show (usually the finale or season premiere) to set up the "previously on" segments. For both premieres and finales, these are usually set to music; after season one, "Carry On Wayward Son" was the go-to song for the "previously on" round-up. "A Single Man Tear" speaks to a particular episode of the series, "Heart," in which Sam had to help a woman he was falling in love with take her own life after she was infected by a werewolf. While the audience doesn't see the shot, they hear it, along with Dean, who sheds a single tear before the credits. (The scene itself is also set to music; there is no dialogue, and Queensrÿche's "Silent Lucidity" plays quietly.[19]) Lyrically, "A Single Man Tear" is sung by the play's Sam about Dean about his brother's repressed but still strong emotional core; Dean's verse about the ways he feels the need to hide that aspect of himself.

The episode also served as something of an apology to the series' fandom, which the series did not always portray in the best light. While certain elements are understandable, such as Dean and Sam's shock at the discovery of *Supernatural* fandom and fan fiction in its various iterations in "The Monster at the End of This Book,"[20] some characterizations seemed both more gratuitous and pointedly cruel. This was particularly embodied in the character of Becky Rosen (Emily Perkins), a *Supernatural* superfan who not only consistently violates Sam's personal space, but in her second-to-last appearance on the show makes a deal to magically ensnare and marry him without his consent.[21] Given that Becky is the fan the viewer sees the most of, it does suggest a certain disdain for the fandom or the works that it produces. (The final season offers a redemption of sorts for Becky, who'd built a life in which fandom was a part rather than her whole life, only for God [Rob Benedict] to make her and her family disappear.[22]) "Fan Fiction," on the other hand, actually offers tacit approval for these types of works, with Dean telling the cast:

> I know I have expressed some differences of opinion, regarding this particular version of *Supernatural*. But tonight, it is all about Marie's vision. This is Marie's *Supernatural*. So, I want you to get out there, and I want you to stand as close as she wants you to, and I want you to put as much sub and add text as you possibly can. [23]

It also adds an additional self-aware moment; when Dean quotes from "No Day But Today" from *Rent*, Marie assures another cast member that he didn't quote enough of it to "get us in trouble." This moment, and the musical itself, offers not only a brief reimagining of the series but a different way to revisit these characters and see how much they've developed over the course of the series' road thus far, and a fitting way for the show to celebrate its unprecedented (for a genre series) two hundredth episode. In particular, its focus on the act of writing and creation also offers the show a way to reflect on itself from the perspective of its creators.

"I really hope it's like a big Broadway musical": Tapping the Professionals

One potential way around the challenges of the single-episode original musical, particularly if music or performance isn't an integral part of the series, is to bring in outside lyricists and/or composers. This can represent some degree of risk, as the newcomers may not have the same sense of the characters, setting, or narrative. The best case scenario is for the individual series to collaborate with lyricists and composers whose previous work shares a similar aesthetic. Such was the case for both *Once Upon a Time* (2011–2018) and *Scrubs*' musical episodes, although the two worked in different genres.

Given the premise of the series, it was likely only a matter of time before *Once Upon a Time* tapped into the musical genre. That is, it's a fantasy series that shifts between the real world and one in which fairy tales are real; specifically, Disney's interpretation of said fairy tales. At the start of the series, the residents of the small town of Storybrooke, Maine, are revealed to be actual fairy tale characters who lost their memories and were transported to the real world via a curse cast by the evil queen Regina (Lana Parilla) at the wedding of Snow White (Ginnifer Goodwin) and Prince Charming (Josh Dallas). The only one unaffected was their daughter, Emma Swan (Jennifer Morrison), who was sent into the real world before the curse was cast. The series starts when Emma Swan is brought to Storybrooke by her son, Henry (Jared S. Gilmore), whom she'd given up for adoption when he was an infant; his adoptive mother just happens to be Regina. When she does break the curse,[24] these residents remember their real identities. Airing on ABC, which has been owned by Disney since the mid-1990s, *Once Upon a Time* was able to make use of characters not only known from fairy tales (i.e., Rumpelstiltskin [Robert Carlyle]) but also those particular to Disney's interpretation, such as Jiminy Cricket (Raphael Sbarge). (The talking cricket exists in the original story, but is not named and is squashed by Pinocchio early on, appearing as a ghost later in the story.[25]) Indeed, each season would add more characters from the Disney canon, including Belle (Emile de Ravin) from *Beauty and the Beast*, Jasmine (Karen David) and Aladdin (Deniz Akdeniz) from *Aladdin* (1992), and Elsa (Georgina Haig) from *Frozen* (2013), among others. As most Disney films fall into the musical genre, *Once Upon a Time* would not necessarily need a narrative justification for building an episode around the genre. (*Zootopia* [2016], in which Goodwin voices the main character, Judy Hopps, is a notable exception, with only a single pop song appearing in the film. The film flags up its non-musical status—and references *Frozen* [2013]—when police chief Bogo [Idris Elba] tells Judy: "Life isn't some cartoon musical where you sing a little song and your insipid dreams magically come true! So Let. It. Go."[26])

"The Song in Your Heart" shifts between the various realms of the series, from the real world to Oz and Wonderland, as well as into the characters' pasts.

Like the *Buffy* episode discussed previously, the episode is tied into the overall narrative of the season and series, making it work less as a standalone and more as a remix and extension of the show's past and present. In fact, it calls back to the first episode and the curse that made them forget their memories and exiled them from the fairy tale world.[27] That being said, the episode actually starts with Emma as a young girl (circa 1991), living in an orphanage, trying to sing into a tape recorder (she wants to perform in her home's talent show) before being discouraged by another resident. The action then shifts to the present day, with Emma and her mom (Snow White) looking at wedding dresses to prepare for Emma's upcoming wedding (to Killian [Colin O'Donoghue], aka Captain Hook), when the Black Fairy (Jaime Murray) appears to tell Emma she is planning to release a spell that will hurt everyone unless Emma gives in and gives her heart to the Black Fairy (they are destined to battle). The action then transitions to the aforementioned past, with Snow White making a wish upon a star that ends up causing them, and nearly everyone else in the fairy tale realm, to burst into song. Snow realizes that this is what can save them—and their unborn daughter—from Regina's plans. It's an interesting callback so close to the end of the season, and the departure of several cast members, reminding viewers that allies such as Regina and Zelena were once their biggest threats. In the present day, Regina vows to help, saying she won't let Emma and Hook's wedding day be ruined as she'd ruined Snow and Charming's.

Throughout the episode, the narrative shifts between the present threat and the past, with the singing initially being confined to the past sequences. Snow and Charming sing about how their love is a powerful magic itself that can defeat Regina, which Regina counters by singing "Love Doesn't Stand a Chance." When they go seek help from Hook, he agrees to assist only if they help him take revenge on Mr. Gold (Robert Carlyle). (There's also a self-aware moment, when Snow asks who Hook wants revenge against, and he sings "You'll have to wait for the second verse.") It's notable that while Snow and Charming's song ("Powerful Magic") fits more into the expected ballad type Disney's known for, those sung by either antagonistic or morally gray characters (Regina, Zelena, Hook) hew closer to the rock genre, both of which battle for supremacy in the appropriately named "Charmings vs. the Evil Queen" number. In the present day, Emma prepares to face the Black Fairy on her own, not willing to risk her loved ones or the rest of the town, and it is here in which the "meaning" of both the musical interludes and the flashback structure becomes clear: Emma has always struggled with being alone and feelings of abandonment because she was given up to avoid Regina's curse. Another flashback, in which Regina is able to silence the singing and Snow, Charming, and their unborn daughter are now vulnerable again, ends when the Blue Fairy (Keegan Connor Tracy) appears, informing them that the song magic was never meant to defeat Regina, but a bigger threat lies ahead. She uses her magic to place the music in the unborn Emma's heart, but as a consequence, no one remembers anything of it. In a fairy ex machina moment, however, Henry uncovers this fact and rushes to tell his mother. The Black Fairy's attempt to crush Emma's heart is repelled by song, and the episode ends with Emma and Hook's wedding, complete with an ensemble number "Happy Beginnings"—before the Black Fairy's curse is released and engulfs them all.[28]

Each cast member did their own singing, which is a feature of all the episodes discussed in this chapter, but as with *Scrubs* (which I'll discuss later), the series did outsource the writing of the songs to Alan Zachary and Michael Weiner. While they are not part of the regular writing team, Zachary and Weiner have worked on the musical versions of films such as *Trading Places* (1983) and *13 Going on 30* (2004), and wrote an original song for the Disney+ series *High School Musical: The Musical: The Series*. Aside from the connection to Disney that both share, Zachary and Weiner have made a career of re-imaginings and reinterpretations of properties from one medium to another, something that also represents the organizing premise of *Once Upon a Time*. In that respect, it makes them a smart choice that aligns with the narrative and overall aesthetic of the series.

Scrubs, a sitcom (sans laugh track) set in a hospital and following the challenges of interns, residents, and doctors at Sacred Heart Hospital across its nine seasons, seems a less likely venue for a musical episode. That being said, it takes its cue from earlier shows like *Parker Lewis Can't Lose* with its use of cutaways and unexpected turns, primarily filtered through the perspective of John "JD" Dorian (Zach Braff), and earlier seasons offered cast-created musical interludes, mostly through the hospital a cappella group The Worthless Peons. While these weren't full musical episodes, their song choices often reflected the action of the episode: cartoon theme songs in "My Hero," classic television theme songs in "My Nightingale," and commercial jingles in "My Kingdom." In "My Hero," in which Dr. Perry Cox (John C. McKinley) is trying to save the life of his best friend, Ben (Brendan Fraser), they sing "Underdog" to both reflect his actions and their chances of success.[29] For "My Nightingale," in which JD, and fellow interns/friends Turk (Donald Faison) and Elliot (Sarah Chalke), are on their own with no attending physician, and only Carla (Judy Reyes), head nurse and Turk's fiancée, as back-up, the Peons perform the television theme songs from *The Facts of Life* (1979–1988) and *Charles in Charge* (1984–1990), both of which focused on teen characters and the challenges of growing up.[30] While Turk, JD, and Elliot are adults, they are still young in their professional lives and experiences, so these "coming of age" type shows have a narrative resonance. The end of the episode "My Philosophy" features a heart patient named Elaine (Jill Tracy) who hopes the afterlife is like a "big Broadway show"; the final moments of the episode feature the now-deceased Elaine performing "Waiting for My Real Life to Begin" by Colin Hay while standing in a spotlight.[31] In "My Choosiest Choice of All," when a patient, Jeff (Joshua David Jordan), asks if he can perform with his band before the band (unnamed in the episode, but actually the Polyphonic Spree) leaves on tour, Dr. Cox brings them to the hospital, and the episode offers an extended performance of the band's most famous song "Follow the Day."[32]

FIGURE 5.1 ***The Polyphonic Spree performs on* Scrubs. *NBC / Photofest © NBC. Photographer: Danny Field.***

In "My Musical," however, everyone gets in on the act, and the episode, like *Buffy* before it, follows the typical act structure of a play. In the episode's cold open, JD and Elliot are relaxing in a local park when a woman, Patti Miller (Stephanie D'Abruzzo), faints. When she comes out of it, she hears everything said to her, and everything she says, as a song. She's transported to Sacred Heart, where she's taken in via an ensemble musical number ("Welcome to Sacred Heart"). Dr. Cox assumes that it's not neurological but psychological, and JD and Turk decide to run a series of tests to determine whether there is a physical cause ("Everything Comes Down to Poo"); the tests reveal nothing amiss. After Dr. Cox does one of his patented rants at JD ("The Rant Song"), Patti tries to convince him that it is a neurological problem, and he agrees to give her a CT scan; this is proceeded by another ensemble number, "When the Truth Comes Out," referencing both Patti's case, and the interpersonal issues everyone is dealing with (Carla trying to decide whether to take a leave of absence after the birth of her and Turk's daughter; Elliot trying to tell JD she doesn't want him as a roommate at her new house). An aneurysm is discovered in Patti's temporal lobe, and act one ends with Dr. Cox literally closing the curtain around her bed as he delivers the news.

Act two opens not with Patti, however, but with the aforementioned interpersonal problems between Turk and Carla and JD and Elliot, although Elliot believes Turk and JD aren't willing to talk about their feelings. This leads, however, into what became the most famous song from the episode, a duet between Turk and JD called "Guy Love," which is basically two minutes of the two of them sharing their feelings. (The song has appeared in numerous fan videos for shows from *Sherlock* [2010–2017] to *Supernatural*; Zach Braff and Donald Faison also performed it at a screening of Braff's film *Wish I Was Here*.[33]) When both Carla and Elliot finally confront Turk and JD, JD storms off, while Turk makes a mistake he's made several times when he tells Carla "I always thought family was the most important to Puerto Ricans," which prompts her to launch into "For the Last Time, I'm Dominican"; it becomes a duet, and Turk eventually comes around to her point of view, and JD and Elliot make up via an ensemble number that is clearly a riff on "We Go Together" from *Grease*. The final number transitions straight out of "Friends Forever," as Patti asks, via song, "What's Going to Happen?" as she is prepped for surgery. When she wakes up, the singing has stopped, something that JD suggests, via voiceover, she might miss a bit.[34]

While not in the sci-fi/fantasy genre, *Scrubs* shares with shows like *Northern Exposure* and *Ally McBeal* a sense of heightened reality, and the decision to include a musical episode is not as outré as one might expect. Further, like *Once Upon a Time*, the show brought in outside help, although not to the extent *Once* did. Staff writer Debra Fordham wrote most of the lyrics, while the songs were composed by regular *Scrubs* composer Jan Stevens, as well as outside composers Doug Besterman, Jeff Marx, and Robert Lopez, the latter two who also wrote the musical *Avenue Q* (2003), an adult-oriented parody of *Sesame Street* (1969–present) that featured songs like "The Internet Is for

Porn" and "What Do You Do with a B. A. in English?" On a tonal level, it's a good match; while *Scrubs* frequently touched on subjects such as disease and death, it did so with a lighter touch than series such as *ER*, and the cutaways and fantasy sequences (some of which, as discussed previously, contained musical numbers themselves) meant that "My Musical" stayed consistent with the tone of the show and a good match for a production like *Avenue Q*. (Indeed, a season two episode featured a pediatrician, Dr. Norris [Christopher Meloni], who used a puppet to communicate with his patients.[35]) While not necessarily common, episode writer Fordham did research the potential for this condition; musical hallucinations can occur with an aneurysm, as well as other neurological conditions.[36] In that respect, by using its more realistic setting, *Scrubs* managed to provide a narratively justified reason for everyone to break into song, although based on interviews with the cast, few of them needed much encouragement.

These single-episode musicals, whether created in-house or outsourced, offer a way for established series to reflect on both their pasts and what lies ahead. It is significant that all of these musical episodes debuted deep into the individual series' run; not only is the production of a musical episode much more involved, but each of these one-and-done musical episodes requires much more time and money to produce than a regular episode. Yet on a character and narrative level, these episodes work best within the musical genre when the audience is already well-versed and familiar with the show's characters and stories. While each of these episodes falls under the rubric of an "event" episode, none of them can really stand alone without the development of the world with which they are attempting to harmonize.

6

"Bloody Celestial Karaoke Jam": Pop, Rock, and Everything in Between

With the critical and ratings successes of episodes like "Once More, With Feeling" or "My Musical," other series started to incorporate musical numbers—or even an entire episode—to either original music or, taking a page from sources like *Glee* or *Mamma Mia!* (2008), what was known as the jukebox musical. A jukebox musical is essentially one in which most, if not all, the songs it contains are already known and popular, rather than featuring original compositions. While there are a few series in which this is a regular part of the narrative, others, such as *Grey's Anatomy* (2005–present), used the device for a single episode. Serving as a kind of sung soundtrack, the jukebox musical episode often allows series to showcase the vocal talents of its cast that ordinarily aren't on display (e.g., Mandy Patinkin on *Chicago Hope*). Yet, like their original music siblings, jukebox musical episodes can be used to add additional characterization and advance the plot through song choices that would be familiar to the majority of the audience.

Macking the Knife: A Brief History of the Jukebox Musical

While *Mamma Mia!*, both on Broadway and in film, is probably the best known, the jukebox musical has a much longer history than that. Comic operas in the 1700s, for instance, would use familiar songs with new lyrics as part of the libretto. John Gay's *The Beggar's Opera*, in 1728, is probably the earliest example of this, but redoing and remaking the music of one's contemporaries was not uncommon in the musical community. (A scene in the 1984 film *Amadeus* highlights this; when court composer Salieri [F. Murray Abraham] composes a welcome march for Wolfgang Mozart's [Tom Hulce] first appearance at court; Mozart rewrites it on the spot,[1] and it later appears in *The Marriage of Figaro*.) *The Beggar's Opera*'s goal was to "satirise the conventions of contemporary Italian opera of which Handel was the master and lampooned famous figures of the age";[2] an element facilitated by using well-known music. While satire is not the goal of every jukebox musical, listeners/audience would already be familiar with the songs, which means that the songs don't have to build a connection with the audience; the connections and associations would already be there. Instead, the chosen songs only have to reveal plot and character rather than establish themselves first.

There are several films, particularly in the 1940s and 1950s, that a contemporary audience wouldn't have labeled as jukebox musicals, as the songs they contain are more familiar in that context. *Singin' in the Rain* (1952) is based on Arthur Freed/Nacio Herb Brown's back catalog of songs from early cinema. Given the time period the songs were written in (the transition from silent films to "talkies"), the premise of *Singin' in the Rain* practically writes itself: a comedy about the challenges of transitioning from silent film to sound.[3] While *Rock Rock Rock!* (1956) uses a variety of early rock stars (both soundtrack and live performances), including Chuck Berry, *An American in Paris* (1951) exclusively uses famous songs from the Gershwins in a new context.[4] (One critic referred to *A Hard Day's Night* [1964] as a jukebox musical, but that is really stretching the definition, considering it was a film featuring both the Beatles and their music. A better case could probably be made for *Yellow Submarine* [1968]; it was based on their music, but didn't actually feature their voices.) And while biopics could be considered a type of jukebox musical (the artist's songs generally being performed by someone cast as them; e.g., Joaquin Phoenix and Reese Witherspoon as Johnny and June Carter Cash), that seems to stretch the definition a bit too far, and shows like *Ain't Misbehaving* (1978), which focuses solely on the music of Fats Waller, is more a revue of his work than building a plot around the song choices themselves.

In that respect—using known songs to build a story around—the jukebox musical really started to take off in the 1980s, with shows such as *Leader of the Pack* (1984) and *Forever Plaid* (1989). In keeping with the 50s nostalgia that infused the decade (*Back to the Future* [1985], *Peggy Sue Got Married* [1986], *Happy Days* [1974–1984], etc.),[5] both of these musicals were focused on music from that era. The 1990s, however, expanded on that, with shows like *Boogie Nights* (a British jukebox musical, not the film). *Boogie Nights* (1998), unsurprisingly, featured disco hits and other pop music of the 1970s to tell the story of Deb and Roddy; Roddy wants to be a rock star, while Deb slowly realizes that Roddy might not be the one for her. *Jelly's Last Jam* went back to the 1930s to tell the famous jazz musician's life through his songs. In the 2000s, shows like *Jersey Boys* (2004) told the story of Franki Valli and the Four Seasons through their songs, *We Will Rock You* (2002) offered a dystopian, corporate-controlled future in which an underground group known as the Bohemians attempt to take down the corporate overlords destroying society, while *American Idiot* (2009) focuses on three young men who are trying to make a life for themselves outside of a stifling suburban environment, with most of the featured songs taken from Green Day's *American Idiot* album. *Jagged Little Pill* (2018) used Alanis Morissette's work (with two new songs written by

Morissette specifically for the play) to tell a story about gender identity, assault, and drug use, while *MJ the Musical* (2021) uses the songs of Michael Jackson in a musical purportedly about the singer's life leading up to his 1992 Dangerous World Tour. The form itself has only increased over the past decades, with eighteen different jukebox musicals debuting between 2020 and 2024. (The latest, as of this writing, is a re-conception of the 1990s romantic comedy *My Best Friend's Wedding* featuring the music of Burt Bacharach, whose "I Say a Little Prayer" was featured in a memorable restaurant scene in the original.) In film, *Yesterday* (2019) imagines a world without the actual Beatles but with their songs,[6] and British rom-com *Walking on Sunshine* (2014) features versions of 80s pop from Madonna, Whitney Houston, Wham, Duran Duran, and others.[7] What most of these share (outside the biopic ones) is using these songs to tell an entirely new story informed by them, in a similar way to how certain songs can invoke an individual memory that may or may not be related to the song's actual content.

Of all these, however, the most famous is likely *Mamma Mia!*, both as a stage play and film. It was written by British playwright Catherine Johnson, developed with ABBA members Benny Andersson and Björn Ulvaeus, with the film being directed by Phyllida Lloyd. The plot focuses on Sophie (Amanda Seyfried), a young woman about to get married, who hatches a plan to find out who her father is so he can walk her down the aisle at her wedding. She does so by reading through her mom's old journals and realizes there are three likely candidates: Sam (Pierce Brosnan), Bill (Stellan Skarsgård), and Harry (Colin Firth). Armed with that knowledge, she invites all three—unbeknownst to her mom—and hijinks ensue when her mother, Donna (Meryl Streep), figures out they are there, and they figure out why they were invited. Interspersed throughout, the cast sings a variety of songs from ABBA's catalog, ones that coincide with the action in the scene. For example, when Sophie reads to her friends from her mother's diary (kept the year she was pregnant with Sophie), she sings ABBA's "Honey, Honey," a song about love and lust, as if it's part of the entries themselves. "SOS" is re-conceived as a duet between Donna and Sam, neither of whom seems to hear what the other is saying. While some of these work better than others ("The Name of the Game" seems an odd choice for a [potential] father and daughter conversation), they generally work as jukebox musicals are supposed to: the song choices reveal character and advance the plot. While the film eliminated some of the songs and scenes that appeared in the stage version and rearranged a couple of others, the story remains basically the same in the transition.[8] Both the play and the film were massively successful. It is the fifth longest-running show in London's West End, ran on Broadway for fourteen years, and has grossed more than $4 billion worldwide.[9] The film ended up making more than $600 million on a $50 million budget, despite receiving mixed reviews from critics. Despite individual opinions on the quality of the story or performances, it certainly did precisely what a jukebox musical is intended to do: connect (established) music and story in a new context.

"You just made me sing again!": The Jukebox Musical on TV

The twin successes of the *Mamma Mia!* film and Ryan Murphy's *Glee* in 2008 and 2009 seemed to suggest the viability of the jukebox musical in both mediums. While I'll discuss series that leaned into the jukebox musical as part of the overall series in a later chapter, musical episodes of both the original and jukebox variety grew throughout the 2000s, often appearing in unexpected series. The seventh season of *Grey's Anatomy* used the accident and resulting coma of Dr. Calle Torres (Sara Ramirez) as a set piece for several musical numbers based on contemporary songs that had previously appeared on the show, such as The Fray's "How to Save a Life" or Snow Patrol's "Chasing Cars."[10] *The Flash* (2014–2023), which featured actors who'd appeared on *Glee* (Grant

Gustin and Melissa Benoist) and Broadway (Jesse L. Martin, Victor Garber, and John Barrowman) as part of the main cast, used a known DC Comics villain, the Music Meister (played by Darren Criss, also of *Glee*) to put Gustin's Barry Allan and crossover character Kara/Supergirl into a coma, while telling them they can only return to the real world if they follow the script in this dream sequence. Most of the songs featured were standards (e.g., "Moon River"), although fellow CW series star Rachel Bloom wrote an original song for the episode, "Super Friend."[11] As part of a sweeps month promotional campaign called "Fox Rocks" in April 2010, several Fox series featured musical numbers, from the expected (*Glee*, of course, but featuring Olivia Newton-John) and *Family Guy*, to the head-scratching (House [Hugh Laurie] and two of his colleagues visit a karaoke bar;[12] *Bones* investigating a murder at a rock and roll fantasy camp that ends with Booth [David Boreanaz] and Bones [Emily Deschanel] performing "Hot Blooded" by Foreigner).[13] On a critical level, most of these were considered a bit cringe-worthy, with the exception of *Fringe*'s "Brown Betty." A science-fiction show that owes a bit of a debt to *The X-Files* (1993–2002), that offers doppelgangers and alternate realities, actually went with a less scientific (or fictional) reason for incorporating music numbers: Walter (John Noble) smokes his self-created strain of marijuana he calls Brown Betty. When he is tasked with looking after Ella (Lily Pilblad), he tells her a noir-infused detective story to pass the time, which incorporates elements of the ongoing narrative of the show. The sung musical numbers were generally incorporated into the noir story, which ranged from classic psychedelic rock ("Low Spark of High-Heeled Boys" by Traffic) and 80s New Wave ("Head Over Heels" by Tears for Fears) to movie songs ("Candy Man" from *Willy Wonka and the Chocolate Factory*) and Broadway numbers ("I Hope I Get It" from *A Chorus Line*), among others.[14]

The Magicians (2015–2020), however, went to the jukebox well more than once. Based on the books by Lev Grossman, *The Magicians* was a series set in a version of reality in which magic exists in parallel to the ordinary world.

Those who wield it are separated into two groups: those who attend Brakebills, a magical graduate program, and "hedges," those who practice magic outside of the authority of places like Brakebills. The protagonist, Quentin Coldwater (Jason Ralph), struggles with both magic and depression, and finds comfort in the *Chronicles of Narnia*-like books about a land called Fillory, led by two rams, Ember and Umber. Grossman cites Narnia as an influence, as well as T. E. White's *The Once and Future King* (1958) and Ursula K. LeGuin's *A Wizard of Earthsea* (1968).[15] The television series, however, goes far afield of the books, retaining some elements while building on others over its five seasons, particularly around the politics of Fillory and deepening and developing more of the characters beyond Quentin. The magic that the show revolves around made it easy to incorporate a musical element into numerous episodes, as well as using the established vocal talents of Hale Appleman (who'd appeared on musical series *Smash* before *The Magicians*) and Jade Tailor (off-Broadway productions, as well as releasing music during the run of the series). Nearly every season features an episode that includes at least one musical number ("Lesser Evils" offers "One Day More" from the musical *Les Misérables* as Eliot [Hale Appleman] and Margo [Summer Bishil] prepare for battle in Fillory),[16] but others make the use of multiple musical numbers integral to the plot. Season four's "All That Hard, Glossy Armor" features Margo in the desert on a quest to get a weapon that can save Eliot (currently possessed by an ancient god). To help her along, she ingests poisonous toad oil, which leads to her hallucinating her friends as various aspects of herself, expressing themselves in song to help her along her quest. While each character does represent parts of Margo, the songs they choose to sing also reveal elements of their own characters, such as Kady (Jade Taylor), who struggles to accept help, singing "Here I Go Again" by Whitesnake.[17] "All That Josh" features an alternate reality where the party never stops; it is fueled by music (opening with Josh [Trevor Einhorn] singing "Wham Bam" by Clooney), and fixed with a closing ensemble performance of "Under Pressure" by Queen and David Bowie.[18] In the penultimate episode of the series, the group plans a heist at a hotel that does not allow magic to be used and has guards that can sense strong emotions, which can cause the person feeling said emotions to burst into song, or, as Josh says, "Any feelings, and we go full-on *Glee*." To fight this, they use magic to make themselves emotionless; however, circumstances occur that make them have to un-bottle their emotions, leading to solo numbers (David Bowie's "I'm Afraid") as well as a final ensemble version of "I Wanna Be Sedated" by the Ramones.[19]

Long before they finally aired a musical episode, however, the series *Lucifer* (2016–2021) made music and musical performances a regular part of the series, particularly through the character of Lucifer (Tom Ellis) himself. Based on the DC Vertigo comics of the same name, *Lucifer* is a series about the devil who grows bored with hell and elects to move to Los Angeles instead. He opens a club called Luxe and, when a friend of his is murdered, works with the Los Angeles Police Department, and Detective Chloe Decker (Lauren German) in particular, to solve the crime.[20] He finds he has an affinity for, and with, the work, and continues to work with the LAPD as a consultant. While few outside his own cosmic circle—demon friend Maze (Lesley-Anne Brandt) and his angelic brother Amenadial (DB Woodside)—actually believe he is Lucifer, they do make use of his abilities (he can make people reveal their deepest desires). Luxe is often the venue for his musical performances; in season one, he sings Nina Simone's "Sinnerman" and in season two, "All Along the Watchtower," both while accompanying himself on the piano. He sings "I Will Survive" in a duet with a pop star at his club in "Off the Record," and the season four opener offers a more dramatic setpiece, as a depressed and overwhelmed Lucifer sings Radiohead's "Creep" at his club, while both the background, his clothes, and his amount of facial hair shift and change until the club is empty and he's alone.[21] This trend continued both during the time it aired on Fox (seasons one to three) and the final three seasons that aired on Netflix.[22]

Season five, however, finally debuted an episode that got the entire cast in on the act, with its jukebox musical "Bloody Celestial Karaoke Jam." As with any arc-based series, the episode aired at a time when each character's seasonal journey was reaching a peak. In this instance, Chloe has expressed her love for Lucifer (now knowing who he is), but he's struggling to say it back. Ella (Aimee Garcia), the crime technician, has a penchant for bad boys, only to discover the "nice" guy she was dating was anything but.[23] Maze, a demon, wants to be more human (i.e., have a soul), but, denied that, decides to embrace her darker impulses. Amenadial and Linda (Rachel Harris) have recently had a child together; Amenadial worries about the fact that the child seems entirely human, and therefore vulnerable, and Dan (Kevin Alejandro), Chloe's ex-husband and fellow detective, has recently learned demons and angels are real, and is freaked out about his potential afterlife. Into this morass of emotions enters God (Dennis Haysbert), on Earth for the first time to check on his "children" (Amenadial and Lucifer, among others). It is his presence that turns everything, in Lucifer's own words, into a "bloody celestial karaoke jam" that affects humans and angels alike (although only the angels are aware it's happening).

The songs included serve more than one purpose. Some of them move the plot, some reveal character, and some resolve ongoing arcs; many do more than one, and one does none of them. (That would be Queen's "Another One Bites the Dust," sung by most of the cast at a crime scene. Its main purpose seems to be to establish the way that this singing compulsion exists, which the opening song wouldn't necessarily do; as stated above, several episodes feature Ellis soloing.) Maze, who works as a bounty hunter, tries to embrace her dark side by presenting Ella with a variety of "bad" (but attractive) guys Ella might be into; this push-pull dynamic is illustrated in Maze singing George Thoroghgood's "Bad to the Bone" blended with Ella's rendition of TLC's "No Scrubs" ("scrub" being Atlanta-based slang for a loser).[24] While Linda starts out by herself, taking her baby for a walk through the park while singing the

Bill Withers and Grover Washington Jr.'s version of "Just the Two of Us" (joined at times with other moms at the park), Amenadial joins in halfway through, with Will Smith's hip-hop version, which was re-conceived as song about a father's love for his son (specifically, Smith's firstborn, Will Smith III). Its use here is significant, as Amenadial's concern about his son being human is less about having an "ordinary" child and more about his own realizations about the dangers young men of color face in the world, a theme of Smith's version as well.[25] In this instance, it both reveals character and advances the plot, as Amenadial more fully commits to fatherhood going forward.

As for solos, Dan's recent revelation about the existence of a cosmic order, and his subsequent fears about the state of his soul, lead to his number, at Luxe, singing the 1990s swing-inspired one-hit-wonder "Hell" by the Squirrel Nut Zippers. Trixie, Dan and Chloe's daughter, also gets a solo, but hers is not concerned with the state of her own life, but her realization of how sad her mom is, as she quietly sings "Smile," a standard sung by several artists, although Nat King Cole is credited with popularizing it. ("Smile" has its own history; the music is based on the love theme from Charlie Chaplin's film *Modern Times* [1936], which itself was inspired by melodies from Puccini's opera *Tosca*.)

It is Lucifer, however, who participates in four of the numbers (the most of any other character), and thus the focal point of the episode. Most of Lucifer's songs tend to reveal character; he opens the episode singing Chris Isaak's "Wicked Game" as a way to work through his complicated relationship with Chloe. Yet his biggest issue through most of the series is his troubled relationship with God (aka "Dad"). Aside from his opening song, he also sings two duets: The Police's "Every Breath You Take" and "I Dreamed a Dream" from *Les Misérables* (a popular choice for these types of episodes, it seems!). The first is a duet with Mrs. Bitner (Debbie Gibson), the mother of a young man being questioned about the death at the start of the episode. She answers the questions set to her son, barely letting him get a word in. Lucifer feels

FIGURE 6.1 **Lucifer *offers a new take on "Every Breath You Take." Netflix / Photofest © Netflix.***

a particular kinship with the son; his father has insisted on accompanying him to work, and their interactions are tense and full of subtextual critique. Into this environment of an overbearing parent, the scene re-contextualizes the original meaning of the song, which clearly describes stalking behavior, to reflect the nature of certain parent-child relationships.

The episode closes out with a duet between Lucifer and God: "I Dreamed a Dream" from the musical *Les Misérables*. In the musical, the song is sung by Fantine, a young woman who'd fallen in love with, and borne a child by, a man who subsequently left without marrying her. Knowing she can't support both herself and the child (morals clauses in workplaces would likely prevent her from being hired), she leaves her child in the care of others before securing a job to pay for her daughter's care. Unfortunately, the truth comes out, she is fired, and, after selling anything of value to survive and pay for her daughter's care, turns to prostitution. The song itself, sung after she is fired, is a lament for the life she expected versus what actually happened. In the context of the series' character and narrative, it remains a lament, although for Lucifer it is a lament for the hope that he could love and be loved in return, and for God, the distance and misunderstandings that have made their father/son relationship so fraught. Yet the final moments add an additional layer to God's motivation; when Lucifer berates him for making him "sing" again (i.e., reveal himself), God breaks down and admits that he has little control of his powers, and how much that terrifies him. Indeed, the way it is presented here makes an obvious parallel to the challenges of aging and dementia.[26]

While musicals such as *Mamma Mia!* may have brought it into greater prominence, the jukebox musical has been a part of the media landscape for decades. At its best, it leverages well-known songs that its viewers may already have a connection with in a new context that advances both plot and character; even more average examples, however, can at least be a showcase for the vocal talents of actors in roles that don't usually include singing. (And, as was seen in the *Mamma Mia!* film adaptation, can be an indicator of how little vocal ability an otherwise talented actor may have, like Pierce Brosnan.)

The same applies in television. While musical episodes overall rose following success stories such as "Once More, With Feeling," not all were good or made sense in the context of the series themselves. This can come down to a few important factors. While not a dealbreaker, having more than one strong singer in the cast can make or break an episode. These episodes also work best where there is an external reason why it's happening; that's why so many musical episodes (jukebox or otherwise) appear in the science fiction and fantasy genre (*The Magicians*, *Lucifer*, etc.). Those that don't, such as *Fringe* or *Grey's Anatomy*, use tropes such as an altered consciousness due to drugs (*Fringe*) or coma (*Grey's Anatomy*) to "justify" this single-episode genre shift. It can also be a handy way to offer a special episode that nonetheless fits into the arcs of a particular season, as with the *Lucifer* episode discussed previously, with the sung elements driving the season's stories as they reached their conclusion.

7

A Swing and a Miss: *Cop Rock*

Speaking to the National Association of Broadcasters in 1961, then-Federal Communications Commission (FCC) head Newton Minow referred to American commercial television as a "vast wasteland."[1] Minow was responding, in great part, to the scandals that rocked television in the late 1950s, in which game shows like *Dotto* (1958) and *Twenty-One* (1956–1958) were found to have been rigged and yet still proliferated on prime-time television in the early 1960s. Yet he was also nostalgic for the anthology dramas that were in decline by 1961, which featured up-and-coming writers (like Rod Serling and Paddy Chayefsky) and established actors (like Ida Lupino or Charles Bayer) rather than the sitcoms, variety shows, and game shows that were the biggest part of the television schedule at the time. In 1987, the FCC chair under Ronald Reagan, Mark Fowler, referred to television as nothing but a "toaster with pictures"; that is, an appliance like any other and should be treated as such.[2] Its job was to sell the products it advertised, not necessarily to innovate or be creative.[3] Although nearly twenty years apart, both hold a dim view of television's ability to be creative or break new creative ground. It was viewed as risk-averse (not an unfair accusation; even in its supposed Golden Age that Minow was nostalgic for, writers like Serling faced significant pushback on their work and ideas from both networks and sponsors[4]) and content geared toward the lowest common denominator existed alongside the more critically acclaimed material.

Unfortunately, these views erase a portion of television history, in which creators and showrunners did attempt to try new concepts, diversify television, and broach controversial subjects. Series such as *The Mary Tyler Moore Show* (1970–1977) or *All in the Family* (1971–1979) used a typical sitcom structure, but still managed to foster discussions about gender, race, and bigotry. Shows like *I Love Lucy* (1951–1957), *Room 222* (1969–1974), *The White Shadow* (1978–1981), or *Julia* (1968–1971) broke out of the overwhelming whiteness in casting; despite network pushback, Lucille Ball won the fight to have the couple on her series reflect her own life.[5] The 1980s represented something of a step back in these terms, but there was still some forward momentum in surprising areas. Steven Bochco was a fixture of 1980s television, with hits like *Hill Street Blues* (1981–1987) and *LA Law* (1986–1991) cementing his legacy, reinvigorating the cop show and legal drama without necessarily breaking new ground. (His sitcom *Doogie Howser, MD* [1989–1993], however, was somewhat innovative in the way it blended comedy and drama and eschewed the laugh track.) In 1990, based on an earlier remark from a Broadway producer interested in adapting *Hill Street Blues* as a musical, Bochco took a risk and created a new series that would combine the police procedural and musical genres, aptly named *Cop Rock* (1990). Featuring music and lyrics by Greg Edmonson and Mike Post, both television composer veterans, as well as Randy Newman, the series nonetheless suffered from numerous challenges, including actors who couldn't sing, singers who couldn't act, and, most importantly, no narrative justification for its musical numbers. I'll examine the series as an interesting failure that nonetheless set the groundwork for series that followed in its wake.

Damn Good Coffee and Teen Angst: The Wonderful Weirdness of 1990

There are certain years that, in retrospect, suggest elements of the pop cultural future. In 2005, for example, the first *Twilight* novel was released, which sparked a huge YA upsurge; YouTube went online for the first time, and *Supernatural* debuted on the soon-to-be-defunct WB, which would become the longest-running genre show in US television history. While perhaps not as dramatic, 1990 had a few firsts that pointed the way forward, at least for television. Fox debuted as the third network in 1986, and had its first major hit in the animated series *The Simpsons*, spun off from sketch comedy series *The Tracey Ullman Show* (1987–1990). By 1990, it was enough a part of the cultural zeitgeist to not only have a novelty album ("The Simpsons Sing the Blues") and endless merchandise (e.g., T-shirts reading "Eat My Shorts") but to have then-First Lady Barbara Bush call it the "dumbest" show she'd ever seen; two years later, her husband, George H. W. Bush, suggested on the campaign trail that it didn't display proper "family values."[6] This was on top of the backlash they'd received for *Married . . . with Children* (1987–1997), which took aim at the more family-friendly 80s sitcoms by featuring disappointed, and disappointing husband Al (Ed O'Neill), his restless and scheming wife, Peggy (Katey Sagal), and two children (Kelly [Christina Applegate] and Bud [David Faustino]) with little reason to respect or obey their parents. The duo who created the show, Michael G. Moye and Ron Leavitt, had tried a similarly slightly subversive sitcom with NBC's *It's Your Move* (1984–1985), with Jason Bateman as an amoral teen grifter antihero a few years ahead of its time, sparking similar parental complaints to those *Married* would receive a couple of years later. NBC canceled it. The other way they differentiated themselves from what was then known as The Big Three (ABC, CBS, and NBC) was to focus on the teen audience, starting with *21 Jump Street* in 1987, but really kicking off in 1990 with the debuts of *Parker Lewis Can't Lose*, a semi-surreal, laugh-track-less teen sitcom loosely based on *Ferris Bueller's Day Off* (and which inspired later sitcoms such as *Scrubs*) and *Beverly Hills, 90210* (1990–2000), which like *The Simpsons* became part of the cultural consciousness of the decade, with the cast appearing in commercials or the covers of teen magazines like *YM* (1932–2004) and *Sassy* (1988–1996). Even the do-it-yourself zine culture of the early 1990s responded; an "I Hate Brenda" zine was launched in 1993, responding to the shifts in the character Brenda Walsh (Shannen Doherty) before Doherty's ouster following the third season. The zine was popular enough to launch its own merchandise and garner interviews with 90s icons like Eddie Vedder.[7] *The Fresh Prince of Bel-Air* (1990–1996) debuted on NBC, launching Will Smith's career beyond music, and *Northern Exposure*, on CBS, offered an ensemble dramedy in a rural setting uncommon on television at the time: Alaska. Its humor was quirky, and it stood out at the time not only for acknowledging the indigenous population of Alaska but also for casting indigenous actors to play the roles, still a rarity in 1990. (For every Jay Silverheels in *The Lone Ranger* [1949–1957], there was an Iron Eyes Cody, who claimed Native ancestry and played Native roles but was actually Italian.)

The series, however, considered the most avant-garde and unexpected hit of the 1990s was *Twin Peaks* (1990–1991). Created by Mark Frost and David Lynch, the simple description doesn't seem radically different from most procedural dramas: a young woman is murdered, and when the local police struggle to close it, FBI Agent Dale Cooper (Kyle MacLachlan) arrives to work with them to solve the case. While Laura's murder (among other things) is the driving plot of the first (and part of the second) season, its execution diverges both narratively and visually. Broken down to its bare bones, *Twin Peaks* would likely be considered a hybrid of police drama and soap opera, but that doesn't account for its demonic entities, doppelgangers, mysterious other dimensions, or cryptic clues. The quirkiness of *Twin Peaks*' small-town population superficially resembled that of *Northern Exposure*, but the cinematic visuals and unexpected twists gave their performances a far darker twist.

While there's been a significant amount of scholarly—and cultural—discussion about the big television shifts in the 1950s, 1970s, and throughout the 2000s, 1990 has been relatively ignored as an inflection point. It may have been the rise of Fox pushing the Big Three to expand their repertoire when shows like *The Simpsons* (the first animated prime-time success since the debut of *The Flintstones* in 1960) and *Beverly Hills, 90210* racked up viewers and cultural cachet. Networks such as CBS, known as the Tiffany Network for their highly regarded news department (Edward R. Murrow was one of their early journalists), rarely took risks with programming, except in the 1970s when they canceled and replaced their whole slate of programming in favor of more socially relevant comedies like *All in the Family*. *Northern Exposure* was an unlikely hit for a network that even in 2025 is keeping the multi-camera sitcom alive. NBC, with one exception, made no significant programming changes in 1990, which I'll discuss later. That being said, ABC, often in third place behind NBC and CBS, had a history of taking chances with its programs; *Moonlighting* was expensive and fraught with backstage drama, but it was also unlike anything else on television in 1986. *Twin Peaks*' next-level weirdness was a good fit and unsurprising choice for ABC. They would take another big swing for their fall schedule, however, that garnered the opposite of *Twin Peaks*' critical and commercial success: *Cop Rock*.

"He's guilty, Judge, he's guilty": Bochco's Big Swing

Having served as creator and showrunner for some of NBC's biggest drama hits in the 1980s, *Hill Street Blues* and *LA Law*, Steven Bochco may not have been untouchable, but had certainly built up enough goodwill amongst network executives—and audiences—to try something new. Yet even before *Hill Street Blues* was a hit, Bochco's first series as executive producer was *Paris* (1979–1980), starring James Earl Jones as a police captain in Southern California (who also moonlights as a criminology professor), trying to navigate home and work life—still a rarity in the police procedural—and the morally gray world in which he is forced to operate, featuring a diverse cast in a broadcast era still blindingly white. Bochco would carry these elements into his next project, *Hill Street Blues*. Sadly, *Paris* was saddled with a terrible time slot (Saturday nights) and was quickly canceled. *Hill Street Blues*, however, more than made up for it, using the same mix of personal, professional, and morally gray situations or individuals, winning dozens of Emmys and remaining a hit series throughout its run. *LA Law* moved this formula into the law genre, but Bochco's addition of David E. Kelley as writer, and later executive producer, gave *LA Law* more of the off-beat and quirky vibe that were the stock and trade of Kelley's later shows like *Ally McBeal*, *Boston Public* (2000–2004), and *The Practice* (1997–2004) (among many others). (That Kelley was one of the writers for the "Good to the Last Drop" episode of *LA Law*, in which antagonist Rosalind Shay falls down an elevator shaft,[8] is not surprising.) Given his success, ABC offered Bochco a deal to create and produce ten series. Shifting away from drama, he created the sitcom *Hooperman* (1987–1989), starring John Ritter as a police inspector and the series responsible for the coining of the word "dramedy."[9] *Hooperman* only lasted two seasons, and his 1992 animated comedy series *Capital Critters* only thirteen episodes. His first big success with this deal, however, came from his second foray into sitcom territory, *Doogie Howser, MD*, about the trials and triumphs of Doogie Howser (Neil Patrick Harris), a genius 16-year-old surgical resident who must find a way to balance being a physician and being a teenager. The nature of his deal with ABC gave Bochco a significant amount of power; while the executives didn't care for *Doogie Howser*'s pilot, they had to air it anyway or pay a substantial penalty.[10]

Bochco's deal with ABC also made it easier for him to take chances with the programs he proposed. It was likely this was a reason why he went forward with an idea presented to him a few years earlier to turn *Hill Street Blues* into a Broadway musical. In an interview, he stated: "If you have the guarantee of getting that many shows on the air and you don't do something bold and adventurous and experimental, then shame on you."[11] While he declined to adapt the original, *Cop Rock* used many of its signatures: gritty setting, morally ambiguous cops and officials, and interpersonal drama. He brought in Mike Post, a composer he'd worked with on *Hill Street Blues* and *LA Law*, even though, according to Bochco himself, Post thought that the cop/musical hybrid was a terrible idea,[12] as well as Randy Newman to write the five songs included in the pilot episode. In terms of casting, more emphasis was placed on singing rather than acting ability. Composer Greg Edmondson, who had also worked with Bochco before, was joined by songwriters Ron Boustead, Brock Walsh, and Donny Markowitz. Boustead and Walsh had worked with either Bochco or Edmondson on past projects, and Markowitz had won an Oscar in 1987 for Best Song "(I've Had) The Time of My Life" from *Dirty Dancing*. It is significant, however, that none of these songwriters had worked in the musical genre prior to *Cop Rock*.

This pilot episode sets up the main stories for the eleven episodes of the series, including a public official on the take, Officer Vicki Quinn (Anne Bobby), who is torn between her husband and her feelings for her partner, and a young drug addict, Patricia Spence (Kathleen Wilhoite) who ends up selling her baby at the end of the first episode to both buy drugs and give her daughter a chance at a better life. The main story, however, revolves around Detective Anthony LaRusso (Peter Onorati), who murders an unarmed Black man, Tyrone Weeks (Art Kimbro), suspected of shooting a cop, while Weeks is handcuffed and sitting down.[13] All of these elements were part of Bochco's aforementioned signature style. The series had professional composers and lyricists, singers, and a showrunner with a proven track record. While it did represent an outré premise to set it to music, it could have worked. So why didn't it?

There is no single reason, but rather a collection of them. Without judging the quality of the songs, which can be hit or miss, there are several elements that worked against the series. The first is a compelling reason for the cast to break into song in the first place. While this isn't strictly necessary—musicals from *Oklahoma!* to *Hamilton* don't stop the action to explain why they're singing—both the genre (police procedural) and the medium (television) essentially demand it because it is uncommon in both. In terms of genre, the tonal shift from gritty drama to, for example, a pensive love ballad in the pilot episode is jarring. Others are even worse: in "Marital Blitz," Officer Campo's (David Gianopoulos) new partner, Officer Petrovich (Diane Delano), gets sexually charged at a crime scene, performing the highly uncomfortable song "Bumpty Bumpty" while grinding on Campo on the trunk of their police car in a way that borders on assault.[14] On the medium level, while musical series and episodes are more common now both episodically and series-wide, they were not so in 1990. Series like *The Monkees* featured at least one song per episode, as did *The Partridge Family*, but that was baked into the premise of the show. Later series, such as *Crazy Ex-Girlfriend*, *Schmigadoon*, and *Zoey's Extraordinary Playlist*, either made it clear that the musical numbers were either a matter of perception (*Crazy Ex-Girlfriend*/*Zoey*) or took place in an alternate reality (*Schmigadoon*, *Galavant*). *Cop Rock* failed to clear the suspension of disbelief required of its premise from the outset.

There was also the pressure of needing to feature at least five songs in each episode. The strictures of television production and the time constraints involved in filming (a single episode is usually shot in 8 to 10 days[15]) were often cited as the reason why, as discussed previously, television was considered the lesser medium compared to film. That is, creating content at that speed necessitates cutting some corners, whether in terms of scripting, blocking, or rehearsal time. Single-episode musicals, like those discussed in Chapter 5, required weeks if not months in the planning, writing, rehearsing, and choreographing, even if the material or production is entirely in-house.[16] In that respect, adding five musical numbers per episode requires unreasonably quick work on the part of the lyricists and composers, with little time for revision or recomposition.

Further, as Katharine Coldiron writes, while the series delivered well on the procedural side, it displayed a fundamental lack of understanding of the musical genre. The songs in most musicals "expand on character, capture a ceremony, gather a crowd under a particular purpose, or explain a circumstance. Most importantly, songs and arias illustrate transitional emotional moments."[17] Too often, the songs in *Cop Rock* merely underlined what had already been established. "You're the One for Me," a song about bribing Mayor Louise Plank (Barbara Bosson), establishes her corruptibility before the song starts, meaning the subsequent performance adds nothing. "Baby Merchant," sung by Glen, the aforementioned baby merchant, to two undercover cops trying to catch him in the act, is about being a baby merchant.[18] Given the strictures under which the show operated (five songs per episode were required), too many sounded similar, relying on synth/pop elements overall; see "Choose Me," a pop number that puts nearly every female officer in skimpy clothes dancing for the other officers to convince them they'd do well going undercover as prostitutes, which plays like a low-rent Madonna video.[19] Exceptions such as "He's Guilty" or "We've Got the Power," which used gospel and hip-hop, respectively, or "Hear the Doggy," inspired by country music, were fairly rare.[20] As I suggested above, this isn't entirely surprising, given that *Cop Rock*'s composers and lyricists came from different musical specialties (pop, film composition, etc.). Coldiron goes on to suggest that a "membrane" (another term for suspension of disbelief, in many respects) exists between fiction and audience. Said membrane allows the audience to accept what's happening on screen, as long as nothing ruptures it, either accidentally or deliberately. With two exceptions (the show's theme song, which features the cast out of character in a dark studio listening to Randy Newman singing, and the final song of the series, which focuses on the show's cancellation),[21] *Cop Rock* does not intentionally break the fourth wall. Instead, Coldiron contends, the genre-blending and musical choices does it for them.[22]

With all the focus on the songs' qualities, the oddball genre blend, and the challenges of taking it seriously, few, if any, of the reviews and analyses of the

FIGURE 7.1 ***Choreography wasn't* Cop Rock's *strong suit. ABC / Photofest © ABC.***

series mention movement. Choreography encompasses more than simply dance numbers; it is how the performer moves, whether in ballet, a runway, or a musical. If *Cop Rock* did employ a choreographer, it is not readily apparent in most of the musical numbers. "Since She Chose Me" and "You're the One for Me" from the pilot are a case in point; in "Since She Chose Me," Ralph Ruskin (Ron McLarty) sings a pensive ode to his much-younger wife without moving from his chair, which at least fits the downbeat tone of the song. "You're the One for Me," however, is a lively song about bribery and corruption, and yet what little dancing or movement there is remains stiff and expected, with little flourish.[23] While it would be tempting to blame this on the time period and the relatively few examples of how a musical series could work, NBC debuted *Hull High* in 1990 as well, a musical comedy set in a high school. While largely forgotten—compared to *Cop Rock*—*Hull High* actually worked much better despite similarly offering no justification for its musical numbers, although some, such as "Figures of Speech," were clearly meant to be dream/fantasy sequences.[24] This may be due to the fact that teens and music are a natural combination. On a tonal level, the blending of teens, musical numbers, and comedy worked much better; neither the songs nor the actors performing them took themselves too seriously. Yet, what really set *Hull High* apart was the presence of Kenny Ortega, who'd started as a stage actor before transitioning into choreography. Before *Hull High*, he'd worked on *Xanadu* (1980), *Pretty in Pink* (1986), *Ferris Bueller's Day Off*, and the film that made his name, *Dirty Dancing*, as well as arena tours for Cher and Kiss and the music videos for Olivia Newton-John's "Physical" and Madonna's "Material Girl." The difference is obvious from the opening scene of *Hull High*, with its hip-hop Greek chorus dancing through the campus before ending up on the bleachers near the football field holding tridents. While silly, their movements blended well with the music and elevated the scenes, underscoring the importance of how the performers exist in and move through the space.[25] The series embraces the basic staged-ness of the genre; the aforementioned Greek chorus opens each episode by commenting on the action and suggesting the episode's theme and plot (which, of course, is the function of the chorus in classic Greek dramas).

The year 1990 was a strange time, not just for television, but on a broader social scale. The earliest part of Generation X was coming of age, the Reagan era had been extended through the election of George H. W. Bush, who, like his son would do a little over a decade later, had gone to war with Iraq. Like Vietnam two decades earlier, it was heavily televised on the still fairly new 24-hour news channels as well as broadcast television. Combining this with teen dramas, comedies, and singing cops made for a surreal viewing experience, particularly since the conflict's coverage employed newer technologies, like night vision shooting, that made many of the televised battles resemble video games. It was an early sign of the shifts to come, and a chance to try new things. With *Cop Rock*, Bochco could certainly not be accused of not trying new things, but there was and remains a reason why certain genres are simply too incompatible to work together. While the BBC's *The Singing Detective* was cited as an inspiration for the series,[26] its noir drama is set up as an escapist fantasy created by a suffering and blocked Philip Marlow (Michael Gambon). Given its status as fantasy and the (already) highly stylized world of noir, the period-appropriate musical numbers blended rather than clashed. While *Cop Rock* was, by most accounts, a failure, it nonetheless paved the way for later series, both as an opening for the genre on television, and a cautionary tale on how *not* to make a musical.

8

"Got Any Song Requests?": *Zoey's Extraordinary Playlist* and *Glee*

It's hard to tie down a firm date on when television decided to go more niche and focus on which audiences were watching as well as how many. Being commercially funded, US television has always had its eye on the type of audience engaged with the particular shows and whether they were buying the advertised products. That being said, a big moment in this shift occurred in 1970, when CBS enacted what was known as the "rural purge"[1] and canceled *Green Acres* (1965–1971), *The Beverly Hillbillies* (1962–1971), *Mayberry RFD* (1968–1971), and *Petticoat Junction* (1963–1970). These shows were canceled not because their ratings were bad (all were still in the top 10 in the Nielsen ratings), but because they attracted older and less affluent audiences (among other reasons). While the rural purge didn't keep US television from chasing after big audiences, networks did seem to get a bit more comfortable in greenlighting—and renewing—shows that might have more niche appeal than mainstream (e.g., *thirtysomething* [1987–1991], *Northern Exposure*), especially if the average income of a viewer of *thirtysomething* was about $65,000 a year (about $150,000 in 2025).[2]

As has been clear throughout, musical shows can be a hard sell outside of particular circumstances (variety shows, etc.). The incorporation of music can add a level of difficulty to a process that is difficult enough already: finding actors who can sing (in multiple episodes) is one hurdle, as is the double duty of writing songs and scripts. The jukebox musical, as discussed in Chapter 6, eliminates at least one of those difficulties, as original songs are not required, and, as a bonus, are familiar and may resonate with audiences. Using this format was one way that 2009's *Glee* broke the *Cop Rock* curse of musical series on television, through one simple change: a reason to sing. Created by Ryan Murphy and focused on the misadventures and challenges of a high school glee club, mixing drama, music, and hijinks in a way that proved massively successful (in 2000s terms), with good ratings and a huge amount of ancillary material that made the show profitable. While not as successful in ratings (although garnering a devoted fanbase), *Zoey's Extraordinary Playlist* used the jukebox format less for in-narrative performance but rather as an indicator of the main character's state of mind, which owes more to series such as *Crazy Ex-Girlfriend* than *Glee*. Thus, this chapter examines the different ways that the two series use the jukebox format to create their overarching narratives and develop—or stymie—their characters.

"There is nothing ironic about show choir!": Singing Out the High School Drama

In its third season, the series *Community* (2009–2015) took on *Glee*, the show that had been trouncing it in the ratings. "Regional Holiday Music," which featured five original songs, has the study group, who a previous episode revealed had filled in for Greendale Community College's glee club after a fatal bus crash,[3] targeted by the head of the glee club, Mr. Rad (Taran Killam), to fill in once again, after Jeff (Joel McHale), a former lawyer, had them served with a cease and desist from the American Society of Composers, Authors and Publishers, prompting the club into a collective nervous breakdown. Mr. Rad, who Killam plays as, in Jeff's words "equal parts Manson and Hanson," convinces Abed (Danny Pudi), who wants nothing more than a nice Christmas, to join and then convince the others, with a song appropriately titled "Glee." Playing out like a comedic *Invasion of the Body Snatchers* (down to replicating Donald Sutherland's scream and point at the end of Philip Kaufman's adaptation),[4] most of the study group is brought down by songs targeted to their weak points. Troy (Donald Glover), Abed's best friend, was raised as a Jehovah's Witness, which prohibits celebrating holidays such as Christmas; he and Abed perform a hip-hop song called "Jehovah's Secret Witness"; afterward, the two of them target Pierce (Chevy Chase) with "Baby Boomer Santa," which "pander[s] to your demographic's well-documented historical vanity." Pierce ropes in Shirley (Yvette Nicole Brown), who is militantly Christian, with a choir of children singing about how they are not allowed to say "Merry Christmas" in school, and Annie (Alison Brie) performs a Marilyn Monroe/Betty Boop-esque "Teach Me How to Understand Christmas" in a sexy costume to play on Jeff's attraction to her. Once all of them are on board to perform in the Christmas pageant, Mr. Rad finally reveals his true colors to Abed, telling him, "This is what we do now," and assuring him that "If we win regionals, then it's straight on to sectionals. And then a week later is semis. Then semi-regionals. Then regional-semis. Then national lower-zone semis!" Abed, who only wanted a holiday that wasn't "dark," undermines the performance by sending out Britta, who has a weak singing voice, to perform an original song. Mr. Rad flips out, yelling: "This show is supposed to be gleeful and bright and fun, and you can let me do that, or there can be another bus crash!" before fleeing the stage.[5]

Dan Harmon, creator of *Community*, has made no secret of how much he disliked the show,[6] although both *Community* and *Glee* were based on the authors' own experiences; Ian Brennan, who brought the idea to Ryan Murphy, had been in the glee club at his own high school, as had Murphy, while Harmon based Greendale on his time at Glendale Community College in Los Angeles. "Regional Holiday Music" pulled no punches, particularly in the way it presented Mr. Rad as the parallel to Glee's Will Schuester (Matthew Morrison), known to the William McKinley High School glee club as Mr. Schue. The premise of the series revolves around Mr. Schue's takeover of the glee club after its previous head, Sandy Ryerson (Stephen Tobolowsky), is fired. (Schue had been in the glee club during his own high school days.) He faces significant pushback, both at the school and at home; Sue Sylvester (Jane Lynch), who heads up the popular Cheerios (a cheerleading squad) sets herself against Schue's attempts to rebuild and rebrand the glee club, now known as New Directions, and participation has a geeky stigma within the world of McKinley High that keeps membership down. At home, his marriage is struggling as he and his wife, Terri (Jessalyn Gilsig), are attempting to have a baby, and she is pressuring him to get a better-paying job. The moment, however, in which Harmon's characterization of Schue stand-in Mr. Rad hits the mark occurs in the very first episode, when he overhears quarterback Finn Hudson (Cory Monteith) singing in the shower and, in order to get him to join New Directions, plants marijuana in his locker and then blackmails him into joining, only to quit when his wife reveals she's pregnant to get a job as an accountant. Of course, New Directions attempts to carry on, and when he hears their rendition of "Don't Stop Believin'" by Journey, he changes his mind.[7] The rest of the first season combines these various storylines—getting New Directions ready for competition, Sue Sylvester's attempts at sabotage, teen pregnancy and coming out, and Mr. Schue's home life and deteriorating marriage—with musical numbers.[8]

In many respects, *Glee*, as a satire on the dramas of high school, is a natural continuation of Murphy's previous series *Popular* (1999–2001), which eked out two seasons on the WB ten years before *Glee*'s debut. The main story revolved around popular Brooke (Leslie Bibb) and geeky Sam (Carly Pope) as stepsisters after their parents marry, with campy characters like Mary Cherry (Leslie Grossman) and the way it "celebrated the value of outcasts and portrayed overplayed topics—Homecoming Court, sex, and secrets—through an absurdist lens."[9] However, *Glee* was able to tackle some of these topics more openly, as the WB seemed to struggle with LGBTQIA+ storylines in particular; strictures were placed on shows like *Dawson's Creek* and *Buffy the Vampire Slayer* in terms of their portrayals of same-sex couples, and Murphy himself revealed both being the victim of homophobic remarks from WB executives and the policing of certain storylines.[10] The Fox television network, which made a name for itself since the 1980s in going against the grain in terms of content, gave Murphy and company more freedom on *Glee*, with storylines around gender transition (starting with the introduction of Unique [Alex Newell] in "Saturday Night Glee-ver") and coming out among others (teen pregnancy, mental health).[11]

In terms of the music, *Glee* managed not only to provide a narrative reason to sing, but also, like *Lucifer* would later do in its jukebox musical episode, generally had its glee club members performing songs that were thematically resonant, either in terms of the episode or the character. "Silly Love Songs" was, appropriately, a Valentine's Day episode, with the characters of Artie (Kevin McHale) and Mike (Harry Shum Jr.) serenading their girlfriends with "PYT" by Michael Jackson, which moved both of them, while Puck (Mark Salling) makes a serious misstep when he sings "Fat Bottomed Girls" by Queen to his crush Lauren (Ashley Fink), a mistake that is in line with his character thus far.[12] A later episode in season two, however, takes on some significantly problematic dimensions in both storyline and song choice. "Sexy" features a plot in which Lauren and Puck want to make a sex tape that would hopefully further Lauren's career before substitute teacher Holly Holiday (Gwyneth Paltrow) informs them that, since they are both underage, it would be considered child pornography.[13] Not only did this episode cause controversy in the United Kingdom upon airing through its use of a cover of Gary Glitter's "Do You Wanna Touch Me (Oh Yeah)" after Glitter was jailed for possession of child pornography, but Salling, who played Puck, was later indicted for the same crime before taking his own life.[14] This was just one of the tragedies associated with the show, including Cory Monteith's overdose and Naya Rivera's 2020 drowning death. Other times, however, some critics considered that the song choices drove the narrative in ways that made little sense in terms of established characterization and plot progression. This seemed a particular issue with "theme" episodes, as with "Michael," which was intended to be a tribute to Michael Jackson.[15] Richard Lawson, in his review, wrote: "The writers, in this case Ryan Murphy himself, are forced to create a story in service to songs," rather than the songs being in service to the story.[16]

Like the teen dramas of the 1990s, *Glee* did not ignore or fudge the passing of time; many of the established members of New Directions—and their rivals at other schools—graduated at the end of the third season, allowing the series to introduce several new characters to McKinley as well as following the post-high school stories of Rachel (Lea Michele) or Kurt (Christopher Colfer) as they attempt to navigate life at the (fictional) New York Academy of the Dramatic Arts. The remaining three seasons do find ways to bring back any number of cast members to, for example, reconstitute the glee club at McKinley after Sue Sylvester shuts it down due to budget cuts.[17] One can also see the influence of shows like *Fame* in McKinley's eventual fate at the end of the series, when it is reconstituted as a performing arts magnet school with Mr. Schue as principal.[18] (The popularity of the show also led to another *Fame*-based element: the Glee Live! In Concert! tour across the United States and parts of Europe.)

While *Glee* seemed to break the musical series' curse and was a ratings—and soundtrack—hit, it was not without detractors. While purportedly a satire, the tone often veered into "very special episode" territory that undermined that assertion and thus provided little cover for racist, ableist, and sexist jokes that too frequently crept into the series. Further, some moments could be remarkably tone deaf or cringeworthy, including Mr. Schue's response to the valid complaints of minority students in the club by saying "You're all minorities. You're in the glee club," a moment that likely inspired Jeff's line in "Regional Holiday Music": "Not liking glee club doesn't make us bullies, and implying that is reverse bullying."[19] Characters of color, both in *Glee* and in other Murphy productions, were too often relegated to the background, and there were accusations of racist behavior on the set.[20] The show was capable of calling out behavior in its characters within the narrative, as when Santana (Naya Rivera) calls out Mr. Schue for his egregious performance of "La Cucaracha" for his Spanish class dressed in a sombrero and serape, as well as the horrified looks of his students, but less so in "Wheels," when New Directions performs "Proud Mary" in wheelchairs to show solidarity with wheelchair user Artie (Kevin McHale).[21] None of the actors, including McHale, are wheelchair-bound in real life, suggesting to some commentators "caricatures and appropriation, not understanding" despite the show's intentions, although others felt it worked and was "thoughtfully handled."[22]

Despite some significant missteps, *Glee* was at least a step beyond, in terms of LGBTQIA+ representation, the teen dramas of the WB ten years earlier, including the introduction of Unique as one of the first transgender main cast members in television and one whose portrayer identifies as genderfluid. Its popularity, moreover, exposed a wide swathe of audiences to concerns and identities they either were unaware of or misunderstood, even if *Glee*'s writers or performers didn't themselves always understand the nuances or challenges of certain portrayals or jokes. It also proved that shows with a musical premise—particularly one with a narrative justification for all that singing—could work on television.

"Good music can make you feel things you can't express in words": Heartsongs and Heartbreak in *Zoey's Extraordinary Playlist*

While shows like *Glee*—or *Fame*—set their musical interludes as appropriate parts of performing arts or performance more generally, other series went mystical (*Lucifer*), medical (*Scrubs*), or, in the case of *Zoey's Extraordinary*

Playlist, a combination of both. The premise of the series involves Zoey (Jane Levy), a computer programmer in San Francisco whose family has been rocked by her father Mitch's (Peter Gallagher) diagnosis of Progressive Supranuclear Palsy (PSP), a degenerative disease that affects movement and speech, among other things. Given its genetic nature, Zoey, who'd been experiencing headaches, elects to get an MRI to make sure she's not developing the same illness. The technician puts on a playlist to help keep her calm during the procedure—although she claims she doesn't need it—but when an earthquake hits halfway through the scan, all of the songs are seemingly downloaded in Zoey's head, and she subsequently discovers she has the ability to hear what people are thinking or feeling through songs only she can hear.[23] Given that Zoey's not well-versed in popular music, she often has to figure out exactly what they are trying to tell her by enlisting the help of her neighbor Mo (Alex Newell). This ability has both downsides, including learning things about people that she'd rather not be privy to, and upsides, such as allowing her to communicate with her father in a new way, particularly since he is unable to speak.

Debuting as a midseason replacement in 2020, the series as a whole reads like an exercise in empathy and a lesson in communication. While the Zoey of the pilot episode is neither unkind nor unaware of the people around her, she nonetheless struggles to connect with others. The first episode opens with Mo singing, and Zoey simply covers her ears, annoyed at the sound, before knocking on Mo's door and asking her to keep it down.[24] While she is adept at picking up flaws in code (she works as a coder at SPRQ Point, a company that seems equal parts Meta and Apple), she is not always the best at reading or communicating with other people. This is set up in two ways (professional and personal) in the pilot episode: she struggles to communicate with her boss Joan (Lauren Graham) as to why she should be promoted (professional) and is completely unaware of her best friend Max's (Skylar Astin) obvious feelings for her until she hears him sing "I Think I Love You" by The Partridge Family. Her newly acquired power lets her see beyond the surface of the people around her and provides insight into herself. This includes seeing beyond the handsome and confident exterior of her coworker (and crush) Simon (John Clarence Stewart) when she hears him singing the slowed-down cover of "Mad World" by Gary Jules, or her boss Joan's personal unhappiness as revealed through "(I Can't Get No) Satisfaction" by the Rolling Stones.[25] That no one else can hear or see these song (and often dance) numbers forces Zoey to find creative ways to communicate with or assist them without revealing how she knows something is on their minds—or in their hearts (she dubs them "heartsongs"). If she doesn't reach out immediately, however, the song will follow her until she takes action.[26] With the help of Mo, herself a singer and the only one who believes what Zoey is experiencing is real, Zoey decides to use her gift to help others.

This is underscored by the ways in which this particular gift helps her communicate with her much beloved father. The entire first season sets up the ways that Mitch is the pivot around which the family turns, and his illness, which literally makes him unable to communicate, is a potentially fracturing event for Zoey, her mother Maggie (Mary Steenburgen), and her brother David (Andrew Leeds). In this respect, the use of music takes on an additional emotional resonance when used with Mitch, as Zoey and her ability is initially the only conduit through which he can convey his wants, feelings, or needs to others. She hears him singing "Moondance" by Van Morrison while staring at Maggie, which Zoey correctly interprets as his desire to be close with his wife; later, when Maggie considers shutting down the business she and Mitch created together, his performance of "It's Your Thing" makes Zoey understand he only wants his wife to be happy.[27] It also allows him to say good-bye to Zoey, singing Billy Joel's "Lullaby (Goodnight, My Angel)" to Zoey; her brother David sings the same song to his son Miles in a later episode.[28]

Like *Glee*, the chosen songs are intended to, if not advance the plot, then illuminate character. While this is also the intention of episodes or shows that feature original songs, the use of popular or well-known music has the possibility of adding additional dimensions based on the viewer, particularly the associations they may have with the song in their own lives or from other media. For example, Simon's rendition of "Mad World" in the pilot episode in the slowed-down style of Jules' cover (rather than the quicker New Wave original by Tears for Fears) was actually released as part of the soundtrack for *Donnie Darko* (2001), and plays over the final scene that resets the timeline and trades one death for another.[29] By choosing to perform it in a similar style, it retains those associations with loss and death, setting the stage for Simon's reveal to Zoey that he is still grieving for his father, who'd taken his own life.[30] "Kiss Me" by Sixpence None the Richer was used so frequently in 1990s teen rom-coms and dramas (most famously in *She's All That* [1999]) that an ensemble performance by much of the cast in an episode focused on new couples makes sense.[31]

One could slot the series into the dramedy category, as it mixes bright and lively production numbers—and the series palette overall is colorful—with poignant and heartfelt narratives. This is more pronounced in the first

FIGURE 8.1 **Zoey *(the show and the character)* goes big in production numbers. © NBC / Photofest © NBC.**

season, with Mitch's illness and eventual death an obvious inevitability. In a review of the series, Amal Awad highlights the way that the series deals with the challenges of chronic illness, concluding that "the discussions, the fatigue, the ways in which they try to maintain ordinary life amid extraordinary circumstances have a refreshing authenticity to them"[32] amidst the bright and campy musical numbers that are a vital part of the series' narrative. Because it is not limited to a single episode or scene, these musical numbers are essentially embodying what would be the series' soundtrack, indicating the inner lives of the characters through the use of its music, not through non-diegetic songs but having them actually perform it. This can lead to some unexpected character moments and growth, as when Mo, who appears to the world as confident and comfortable in their identity, sings "The Great Pretender" by The Platters. When Zoey confronts Mo about it, Mo refuses to acknowledge any feelings of the sort. It is only when Zoey follows her to the church where Mo performs in the choir in male attire rather than the female-presenting looks they usually wear that she understands.[33] In this instance, Zoey's meddling (eventually) helps her friend; yet her abilities can also alienate. When she hears her brother and sister-in-law singing Pink's "Just Give Me a Reason," about a relationship that's struggling, her interference alienates her from her brother, and when she confesses to Max about her ability to hear "heartsongs" and her subsequent awareness of his feelings for her, they become estranged.[34] It can even create a sense of connection that is easy to mistake for love or permanence.[35] Even after the two embark on a relationship, Max struggles with this element of Zoey until he is temporarily granted her power and realizes the challenges of both knowing and interpreting what he learns.[36]

Glee and *Zoey's Extraordinary Playlist* were separated by a decade and a half, with *Glee* debuting on Fox before streaming became ubiquitous and *Zoey's Extraordinary Playlist* on NBC right before the COVID-19 pandemic hit in 2020. Both made strides in representation; Newell was added to the cast in the third season (2012) of *Glee* as Unique, with the initial storyline centered on coming out as transgender.[37] By 2020, Newell's Mo has plots centered on their relationships, including the challenges of dating a man with kids and professional interactions, like partnering with Max on a restaurant rather than being limited to coming-out narratives.[38] While *Glee* had an able-bodied actor playing the wheelchair-bound Artie (as discussed previously), *Zoey* presented "Fight Song" by Rachel Platten performed entirely in American Sign Language by Deaf actress and activist Sandra Mae Frank as she tries to convince her father, Howie (Zak Orth), not to be so overprotective.[39]

Both, then, are influenced by the era in which they debuted, with *Glee* as one of the last big broadcast hits before streaming, and *Zoey* benefiting from streaming in getting a follow-up film after its cancellation in 2021. They also shared not only the ability of the jukebox musical format to keep musical television in the public consciousness, but also the benefit of using known work to connect with audiences.

9

"It's a Lot More Nuanced Than That!": *Crazy Ex-Girlfriend*'s (and *Galavant*'s) Subversive Songs

By 2015, one-off musical episodes had been normalized to the extent that they were showing up in shows that seemed as much of a strange fit as the late, little-lamented *Cop Rock*; *Grey's Anatomy* offered a jukebox musical episode in "Song Beneath the Song" (2011), and *7th Heaven* (1996–2007) debuted "Red Socks" in 2005 and secured its place on multiple lists as the worst musical episode ever.[1] Some, however, utilized the vocal talents of their regular cast and the mythology of their shows to good effect. The CW's *Legends of Tomorrow* (2016–2022) never had a full musical episode, but musical numbers appeared in episodes such as "Séance and Sensibility," which ended with an original Bollywood-inspired number featuring the characters of Zari Tomaz (Tala Ashe) and Sunjay/Kamadeva (Sachin Bhatt) and the wisdom of opening one's heart to new experiences.[2] While that was the most elaborate, other *Legends* episodes featured original songs, including a fake David Bowie song called "Space Girl" and the Mr. Rogers-inspired ensemble piece "Sad Feelings."[3] Fellow superhero series *The Flash* offered the aforementioned full musical episode with "Duet";

the signature original song of the episode, "Super Friends," was co-written by Rachel Bloom, co-creator and star of another CW show, *Crazy Ex-Girlfriend.*

Unlike these single-episode events, *Crazy Ex-Girlfriend* embraced the musical genre for its entire run. Co-created by rom-com veteran Aline Brosh McKenna and Rachel Bloom, the series centers on Rebecca Bunch (Rachel Bloom), a high-powered New York-based attorney about to make partner when she runs into ex-boyfriend Josh Chan (Vincent Rodriguez III) and decides to quit her job and move to his hometown of West Covina, California. Continuing with the rom-com premise, the series also features quirky co-workers, an older, mother-hen-like sidekick, a romantic rival, and a "nice" guy who might be "the one," with certain scenes and interactions visualized by Rebecca, and later others, as musical numbers. All seems to be set up as a typical romantic comedy series with a musical twist. Yet the subversion of its own premise is apparent from the first episode, deconstructing the often toxic relationships and gender roles of the genre (for both women and men). The songs not only aid characterization and move the plot, but do double duty in frequently parodying rom-com tropes through both exposure and by simply allowing each character dimension, as well as subverting expectations of relationships, sexuality, gender, and mental illness through original songs that simultaneously acted as parody and tribute to their source materials. While operating at a less subversive level, a fellow 2015 debut series, *Galavant,* took a similar tack with the Disney musical.

"Damn it, why do musicals always get me so worked up?" *Galavant* and the Disney Musical Genre

An additional, if low-key, element that both *Crazy Ex-Girlfriend* and *Galavant* share is their connections to the subgenre of the Disney musical. While this represents only some of what *Crazy Ex-Girlfriend* works to subvert throughout its run, it is perhaps the most representative element of *Galavant.* This is underscored in multiple ways, from production to narrative and characterization. On a production level, the most obvious connection is Alan Menken, who served as composer, songwriter, and executive producer for the series. Menken's collaboration with Disney started with *The Little Mermaid* in 1989; he and Howard Ashman cowrote both that and *Beauty and the Beast* before Ashman's death in 1991. He went on to compose the music for *Aladdin* (1992), *Newsies* (1992) (a live-action Disney musical), *Pocahontas* (1995), *The Hunchback of Notre Dame* (1996), *Hercules* (1997), *Home on the Range* (2004), *Enchanted* (2007), and *Tangled* (2010). The series aired on ABC, which had been owned by Disney since the mid-1990s. Even casting owed something of a debt to Disney, as Luke Youngblood, who appears as squire Sid on the show, was the original Simba in the West End production of *The Lion King.*

Beyond these production-level correspondences, however, is the way that *Galavant* both plays with and subverts the Disney musical, through both characters and the music itself. It starts with a simple premise: Galavant (Joshua Sasse) is the most charming and bravest knight in the land, who has found the love of his life, Madalena (Mallory Jansen), all told through the introductory song, "Galavant." However, trouble arrives in the form of King Richard (Timothy Omundson), who sets his sights on Madalena, kidnaps her, and vows to marry her. Unfortunately, when Galavant successfully breaches the castle to rescue her, she's decided that the money and power that come with being queen are attractive to her, even if Richard isn't, breaks up with Galavant, and marries Richard. Galavant spirals while Richard invades the neighboring kingdom of Valencia and imprisons its king, queen, and Princess Isabella (Karen David). Scared that Madalena still has feelings for Galavant, Richard tells Isabella to lure him to the castle or he'll kill her parents. Against her better judgment, she seeks out Galavant and convinces him Madalena still loves him, and he agrees to aid Isabella in rescuing her parents and his love, with the help of his squire Sid.[4] The rest of the season is focused on their journey to the castle, and the politics and shenanigans going on inside of it.

The tone of the series is lighthearted, sarcastic, and self-aware, and is aided by the fact that each episode is only thirty minutes long. Given the high-concept fantasy premise, the shorter run time keeps each episode from overstaying its welcome, featuring, at most, three songs per episode. In the first minute of the episode, as the village sings of Galavant's virtues, these include "cojones out to there" and "mess with him, he'll disembowel you," and his "lady love" was one he loved to "excess, thrice daily more or less, and she'd be screaming 'Galavant,'"[5] it makes obvious what Disney's animated musicals barely imply. Yet one can see Disney's inspiration in characters such as King Richard, portrayed as an overgrown man-child with a more impressive (i.e., violent) older brother, as a direct descendant of King John in 1974's *Robin Hood*.[6] The narrative is expected, and yet consistently undermined, as with Galavant's big rescue ending in Madalena choosing money over love, or Galavant winning a tournament not because of hard work but because Isabella sabotages his opponent.[7] When Galavant gets over Madalena and Isabella confesses her potential betrayal, their first kiss, which Galavant promises will be "one of those forever sort of kisses," is, in reality, "awkward," "moist," and "slightly yeasty/ oddly musty."[8] Even the "I want" song is not sung by the hero or love interest, but King Richard, effectively combining it with a villain song.[9] Musically, the songs could easily slot into either a Disney renaissance or contemporary film, but lyrically, the series' songs and narratives take explicit aim at the tropes of the genre: the damsel in distress is a social climber and possible evil sorceress by the second season, the brave knight who quickly sinks into despair and takes most of the first season to get back into fighting shape; even the fabled conflict between dwarves and giants reveals that both groups are roughly the same size, leading to an extremely confusing battle.[10] One of Galavant's hero moments is brutally undercut when his squire Sid tosses him his sword to continue the battle, only for it to impale and kill Galavant (he gets better).[11]

All of this is part of the series' overall self-awareness of itself as a created object. In the big ensemble number that opens the second season, the cast sings about what will change in the narrative, their shock at being renewed, and ending with the admission that "there's still no reason why we burst into song,"[12] addressing the frequent complaint discussed throughout this book. Even the episode title acknowledges its status as a television show: "A New Season aka Suck It Cancellation Bear" (a reference to the now-defunct TV by the Numbers website). The first season itself ends with an ensemble reprise of "Galavant," with the cast asking, "Will all the singing kill our Nielsen ratings?" It knowingly borrows from any number of sources, from Disney (as discussed above), to JRR Tolkien and George RR Martin, both in the final battle of three armies, a throwaway reference to sacrifices to the White Walkers, and Galavant's untimely death and resurrection paralleling that of Jon Snow (Kit Harington) in *Game of Thrones* (2011–2019).[13] The final episode references the series' composer; in a flashback, when an off-screen voice asks a young Richard whether he'd like his own "theme song," Richard's valet/bodyguard Gareth (Vinnie Jones) yells "Shut up, Menken!"[14]

The series debuted in January of 2015, taking over the timeslot for the thematically—if not tonally—similar *Once Upon a Time*, but which also pitched it against *The Simpsons* on Fox. Its ratings remained low in live viewings, but improved in DVR playback (something referenced in "A New Season").[15] It was filmed in parts of Wales as well as England (Bristol, primarily), making use of a recently implemented TV tax credit to keep the per-episode costs down; *Galavant* was produced for a little over a million an episode, which was relatively low for 2015.[16] The ratings, however, were not what ABC hoped for, and it was canceled after two seasons.[17]

"It's where dreams live": *Crazy Ex-Girlfriend* Goes for Broke

Timing can be everything in terms of a series' success, particularly those that fall outside of the expected broadcast genres: procedurals, soaps, and sitcoms. *Pushing Daisies*, for instance, aired on ABC between 2007 and 2008. It was critically acclaimed but expensive to make, and when the 2007 writers' strike shut down production for months, its ratings couldn't justify its renewal once the strike was settled. Given that from the mid-1980s on, broadcast channels had expanded from three to (at least) six, the competition even with broadcast alone generally meant that shows had to succeed quickly or not at all.

The CW Network, co-created by Warner Brothers and Paramount after the WB and UPN shut down in 2006, eventually went with a different approach, driven partly by economics and partly by the paradigm shift of streaming. From 2011, when Mark Pedowitz took over from Dawn Ostroff as the president of entertainment, the slate of programming on the network remained fairly stable compared to other networks. There were a few reasons why the network went in this direction. As a smaller network (known as a netlet), the CW did not have the reach of ABC, CBS, NBC, or even Fox. Pilots can be expensive to make, and following rules changes in 1996, networks affiliated with studios tended to focus on creating them in-house, which meant they assumed all the risk but also all the potential reward (syndication money, ancillary deals, etc.). In its first half-decade, the most stable program on the network was a holdover from the WB: *Supernatural.* Two things happened during Pedowitz's first year, however, that changed the landscape for the network. First, he made a billion-dollar deal with Netflix to air its shows on streaming, generating income for the network (if not necessarily for the showrunners, writers, or actors[18]). This allowed new viewers to be able to discover shows like *Supernatural* and *The Vampire Diaries* (2009–2017) while they were still airing, driving viewership both ways. The second was the debut of *Arrow* in October 2012. Not only did *Arrow* bring in the elusive 18-to-24 male demographic that had disappeared following *Smallville*'s ending of its 10-season run, but it created its own mini-network with a series of spin-offs of varying degrees of success: *The Flash* (9 seasons), *Supergirl* (6 seasons), *Legends of Tomorrow* (7 seasons), *Black Lightning* (4 seasons), and *Batwoman* (3 seasons). The success of both the streaming deal and the DC universe shows propped up other, riskier ventures, like the telenovela-inspired *Jane the Virgin* (2014–2019), DC Vertigo's *iZombie*, and the musical *Crazy Ex-Girlfriend*, all of which ran multiple seasons and were able to finish their runs on their own terms; the CW renewed more shows than it canceled. (At least until 2022.[19])

It is likely that on any other broadcast network, *Crazy Ex-Girlfriend* would have been lucky to last a single season, never mind four. Co-created by Aline Brosh McKenna, who at the time was best known for her adaptation of *The Devil Wears Prada* (2006), and Rachel Bloom, who'd hit internet stardom with her original song/video "Fuck Me, Ray Bradbury," it was originally pitched to Showtime, a fact that one can see in what eventually made it to air on the CW. That is, the show often touched on topics that would be considered taboo, particularly around women's biology and sexuality, and the songs were often reedited for broadcast but released unedited on YouTube via Bloom's YouTube page (e.g., the song "Buttload of Cats"[20] was released under its original title "Fuckton of Cats" online). The inciting incident of the series takes inspiration from films and television shows like *My Best Friend's Wedding* (1997), where Julianne (Julia Roberts) tries to break up her best friend Michael's (Dermot Mulroney) impending nuptials when she realizes she's in love with him, to *Felicity* (1998–2002), where the titular character gives up her spot at Stanford to follow her high school crush Ben (Scott Speedman) to New York when he signs her yearbook "wish we'd gotten to know each other better."[21] In *Crazy Ex-Girlfriend*, the first episode starts ten years in the past (2005), setting up Rebecca's two big loves: Josh Chan (Vincent Rodriguez III) and musical theater, at the summer camp both attend. The two date over that summer, only for Josh to break it off at the end of camp, saying she's "dramatic" and "weird." The narrative fast-forwards ten years to a successful, if not particularly happy Rebecca who is about to be made partner at her law firm in Manhattan. She tells herself that "this is what happy feels like" while she runs out of the building and has a small panic attack. In a stunning coincidence, she sees Josh for the first time in a decade, and unlike their initial parting, he seems happy to see her. He tells her he'd been living in New York, but was heading back to his hometown of West Covina, California, where people are "happy." Following this, she turns down the partner position and relocates to West Covina, singing about all its virtues while the visuals tell another story ("West Covina"), telling herself and everyone around her that it's because the struggling law firm Whitefeather and Associates made her a better offer than New York. This particular bit of fiction holds out until the end of the episode, when coworker Paula (Donna Lynn Champlin) confronts her and Rebecca finally admits that Josh may have played a role in her decision (something she won't admit again for another eight episodes). Paula agrees to help her get Josh, and the episode ends on a reprise of "West Covina" sung as a duet between them both.[22]

The series as a whole charts Rebecca's—and her friends'—progress through various phases of adulthood and relationships, as reflected in the conventions of titling the episodes from season to season. That is, the episode titles in season one all feature Josh's name and end in an exclamation point, suggesting her manic hyperfocus on him. Season two's episodes all end with a question mark, indicating that Rebecca is confused as to the status of things between them. Season three expands her perspective as things with Josh fall apart and Rebecca spirals into suicidal depression; the first half of the season returns to the "Josh" format of episode names, before she begins focusing on others as she puts her life and mental health back together. By season four, each episode begins with "I" rather than someone else's name, indicating she's not using other people and her relationships to define herself. Each episode features at least two musical numbers; at the beginning, all of them were from Rebecca's perspective, but starting with the sixth episode, musical numbers appeared in scenes Rebecca was not a part of.[23] By the end of the series, even minor or recurring characters have had at least one solo musical number.

The final episode of the series reveals what is already obvious: that her musical numbers are occurring in Rebecca's head. While this is complicated by the aforementioned fact that several of these occur without her presence, it ends up working as part of the heightened reality of the series. Rebecca is the fulcrum of the series, but everyone around her is dealing with their own issues, whether it's Josh and his immaturity and struggle to commit, or Paula, approaching middle age and unhappy both personally and professionally. Like *Galavant* and other modern musical series, *Crazy Ex-Girlfriend* is highly aware of its status as a created object, but is not as overt as others in breaking the fourth wall. It's an element it plays with rather than fully embraces, as in the song "Who's the New Guy?" with its references to "ratings" ("you mean our terrible ratings on legalscores.com?") or how many "episodes" he'll be there for (that is, "Karen's manic episodes").[24]

And yet, more so than some of the other series discussed, *Crazy Ex-Girlfriend* is in fact hyperaware of multiple elements of narrative, characterization, and genre. The series' title is itself a commentary on the way women tend to be portrayed in some romantic comedies, particularly the ways their behavior can be both romanticized (doing anything for love) and condemned (doing *anything* for love). Yet it also is an indicator of Rebecca's mental health; in the

FIGURE 9.1 ***Rebecca imagines a sexier version of getting ready for a date. The CW Television Network / Photofest © The CW Television Network.***

first episode, she is shown throwing away several bottles of medication.[25] When Josh leaves her at the altar at the end of the second season, the first four episodes of season three show her slow descent into morally and ethically problematic actions before she bottoms out, seemingly alienating all of her friends before they can reject her and tormenting Josh, finally giving up and returning to her mom in New York.[26] When that only makes things worse, she attempts suicide.[27] It's only after this that she realizes that it is less about Josh and more about what he represented, and she finally starts to rebuild her life and herself, and is properly diagnosed and treated for borderline personality disorder.[28]

Despite the darkness of many of its storylines, the series maintains its irreverent touch, of which the featured songs play a crucial part. On a music genre level, an episode can feature songs that suggest Broadway musicals ("The Buzzing in the Bathroom" and "Flooded with Justice" echo the ballads in *Les Misérables*; "Cold Showers" is a direct tribute to "Ya Got Trouble" from *The Music Man*), heavy metal ("What a Rush to Be a Bride"), R&B/hip-hop ("The Sexy Gettin' Ready Song," "JAP Battle"), and 50s doo-wop ("Maybe She's Not Such a Heinous Bitch After All"), among many others. Disney musicals get a sideways nod through Rebecca's love of an off-brand animated musical called *Slumbered*, with its signature song "One Indescribable Instant." This moment carries through multiple episodes, including the first season finale featuring Lea Salonga (who voiced Jasmine in *Aladdin* and sings this original song in the series) as one of Josh's family members performing the song at a wedding.[29] Disney's influence can also be seen in Rebecca's song "The Villain in My Own Story," in which she (briefly) realizes that in the triangle between Josh, Josh's girlfriend Valencia (Gabrielle Ruiz), and herself, she is the bad guy: "I told myself I was Jasmine/But now I realize I'm Jafar."[30] Even the setting of her fantasy resembles the Evil Stepmother's lair from *Snow White* (1937), as do the prosthetics and costume she wears.

These songs can be used in a variety of ways, although primarily they reveal character, both lyrically and through the songs' genre. The aforementioned "new guy" the cast sings about, Nathanial Plimpton III (Scott Michael Foster), a tall, handsome preppy-looking guy from a wealthy family, sings a song in season three that sounds, musically, like mid-2000s slow jams about beautiful women and hitting clubs, but in fact is about how he loves going to the zoo to see the animals and gain some perspective, adding depth to the same character who spent an entire song in the previous season negging Rebecca in "Let's Have Intercourse," which parodies Ed Sheeran's "Thinking Out Loud."[31] Greg Serrano (Santino Fontana/Skylar Astin), who works in a bar but wants to escape West Covina as much as Rebecca wants to embrace it, sings about how stuck he is in a spot-on parody of Billy Joel's "Piano Man," including a piano appearing in the middle of the bar for him to play. The song expertly reveals both his discontent and belief that he's better than those around him;[32] this is underlined later when he takes a class at the community college and doesn't do as well as he thought he would. His song "I Could If I Wanted To" is a take-off on the spoken/sung songs that cropped up in the 1990s, like Nada Surf's "Popular" or King Missile's "Detachable Penis" that bristle with a similarly Gen X "whatever" vibe: "Sure, I could get an A if I wanted to get an A/But who cares about an A?/I don't/I don't care/Although I coulda made that grade if I did care/But I don't."[33] Taken together, they paint a fairly accurate portrait of Greg's cynicism and self-delusion that, in many ways, makes him a mirror of Rebecca's own penchant for delusional or grandiose ideas about herself or those around her.

This is the case for many series, in which traits of the main character are often reflected in those around them. *Crazy Ex-Girlfriend* is well aware of this, both highlighting and subverting the idea through Rebecca's own penchant for main character syndrome: that is, not only considering yourself the main character in your life (which is true) but reducing those around you to sidekicks or villains. The show offers characters that are intentional mirrors, such as Trent (Paul Welsh), whose behavior toward Rebecca is almost exactly like Rebecca's toward Josh, reflecting her unhinged actions in relationships, or

Audra (Rachel Grate), who grew up with Rebecca in New York in a remarkably similar upbringing and represents her competitive nemesis who seems to have done everything right in her life.[34] There are also those who either cast themselves (Paula) or are cast by Rebecca (Valencia) as sidekicks or villains; part of the trajectory of both the series and the characters themselves is the ways in which both they and Rebecca discover the ways in which not only do they outgrow these labels but that they never quite fit in the first place. Paula, who works as a paralegal, actually wants to become a lawyer, and her dissatisfaction with her life drives her to help Rebecca scheme to get Josh, slowly realizing that she's using that to defer her own story and enabling (and enacting) bad behavior. Valencia, who's been dating Josh since high school, comes across as condescending and bitchy to almost everyone, making her seem like the perfect rom-com villain (the girl the guy doesn't belong with), only to reveal her vulnerability and strike out on her own, without Josh.[35] The songs they perform reflect this growth: Valencia, who in season one sings "Women Have to Stick Together," in which she insults every woman she comes across, actually makes friends with Rebecca and Heather (Vella Lovell) by season two, reflected in "Friendtopia," a Spice Girls-inspired song sung by Rebecca, Heather, and Valencia.[36] Paula's personal and professional discontent and hopes are expressed in "Maybe This Dream," in which she sings about what she wants and what's standing in her way; by season three, she is in law school and dealt with at least one of the issues that led her to over-invest in Rebecca's relationship with Josh: her own heartbreak with her first love, Jeff (John Gatins) in "First Penis I Saw."[37] Indeed, by the fourth season, nearly everyone around Rebecca has made significant progress, so much so that Rebecca herself feels left behind.[38]

Unlike shows like *Galavant*, which was canceled after two seasons on something of a cliffhanger, *Crazy Ex-Girlfriend*'s position as a CW show—along with the critical praise and accolades the series received—allowed Bloom and

McKenna to complete the show's journey. Rather than ending with Rebecca finding love with Josh, Nathanial, or Greg, something that the penultimate episode teased by having Rebecca go on a date with each of them,[39] it instead brings Rebecca full circle. That is, her love of music and musical theater, present from the first season of the first episode, leads her to start composing and singing the music that until then had only existed in her head, putting her efforts into learning how to play and sing rather than hyper-focusing on something or someone else to her own detriment. The final shot of the series is her seated at a piano, ready to share her music with the community she built around her.[40]

The 2015/2016 season offered two musical series that shared some significant commonalities, despite differences in execution and their ultimate fates. It is perhaps surprising that the more pedigreed *Galavant*, featuring Disney composer Menken and airing on the Disney-owned ABC, with its light and comedic tone, struggled to last two seasons, while the more unknown Bloom and McKenna were able to complete a narrative that featured difficult or cringe-inducing topics and often-unlikeable characters and situations. Yet the smaller canvas of the CW, both in terms of reach and revenue/budgets, worked for series that were unlike their contemporaries on the larger broadcast networks. Both series, however, simultaneously embraced and subverted the musical genre that inspired them; that is, using the now expected self-awareness to send-up and skewer particular conventions while delighting in the song-and-dance of it all.

10

Where the Past Meets the Future: *Schmigadoon!* and When Musicals Go Streaming

The history of streaming is a long, involved one that could fill its own book, starting with the invention and use of the théâtrophone in 1890, which allowed customers to stream music from local operas and other productions if they subscribed to the service.[1] In the contemporary era, however, streaming started in the 1990s, with companies like RealNetworks broadcasting baseball games, and Microsoft and Apple developing the web players Windows Media and QuickTime, respectively. Technology, particularly around bandwidth and file compression, still needed to catch up before it was a viable alternate platform. Netflix launched in 1997, offering physical media for rental (DVDs), before getting into streaming in 2007, along with Apple, Amazon, and Hulu, which was cofounded by NBC and Fox. Until 2013, however, when Netflix debuted *House of Cards* (2013–2018), none of the existing services offered original programming. Twelve years later, watching programming on streaming has overtaken television (both broadcast and cable).[2] Because streaming isn't necessarily subjected to the same standards and practices of broadcast, as well as not wholly reliant on advertising means that risky subjects, formats, and genres can—if not always do—thrive in a streaming space.

Debuting on Apple TV in 2021, *Schmigadoon!*, about a couple in a troubled relationship that stumble upon a magical land where everyone sings in the style of 40s and 50s-era musicals, offered appropriately escapist fare during one of the many heights of the COVID-19 pandemic. Yet the use of the "Sch" intensifier, a Yiddish construction frequently used to highlight irony, suggests the way the series both honors and subverts its musical forebears, often through its main characters Melissa (Cecily Strong), who adores musicals and finds it easier to navigate this reality, and Josh (Keegan-Michael Key), who can't stand them and remains at odds with the town and Melissa herself throughout much of the first season. I'll conclude this examination of TV, musicals, and everything in between by examining not only the series, but how the transition of the television musical series from terrestrial to streaming nevertheless retains the spirit of its television brethren, starting with a discussion of a product of the 2007 Writers' Guild strike: *Dr. Horrible's Sing-Along Blog.*

The "Death Whinny" of Television? *Doctor Horrible* as Model for Television-Quality Internet Content

In October 2008, Ben Silverman, the co-head of programming at NBC/Universal, applied the method he used during the 2008 May upfront process of "soliciting advertisers to be part of the development process, integrating their brands into scripted shows from the get go" to a whole new set of programs available exclusively at NBC.com.[3] Although this announcement made no reference to the highly successful internet-only series, *Doctor Horrible's Sing-Along Blog*, which debuted July 15, 2008, it is clear that *Doctor Horrible* itself represented the early days of a trend: using the internet as a television-adjunct. Silverman and Cameron Death of NBC's digital studio announced that they were offering a line-up using "name actors and TV-quality production values" that they hoped would be entirely funded by brands.[4]

The stage was set for the rise of internet programming of television quality long before Silverman's plan was set into action; indeed, long before *Dr. Horrible's Sing-Along Blog* debuted. Stephen Bochco entered into an agreement with the site MetaCafe to produce online content in 2006; MetaCafe sought deals from big-name producers to "cut through the clutter" of online videos with "quality" work. Bochco claimed that "People were trying to fit a square peg in a round hole. They were trying to impose our old entertainment model on their new platform. You're looking at a vastly different medium." Yet Bochco saw little appreciable difference in terms of his job as creator and producer: "It's still sitting around a campfire telling stories. It's just a different campfire," thereby affirming the connection between terrestrial television and its new online counterpart.[5] There were, however, problems lying ahead, as executives and writers tended to have differing views on what online content represented.

On November 6, 2007, the Writers' Guild of America (WGA) went on strike over the issue of residuals on DVDs and web-based content. This was an issue that *Variety* had identified as a possible problem in 2004 and again in 2006; it stretched back to the WGA's negotiations and capitulations to the Association of Motion Picture and Television Producers (AMPTP) to end the 21-week strike in 1988 over residuals for VHS releases. When DVD was adopted as the preferred format in 1996, the amount that writers received remained at 4 cents for each copy sold; this despite both the speed of adoption and the volume of DVDs sold, particularly television programs released on DVD. The DVD format, according to the trade publications through the early part of the decade, was vital in offsetting the loss of foreign distribution deals and rising production costs. Further, the internet was still a nascent technology during previous years and thus played no part in any previous contract negotiations. These were the main points at stake for the WGA: to raise the amount of residuals that writers received, as the studios claimed 80 percent of those moneys, leaving 20 percent to be split among: writers, actors, and directors, and to establish that web-based content, such as free episodes online, online actor, director, and writer commentaries, iTunes sales, and web episodes (known as webisodes) was part of the television program and thus fell under the purview of what writers should be compensated for. The AMPTP, particularly on the issue of web-content, claimed that web-based programming and programming adjuncts constituted "publicity," which was covered under the existing contract and thus did not represent additional work requiring compensation, not considering it could be both. Indeed, NBC/Reveille's release of episodes of *The Office* on iTunes and a series of webisodes shown during the 2006 summer hiatus provided the struggling show with enough extra attention from viewers to save it from potential cancellation, making it both content and publicity.

To garner support outside of the industry, the strike captains and assorted writers, producers, and actors made use of the internet to make their case to web-enabled television viewers. The strike captains started a website called UnitedHollywood.com, as well as spearheading a fan movement similar to "save my show" campaigns called "Pencils 2 Media Moguls." Interested individuals could purchase boxes of pencils that would then be sent in bulk to the studios; this, they felt, would indicate to members of the AMPTP how much popular support the writers had outside of the industrial context. They also used YouTube to post videos of the strike, fake "corporate exposure" type pieces intended to highlight what they felt was the disdain and dismissiveness within AMPTP leadership, and supportive videos from actors and crew members. At the forefront of many of these efforts were show creators such as JJ Abrams (*Lost*, *Alias*), Ron Moore (*Battlestar Galactica*), and Joss Whedon (*Firefly*, *Angel*). Joss Whedon, in particular, used the fan-created blog Whedonesque.com to keep fans of his series aware of the progress of the strike and to counteract what he felt were negative portrayals in industry publications such as *Variety* or major media outlets such as the *New York Times*. He wrote on November 7 in response to a *New York Times* piece on the strike that referred to the strike as having "all the trappings of a union protest" except that the writers wore "arty glasses and fancy scarves": "The easiest tactic is for people to paint writers as namby pamby arty scarfy posers, because it's what most people think even when we're not striking . . . (And Hollywood writers are overpaid, scarf-wearing dainties.) It's an easy argument to make. And a hard one to dispute."[6]

The strike officially ended on February 12, 2008, three days before the deadline for production of material for the 2008/2009 television season, with a rise in the DVD residuals for the writers and a metric set up for non-traditional media use of television properties. Not all Guild members were pleased with the outcome; Harlan Ellison felt that WGA leadership, in accepting the terms that ended the strike, allowed the AMPTP to "beat us like a yellow dog" and "make us their bitches."[7] In what he claimed was an effort to "prove" the WGA's claims that programming on the internet was not in fact publicity but could be monetized, Whedon collaborated with his brothers Zack and Jed, as well as Maurissa Tancharoen, during the months of the strike to write the musical *Dr. Horrible's Sing-Along Blog*. In an NPR interview, Whedon described the musical as "an effort to send a message to the community that there was another way . . . that we could create content and ultimately create jobs without the studios."[8] He also cited Felicia Day's web series *The Guild*, which was funded by donations from viewers, as one inspiration for *Dr. Horrible*. *Dr. Horrible* is the story of a nerdy supervillain, Billy/Dr. Horrible (Neil Patrick Harris), tormented by both his crush on Penny (Felicia Day), a girl he'd met at the local launderette, and his self-proclaimed nemesis, Captain Hammer (Nathan Fillion). When not involved in crime as an attempt to gain entrance to the Evil League of Evil, Dr. Horrible is known as Billy; no apparent alter ego exists for Captain Hammer. Although filmed in Los Angeles, the action occurs in some form of alternate existence where superheroes, supervillains, and an "Evil League of Evil" are in charge. Given the fact that "blog" is in the title of the musical, it is similar structurally to an online environment in which a persona is developed within the online community and the individual is thusly referred to as that persona.

Similar to online communities, the world of *Dr. Horrible's Sing-Along Blog* is hierarchically structured; there is the "day-to-day life" that involves mundane tasks such as laundry; the heroic, as represented by Captain Hammer, and his two-tiered opposite number: The Henchmen's Union and The Evil League of Evil. The three-part series revolved around Billy's attempts to get into the Evil League of Evil and win the affections of Penny; both goals are continually thwarted by Captain Hammer, whose social interactions and style of fighting are made obvious by his name. Hammer is reminiscent, particularly apparent in a series of Billy's flashbacks, of an athletic bully. Billy's goal, which, in the guise of Dr. Horrible, is "to rule" a world that he defines as a mess and to disrupt the status quo as represented by "Captain Hammer: Corporate Tool," is thus achieved by exposing the persona of Captain Hammer and revealing him to be weak and cowardly. In the end, he is finally accepted as a high-ranking and respected member of the Evil League of Evil, albeit at great personal cost and a loss of any identity outside of his "Horrible" persona ("Everything You Ever"). In this way, his defeat is soured by becoming what he has despised; the original individual has been supplanted by the persona, a "corporate tool" and celebrity in the same way Captain Hammer was portrayed.[9]

Industrially, *Dr. Horrible* as "internet television" was created as a self-funded collaborative effort among writers, producers, and actors who agreed to participate for no upfront compensation. Further, the conditions under which it was developed were a response to the contract dispute and subsequent strike addressed earlier. Much as information was disseminated and support garnered for the striking writers through the use of the internet and fan communities, so too was the musical publicized freely by fans of Whedon's earlier works. It was later broadcast both nationally and internationally for minimal or no cost upon its release, but it still found a way to make a profit. The soundtrack to the musical was released on iTunes and charted on Billboard's Top 40 at number 39 two weeks after its release. A region-free, on-demand DVD of the musical was released exclusively on Amazon.com on December 19, 2008. It was the second highest selling DVD as of January 5, 2009; it was still the number 23 top-selling item by April of the same year. Proceeds from the sale of the DVD went to compensate the cast and crew.

On both a textual and industrial level, *Dr. Horrible* operated within many of the pre-defined parameters of commercial television. Textually, despite Billy's assertions that he wants to "social change," he also wants money and "anarchy that he runs" ("Brand New Day"). He distrusts that any positive social change can occur at a grassroots level, such as Penny's efforts to garner support to convert an abandoned building into a shelter, preferring to "cut the head" off of humanity. In that respect, *Dr. Horrible* flagged up one of the contradictions of the convergence between the internet and television: Could online content such as *Dr. Horrible's Sing-Along Blog* represent an alternative to television programming when it has been so informed by the medium on an industrial and economic level? Aside from the high quality of the video itself, two out of the three main cast members, Neil Patrick Harris and Nathan Fillion, were known primarily for their television work. In Harris' case, despite his popularity in the show *How I Met Your Mother*, his work on Broadway, and his film work, most of the articles regarding the web musical instead make reference to the show *Doogie Howser, MD*, the 1980s dramedy in which Harris played a 16-year-old physician. Whedon, as well as his brothers and sister-in-law, had or would go on to create for television, including *Deadwood* (2004–2006) (Zack Whedon) and *Agents of S.H.I.E.L.D.* (2013–2020) (Jed Whedon and Maurissa Tancharoen). One of the sets (Dr. Horrible's lab) had been created for the Discovery Channel series *Monster House* (2003–2006), with other filming taking place on Universal's backlot, particularly the "alley" set, used in shows such as *24*. It was hard for a series like *Dr. Horrible* to undermine the primacy of television when it was so informed by it on multiple levels.

That being said, the early success of *Dr. Horrible* seems to suggest that streaming could be a viable alternative, with both television and advertising industries warming to the idea that internet-based programming could at least be an economically sustainable counterpart to terrestrial broadcast and cable programming. Media scholar Amanda Lotz defined the ideas and concepts that cross multiple platforms, such as television and the internet, as one form of "phenomenal television," i.e., a "category of programming that retains the societal importance attributed to television's earlier operation as a cultural forum despite the changes of the post-network era."[10] Depending on one's definition of "societal importance," *Dr. Horrible* could certainly fit under this rubric with the high viewing numbers it generated (more than 200,000 viewers on its first day of release on Hulu.com, crashing the site) as well as the soundtrack's appearance on the Billboard's Hot 100 chart, despite being released only on iTunes. It also fits with Lotz's definition of post-network television being characterized by convergence, theatricality, and mobility, due to its collaborative creation, its musical genre, and its availability for download to multiple platforms.

In its wake, as mentioned earlier, NBC Universal did attempt to solicit content and advertisers to develop web-only programming for NBC.com. At the time, however, this tended to take the form of short webisodes that introduced new programs (*Community* was given a series of webisodes before its debut, in the form of an online student guide to Greendale Community College) or expanded stories or characters from established ones (*The Office*). It would be another five years before original content created for streaming would appear online, and at the time appeared to be a viable alternative to television's structure, particularly the lack of advertising. That being said, it is clear that the same economic issues occurring around terrestrial television have been carried onto the internet. The huge amount of original programming created by Netflix, Hulu, Disney Plus, HBO Max, and the dozens of specialized streaming services that have appeared over the past decade, cannot be paid for merely by their monthly subscription rates, meaning that they've ended up back in the same place as television: incorporating ads, getting sponsors, and engaging in deficit financing in hopes that its success will pay off. The resolution of the 2007 WGA strike allowed internet television to move forward at a greater pace than before, only to lead to a more extensive strike in 2023 addressing many of the same issues, as well as some new ones around smaller writing rooms, lack of mentorship, and royalty payments.[11] Back in 2008, it was unclear whether streaming would develop under the more do-it-yourself, collaborative model that *Dr. Horrible* represented, or the more stylized and commercial model that NBC Universal promoted. As with most things, it ended up being a bit of both.

"It's like if *The Walking Dead* was also *Glee*": *Schmigadoon!* Moves Forward While Honoring the Past

As suggested in the previous chapter, it's challenging to make a TV musical series—or episode—anymore without a high degree of self-awareness; that is, acknowledging the theatricality of it, finding a reason why, or satirizing the conventions of the genre. Within its first episode, *Schmigadoon!* does all three. The series starts with two doctors in New York, orthopedic surgeon Josh Skinner (Keegan-Michael Key), and Melissa Gimble (Cecily Strong), an OB-GYN, and a meet-cute at the hospital candy machine, when Josh's attempts to get Melissa's candy bar loose lead to the machine dumping out its entire supply. While things go well at first, including Josh re-creating that moment on their first anniversary as a couple, after a few years together, they find themselves at odds as to where the relationship is going and whether they are meant to be together. They decide to go on a couples' retreat to reignite the spark in their relationship, only to find themselves in a brightly colored, old-fashioned town they initially think is either part of the retreat experience or some kind of tourist destination. As evidenced by the title of the series, and the town itself, it is a mystical place that is not always accessible, which was the premise of the 1947 musical *Brigadoon*, in which it is revealed that the town is only available to the outside world once every 100 years. Like its predecessor, *Schmigadoon!* also features two lost New Yorkers stumbling upon a place untouched by time or the outside world; in this case, both sets and costumes suggest late 1800s to early 1900s. Josh and Melissa discover this when they try to leave, but the bridge they cross only brings them straight back to the town. A leprechaun (Martin Short) appears to tell them that they cannot leave until they find "true love."[12] The rest of the first season is the two of them figuring out what that means; is it with one another, or someone else in Schmigadoon?

The series creators, Cinco Paul and Ken Daurio, came out of the world of animation (Illumination Studios) including *The Lorax* (2012), *The Secret Lives of Pets* (2016), and the *Despicable Me* franchise, all of which featured some original music, although *The Lorax*, for example, featured multiple original compositions like its Disney forebears,[13] while the four *Despicable Me* films generally only featured an original theme song and a contemporary or near-contemporary popular song as a closing number. *Schmigadoon!* was their first television production, driven by Paul's love of musical theater, with Melissa and Josh representing both their reactions to the genre, as Daurio disliked musical theater.[14] Indeed, Daurio didn't stay with the production; Paul served as primary showrunner for the series' two seasons. Barry Sonnenfeld, who had worked as director and cinematographer in both film (*The Addams Family* [1991]/*Addams Family Values* [1993], *Big* [1988]) and television (*Fantasy Island* [1998–1999], *Pushing Daisies* [2007–2008]) for decades, directed all six episodes of the first season, which shared the colorful and slightly surreal aesthetic of his work in both mediums. Paul wrote the songs and about half of the episodes of the first season; season two, focused on the musicals of the 1960s and 1970s, brought in additional writers.

Paul's familiarity with the genre is clear in the construction of the series. While it does tell its own story, it does so in the context of a mish-mash of characters, songs, and plots that are clearly inspired by classic musicals. For example, from *The Sound of Music*, Dr. Jorge Lopez's (Jaime Camil) characterization as slightly tyrannical but ultimately good-hearted suggests Captain Von Trapp (Christopher Plummer), as does the blossoming of his relationship with Melissa (temporarily in the Maria [Julia Andrews] role). The appearance of his fiancée Countess Gabrielle von Blerkom (Jane Krakowski) is a direct reference to the Baroness Elsa von Schraeder (Eleanor Parker), and "Va-Gi-Na," which Melissa sings to a young unmarried couple expecting a child, is a gloss on "Do-Re-Mi."[15] Of course, the series position as somewhere between satire and homage means that unlike her *Sound of Music* counterpart, Countess Blerkom has no intention of graciously stepping aside; she drives Melissa out into the country and leaves her there, all while singing about all of the men she's loved and lost to other women ("I Always, Always Never Get My Man").[16] "Va-Gi-Na" is also a teaching song, but instead of teaching young people how to sing, as with "Do-Re-Mi," Melissa is using her medical knowledge to teach the scared young couple the intricacies of sex and childbirth. Based on the title of the series and its separation from the regular world, *Brigadoon* is an obvious source, while characters such as Danny Bailey (Aaron Tveit) and Emma Tate (Ariana Debose), as well as their stories and songs, borrow from *Carousel* and *The Music Man*, respectively.

FIGURE 10.1 ***Even Election Day calls for a song and dance. Apple TV / Photofest © Apple+.***

Where the series veers into gentle satire, both in its first and second seasons, is the way it points out the contradictions and omissions of the Golden Age musicals and beyond. Danny Bailey, a carnival barker in the town of Schmigadoon, is a take on the ne'er-do-well Billy Bigelow (Gordon MacRae) from *Carousel*, singing to Melissa that "You Can't Tame Me"; after a single night together, however, Danny's already planning out the rest of their lives, much to Melissa's chagrin. Emma finds her forebears in characters such as Marian (Shirley Jones) from *The Music Man*, complete with a cute little brother struggling with a lisp (as does Marian's little brother Winthrop [Ron Howard]), but, as Chris Murphy suggests, her big musical number "With All Your Heart" parodies "Getting to Know You" from *The King and I* (1956) more than any song from *The Music Man*.[17] ("Tribulation," however, led by the town's self-appointed moral guardian Mildred [Kristin Chenoweth] against the "strangers" [Josh and Melissa], is unmistakably "Trouble" from *The Music Man*.) Season two, known as "Schmicago," which moves into the 60s and 70s, offers takes on *Chicago* (1975), *Sweeney Todd* (1979), *Godspell* (1976), and *Jesus Christ Superstar* (1971) (among others). Bobby Flanagan (Jane Krakowski), Josh's lawyer when he is framed for murder, is clearly the amoral Billy Flynn from *Chicago*, making Josh into a celebrity murderer whose rage was triggered by jazz music, while Topher (Aaron Tveit) and his group of followers are heavily inspired by *Godspell* with a touch of *Jesus Christ Superstar*. Even before her first musical number, "The Worst Brats in Town," orphanage head Miss Codwell (Kristin Chenoweth) is clearly Miss Hannigan from *Annie* (1977), whose "Little Girls" equally expressed her hatred for the kids in her charge. Dooley (Alan Cumming), with his butcher shop and bloody apron, is, of course, Sweeney Todd.

There are a few elements that make the second season less of a retread and more of a re-visioning of the first. This is partly achieved by Melissa being less familiar with this era of musicals, putting her more on par with Josh; for instance, she doesn't realize Dooley's clearly telegraphed plan to use humans for meat in his shop because she never saw the full production of *Sweeney*

Todd, as it scared her.[18] That means they are less prepared for what happens in this reality than back in Schmigadoon. What really differentiates the seasons, however, is not the darker tone of the parodied musicals, but the way they play off one another. When Melissa brings Dooley and Miss Codwell together, thinking she'll be improving both their lives, they hatch a plan to address the meat shortage and her hated orphans simultaneously by fattening the orphans and using them as meat, combining the darker parts of *Annie* with the wholly dark *Sweeney Todd*.[19] When Josh and Topher are stuck in the same jail cell, Topher's followers break him out, dragging Josh along as well. While Melissa is stuck in a musical environment that is part *Cabaret* (1972) and part *Chicago*, Josh finds himself in the bright colors of *Godspell*.[20] This represents another mash-up, when Topher is introduced to Jenny (Dove Cameron), the Sally Bowles/*Cabaret* character, who becomes the Mary Magdalene to his Jesus after he feels outshined by Josh.[21] The season's villain, Octavius Kratt (Patrick Page), is played as a blend of Judge Turpin from *Sweeney Todd* and Caiaphas in *Jesus Christ Superstar*; indeed, his duet with the Narrator (Titus Burgess), "Two Birds with One Stone," is a lyrical and vocal parody of Caiphus's performance of "This Jesus Must Die,"[22] although his ultimate fate, crushed to death under a chandelier, suggests 1980s mega-musical *Phantom of the Opera* (1986).

Finally, if the focus of season one was Melissa and Josh learning the meaning of "true love" before they could leave Schmigadoon—that is, having a greater understanding of commitment and the work that goes into forming a bond with one another[23]—then season two is concerned with what constitutes a "happy ending" in a world that can be dangerous or disappointing or dull. Despite Melissa's avowed love of Golden Age musicals, her own knowledge of them puts her at something of a remove from the town in a similar way to Josh. Conversely, in Schmicago, both of them become fully immersed in the lives of its residents and their own place in the story, which gives Melissa and Josh, as well as the Schmicago citizens, more agency to write their stories. If Schmigadoon helped them make their own lives better, their actions in

Schmicago did more to improve the lives of others, something the series underscores as the two of them return to the real world, which transitions from black and white to color as they move through it continuing to sing the song they started in Schmicago ("A Happy Beginning").[24]

The series was not renewed for a third season, which Paul indicated would've focused on the 1980s and 1990s mega-musicals, like *Les Misérables* and *Phantom of the Opera*, likely due to production costs.[25] The first season was adapted as a stage musical, with a limited run at the Kennedy Center in 2025, with the potential for the second season and the written but unproduced third season to be adapted as well.[26] Yet taken as is, the two seasons bookend one another quite well, ending with Melissa and Josh applying what they've learned in both Schmigadoon and Schmicago to their lives and the lives of others.

It would be hard to imagine precisely what streaming programming would become when *Dr. Horrible* debuted in 2008, or that by 2025, its viewership would outstrip that of terrestrial television. Yet, despite being separated by more than a decade, both *Dr. Horrible* and *Schmigadoon!* share particular elements. *Dr. Horrible*, despite being online, used film sets and television actors, created by writers and performed by actors primarily known for their work in television. It wasn't an adjunct to an existing program but was similarly structured as an episode of television (including being separated into acts, as are commercial television programs). *Schmigadoon!* may have been inspired by Broadway and film musicals, but it was produced by Lorne Michaels/Broadway Video, who created *Saturday Night Live*. Its cast offered a mix of actors/singers who have appeared in all three mediums, and yet visually both its Schmigadoon and Schmicago settings suggest the stage, from the sets to the performances. In this respect, these two series bring the TV musical full circle, from the early variety shows and filmed Broadway productions to the high gloss productions like *Zoey's Extraordinary Playlist* and *Galavant*, honoring past productions and mediums in a new setting.

Appendix

The 20 Must-See Musical Episodes

1. "Marge vs. the Monorail," *The Simpsons*, Season 4, Episode 12 (September 17, 2009)

While they have not done a full-on multi-song musical episode, music has been a part of *The Simpsons* almost since the beginning, from Mr. Burns performing "Be My Vest" ("Two Dozen and One Greyhounds") to the featured acts in "Homerpalooza" (Cypress Hill, Smashing Pumpkins, Sonic Youth). While these tend toward being parodies rather than originals, there are few episodes better than this one to see how well it can be done. Written by Conan O'Brien and using *The Music Man* as inspiration, the episode features the late Phil Hartman as conman Lyle Lanley, who convinces the town to build a monorail, in a delightful riff on "Ya Got Trouble." Unsurprisingly, the monorail quickly goes off the rails, both literally and figuratively: Marge visits other towns Lanley had targeted and finds their monorails are a mess, and Homer, as conductor, is nearly killed when it starts to break down in its inaugural run. Not only is it a fun take on *The Music Man* and the gullibility of Springfield's residents, but it represents a turning point for the show itself, as it became more comfortable breaking out of the standard episode format moving forward.

2. "Psych: The Musical," *Psych*, Season 7, Episodes 15 and 16 (December 15, 2013)

According to creator Steve Franks, the musical had been in the works for some time, but like many discussed throughout this book, it ends up debuting in later seasons. This gives viewers time to get familiar with the characters, especially ones like Shawn Spencer (James Roday), an accomplished cold reader who pretends to be a psychic as a consultant with the Santa Barbara Police. (The early 2000s were big on quirky detectives, and the USA Network, which aired both *Psych* and *Monk* [2002–2009], in particular; they'd rebranded with the phrase "Characters Welcome" during this era.) The series itself, at least in its early days, also was a bit of a riff on another USA program, *The Dead Zone* (2002–2007), re-conceiving Stephen King's horror/political thriller as more of a procedural, with John Smith (Anthony Michael Hall) often assisting the police. (Hall himself would later appear on *Psych*.) Shawn, with the reluctant help of his best friend Gus (Dulé Hill), sells himself as a psychic to the local police with a far more comedic bent than *The Dead Zone*'s drama. The musical set itself apart not only by being twice as long as a typical episode, but also by framing the whole thing as a "story," complete with an illustrated book that opens the episode with "Once Upon a Time." While the vocal performances can be a bit or miss (except Timothy Omundson, who later got to show off his singing ability even more in *Galavant*, as well as Roday and Hill, with their Broadway backgrounds), the episode did what a good musical episode does: provided a context (playwright driven to madness) and fit with the quirky tone of the show.

3. "Zoey's Extraordinary Dad," *Zoey's Extraordinary Playlist*, Season 1, Episode 12 (May 3, 2020)

While the series itself offers music and dancing in every episode, some of the episodes hit harder than others. One of the best parts of the first season was, regardless of the ways that her ability to hear people's "heartsongs" complicated her life, that Zoey's abilities allowed her to communicate with her father, who could no longer communicate for himself, making his final months better than they perhaps would have been otherwise. This, however, is the inevitable episode the first season was slowly building up to: Mitch's death. It offers another grace note in this episode, in a scene with Mitch singing "Lullaby (Goodnight, My Angel)" by Billy Joel to Zoey, a moment that would be paralleled in the next season when her brother David sings it to his newborn child. The episode caps off with the entire ensemble singing "American Pie" in the aftermath of Mitch's death. Despite the on-the-nose song choice, it works as both a gauge for his family's emotional temperature and a metaphor for their loss.

4. "Séance and Sensibility," *Legends of Tomorrow*, Season 4, Episode 11 (April 15, 2019)

Coming out of the *Arrow*verse on the CW, with an origin show that mostly embraced the gritty aesthetic Christopher Nolan popularized with his Batman trilogy, *Legends of Tomorrow* took a bit of time to find its own niche. Its first season, a mix of new *Doctor Who* and *Arrow*, didn't quite gel, as its characters were supposed to be the screw-ups and misfits that didn't quite fit in anywhere else, and the somber and gritty tone didn't work. They course-corrected in season two, leaning into its own bonkers premise (fixing history, time travel, random superpowers) before fully embracing it by the end of its third season (i.e., saving the universe as a giant Beebo doll—the in-universe version of Tickle-Me Elmo). While the show never did a full-on musical episode, several episodes incorporated either original songs or one of the characters performing a known song, "Séance and Sensibility" is perhaps the most elaborate. The action switches between a funeral in the present day and the rest of the crew of the time-traveling Waverider on a mission to a Regency-era England experiencing a "lust" outbreak, with the entire last act of the episode transitioning into a Bollywood musical number. A show about time-traveling superheroes focused on fixing "mistakes" in the timeline (some of which they were responsible for), the third season added Zari Tomaz (Tala Ashe), a Muslim hacktivist living in a dystopian future (around the mid-twenty-first century) who'd lost her family to the same forces that turned her world into a police state; not surprisingly, trust and connection are elements she struggles with, even in the (relative) safety of the Waverider. In this episode, she takes center stage as the crew tries to figure out what is causing this lust outbreak, an event that leads Jane Austen to give up writing. It turns out to be a manifestation of Kamadeva, the Hindu god of passion, who helps Zari let down her guard enough to connect with others . . . and sing and dance.

5. "Regional Holiday Music," *Community*, Season 3, Episode 10 (December 8, 2011)

Less of a parody and more of a slam, "Regional Holiday Music" takes on *Glee* with, well, glee. Keeping with *Community*'s own darker-tinged holiday episodes, the series' first full-on musical episode, starting with the portrayal of Cory Radison, aka "Mr. Rad," the glee club instructor. After the current glee club suffers a collective nervous breakdown, Mr. Rad asks the study group to take over. While they initially refuse, Abed is swept into the moment, being the first recruited by Rad via song, appropriately titled "Glee." That Mr. Rad knows enough about Abed to target him first (Christmas is an important holiday for him) is the first indication that Mr. Rad is, at best, manipulative as hell. Abed then recruits Troy and so on, until Britta is the last holdout. How each of them targets the other is a testament to how well they know each other at this point, with Troy and Abed appealing to Pierce's generational narcissism with "Baby Boomer Santa," Annie (uncomfortably) targeting Jeff by playing on his conflicted feelings toward her, or Pierce recruiting Shirley using a choir of children lamenting that they can't say "Merry Christmas" in their public schools. (My personal favorite is Troy and Abed's Christmas rap, where Troy vows to take down Santa as "Jehovah's most secret witness.") The original songs, scored by series composer Ludwig Göransson, with the writing staff taking lyrics duty, are sometimes hit and miss, but for all the purported "darkness" in the episode, it ends on a touching moment of togetherness.

6. "The Bitter Suite," *Xena: Warrior Princess*, Season 3, Episode 12 (February 2, 1993)

One of the earliest on this list, predating the *Buffy* musical episode by three years, "The Bitter Suite" set some of the elements that became part of the successful musical episodes and series. Torn apart by recent events (Gabrielle's daughter Hope killed Xena's son Solan), Xena's attempt at revenge instead lands both in the musical land of Illusia, where they are forced to deal with their pasts and their current estrangement through song, along with other important figures in their lives (e.g., Ares). Like the later *Buffy* episode, music and lyrics were created in-house, with series composer Joseph LoDuca providing the music and series writers Steven Sears and Chris Manheim penning (most of) the lyrics, and the actors primarily did their own singing (with one exception). The episode provides a narratively appropriate reason for the singing (they are in a musical land), and the songs move both plot and characterization forward. It also holds the distinction of being one of the earliest inspirations for the musical episode in a non-musical series.

7. "Josh Just Happens to Live Here!" *Crazy Ex-Girlfriend*, Season 1, Episode 1 (October 12, 2015)

The show comes out strong from the first episode, with the premise established (Rebecca gives up her high-paying, high-pressure job in New York to follow an old crush to West Covina, California) and simultaneously subverted within the first five minutes (the move was less about Josh and more about herself). The first musical number, "West Covina," goes Broadway big, ending with Rebecca hoisted on a giant pretzel, and the slow-jam style "The Sexy Gettin' Ready Song" points to its deconstructionist tendencies, as the sexy vibes of the song are undermined by the lyrics and the painful realities of trying to mold oneself into particular beauty standards (waxing, girdles, and curling iron burns abound), underscored by a cameo from the late Nipsey Hussle, who stops singing when he sees what Rebecca has done to herself and declares himself "forever changed" by this knowledge. (The stinger of the episode features him calling various women and apologizing.) It does a great job in setting the tone of the series as amusing, satiric, and over-the-top all at once.

8. "Bloody Celestial Karaoke Jam," *Lucifer*, Season 5, Episode 10 (May 28, 2021)

Singing and performance were woven into *Lucifer* from the beginning, although that mostly involved Lucifer (Tom Ellis) performing at his club. This late-series episode gives the rest of the cast their time on the stage, through the literal deus ex machina of God (Dennis Haysbert) being on Earth causing everyone to express their thoughts and concerns through song (including Ellis's duet with 80s pop star Debbie Gibson playing an overbearing mom, with a fresh take on The Police's stalking song "Every Breath You Take"). The episode weaves between more light-hearted numbers (Amenadial and Linda's duet of "Just the Two of Us," which itself blends the original and Will Smith's cover) and emotional ones (God and Lucifer's take on "I Dreamed a Dream" from *Les Misérables*), as well as advancing plot and characterization. The jukebox musical format works particularly well with the tone and aesthetics of the show, with Ellis's previous performances and the nightclub setting of Luxe setting the stage long before this episode aired. Plus, it's just fun to watch.

9. "My Musical," *Scrubs*, Season 6, Episode 7 (January 18, 2007)

Using a mix of outside talent and staff, "My Musical" does a great job of matching the tone of the series, both visually and musically. While the series provides a valid medical reason for the musical interludes, on a tonal level, it fits right in with the show itself, which always featured over-the-top cutaways and fantasy sequences (mostly through JD) that included singing and dancing a not-insignificant amount of times, as well as the occasional inclusion of an a capella group known as the Worthless Peons. Songs like "Everything Comes Down to Poo" suggest the influence of the writers from *Avenue Q* that the show brought on board for the episode, while "Friends Forever" is pure *Grease* from the jump. As would become standard for these musical episodes, everyone does their own singing, and the songs do a great job of reflecting the elements and personalities of both major characters (Turk and JD) and recurring ones (The Janitor's baritone lament is a highlight).

10. "The Nightman Cometh," *It's Always Sunny in Philadelphia*, Season 4, Episode 13 (November 20, 2008)

Not every musical episode can work, and some so cringeworthy they end up at the top of "worst episode" lists even years after airing (looking at you, "Red Socks"). It's a big swing, and easy to screw up. "The Nightman Cometh," which is the name of both the episode and the featured musical, takes a different tack: it is intentionally bad, offering the combination of hilarious and disturbing that the series does so well, written by main cast member Charlie Day and series composer Cormac Bluestone. Closing out the fourth season with a bang, the episode features Charlie (Charlie Day) writing a musical built on his "Dayman" song for "no reason" (it is later revealed to be an elaborate proposal to his crush, The Waitress; she, unsurprisingly, turns him down). While his family questions his motives, they still don't want anyone else playing the roles and decide to go along with it. The plot of Charlie's play makes no sense, and the songs, purported to be about growing up and maturing, are easily misinterpreted as much darker and more sexual to literally everyone but Charlie, but it is a dark delight even outside the context of the series.

11. "Subspace Rhapsody," *Star Trek: Strange New Worlds*, Season 2, Episode 9 (August 3, 2023)

Taking an (acknowledged) cue from *Buffy*'s "Once More, With Feeling" (even the promo poster for the episode resembles the stylized poster for "Once More"), "Subspace Rhapsody" offers a universe-appropriate reason for its musical shenanigans—the obviously titled "improbability field" the ship is trapped in—and uses the episode to advance plot and character beats. Musicals, by definition, offer spectacle and heightened emotion, which can be used in a variety of ways in episodes like these. If *Buffy*'s musical episode was about what everyone was hiding and the interpersonal fractures these secrets were causing, "Subspace Rhapsody" takes the normally stoic crew and puts them in touch with their deeper feelings, allowing them to connect with one another in ways they had struggled to do before. Like *Scrubs*, the series brought in outside help, with the music composed by Tom Polce (who'd also worked on *Crazy Ex-Girlfriend*) and lyrics by Kay Hanley (lead singer of Letters to Cleo) that nonetheless got the character and tone of the series through the musical numbers.

12. "Fan Fiction," *Supernatural*, Season 10, Episode 5 (November 11, 2014)

The main characters might not be the performers in this episode (although the first episode of the season featured Dean singing "I'm Too Sexy" quite badly; a bit of an inside joke, as Jensen Ackles actually has a good singing voice), but that doesn't mean it's not worth watching. The show's love letter/apology to its fans is not only a much better reflection of its fandom than other episodes, but the songs and performances are great and rooted in the mythology of the show. In keeping with the meta element that became part of the show from the fourth season onward, the musical episode was written by staff writer Robbie Thompson and composed by series composer Jay Gruska; in the episode, *Supernatural: The Musical* is written by a fan of the in-universe book series (a stand-in for the show), Supernatural. By making it the work of a "fan"—and featuring an all-female cast in a very guy-centric show—it ends up being both the show's way of giving its blessing to the fanfiction, fanvids, and artwork that had defined its fandom since the beginning and acknowledging the actual make-up of its fanbase. Add in the Muse of epic poetry and a backstage fight that ends up center stage, and it's a fun episode that works for both long-time viewers and those who simply dip in and out.

13. "A New Season aka Suck It Cancellation Bear," *Galavant*, Season 2, Episode 1 (January 3, 2016)

Galavant was always a self-aware musical parody—of Disney musicals in particular—but season two leans into that even harder, with an ensemble opening number that not only catches up any new viewers on the story, but speculates about what they could possibly do differently to grab viewers. The end of the first season scattered the main characters, meaning that each episode juggles at least two stories in its thirty-minute episode time, but the opening number and episode show just how deftly the show balances its stories and characters as it moves toward the big battle that closes out the season (and the show itself). While season two would be its last, this episode sets the stage for the show's "go big or go home" mentality, and expands its gaze to other fantasy series (especially *Game of Thrones*) in ways that served as both homage and parody. Also, it's just fun and silly in the vein of *The Princess Bride*.

14. "Brown Betty," *Fringe*, Season 2, Episode 20 (April 29, 2010)

Despite being created as part of a publicity push by Fox (for *Glee*), "Brown Betty" makes great use of necessity in two ways. It makes the musical parts part of a "story" that a stoned Walter Bishop (John Noble) is telling the young Ella (Lily Pilblad), with the included music both sung or as part of the soundtrack, mixing standards ("Blue Moon") with classic or 80s rock performances, and it subtlety advances the season's plot despite the diversion of the "fairy tale" Walter is weaving. While a musical episode seems an odd fit for the series, the conceit of the noir story Walter tells makes it work within the context of the season's narrative. Given noir's focus on secrets, buried pasts, and things not being as they seem, it blends surprisingly well with *Fringe*'s alternate worlds and secretive investigations.

15. "All That Josh," *The Magicians*, Season 3, Episode 9 (March 7, 2018)

The Magicians, as a series, really took off when it truly embraced the weirdness of its premise—a magic graduate school combined with a darker version of Narnia that's actually real—and both built on and veered off from its source material. (The novel trilogy focuses primarily on Quentin Coldwater, while the series dives into the ensemble a great deal more.) They also clearly loved a good musical episode; they aired three throughout their five seasons. Each one fits into the jukebox musical genre, offering both contemporary and more classic songs. "All That Josh" was the first, and a delight. While impossible to separate from the main storyline of the season (magic has disappeared, and our main characters are on a multi-part quest to bring it back), the episode itself actually primarily occurs in a pocket reality where magic still exists and the party never stops. In order to escape, they all have to work together, no matter which reality they are in, leading to a rousing ensemble rendition of the Bowie/Queen duet "Under Pressure."

16. "Duet," *The Flash*, Season 3, Episode 17 (March 17, 2017)

The CW's *Arrow*verse always offered an event crossover between its many shows at least once a season, featuring some universe-ending threat, but "Duet," an episode of *The Flash* that offers crossover appearances from *Arrow* and *Supergirl*, goes a quieter route using a known DC villain, the Music Meister, to trap Barry Allan (Grant Gustin) and Kara/Supergirl (Melissa Benoist) in a dream world they can escape only if they "follow the script." Not only does it give known Broadway or West End cast veterans like Victor Garber and John Barrowman a chance to sing, but it also offers two low-key (non-narrative) crossovers, first by reuniting Gustin and Benoist with their fellow *Glee* alum

Darren Criss (as the Music Meister) but tapping Rachel Bloom, of the CW's *Crazy Ex-Girlfriend*, to write the episode's sole original number, "Superfriends."

17. "Life Is a Cabaret," *Schitt's Creek*, Season 5, Episode 14 (April 9, 2019)

Schitt's Creek was no stranger to music sequences; local singing group the Jazzagals appeared in multiple episodes, and season four offered two versions of Tina Turner's "Simply the Best," the first sung acoustically, from Patrick (Noah Reid) to his boyfriend David (Dan Levy), the second as a lip-synced apology from David to Patrick. The series, however, decided to close out its fifth season with a community theater production of *Cabaret* that allows Patrick (Noah Reid) and Stevie (Emily Hampshire) to showcase their vocal skills, particularly Hampshire, who hadn't sung on the series before. While obviously not original music, the production and its performances were nonetheless part of the season's overall story and represented a character turning point for Stevie in particular, allowing her to reveal a new side of herself through the heightened drama of the musical.

18. "The Balls," *The Magicians*, Season 5, Episode 12 (March 25, 2020)

Given how much the series enjoyed playing with the musical form, it's no surprise they went there a final time in the penultimate episode of the series. Mixing the heist genre with the jukebox musical, the musical numbers tend to be more individualized, both in terms of performance and narrative, than in "All That Josh," as well as giving a wider variety of characters a chance to shine. Like *Buffy*, to whom the show owes more than a few debts, the songs performed are designed to reveal repressed emotion (literally, in the case of the episode, as each of the heisters has to magically remove them in order to remain undetected), whether relating to the heist itself or ongoing emotional and narrative arcs (e.g., Alice and Eliot's duet of "Don't Give Up" as a product of their shared grief over Quentin's death). It also works as a fitting beginning of the end for the series, bringing together the main cast as well as recurring characters for an (almost) final run.

19. "Dewey's Opera," *Malcolm in the Middle*, Season 6, Episode 11 (February 20, 2005)

One of the most expensive episodes of the series, "Dewey's Opera" goes all in, with elaborate sets and a full chorus. Inspired by a combination of watching an opera on TV and his parents' fight over a new bed, Dewey's desire to write an opera finds its inspiration in his parents' arguing, cutting from the imagined opera (Hal [Bryan Cranston] and Lois [Jane Kaczmarek] in full costume on stage) and an in-school production with his classmates playing his parents. Dewey, however, not only serves as composer and lyricist but also as a Svengali-like director when he manipulates his parents into extending their fight so he can write a better ending. It's a great showcase for Cranston and Kaczmarek's vocal skills, as well as allowing in-house writer Eric Kaplan and series composer Charles Sydnor to go all out, brilliantly ending before we see the school production play out with a focus on the happy—soon to be humiliated—faces of Hal and Lois in the audience.

20. "Once More, With Feeling," *Buffy the Vampire Slayer*, Season 6, Episode 7 (November 6, 2001)

Is this my favorite musical episode? Yes. Yet as a real-time watcher of the series witnessing the hype around the episode (UPN went all out in promos)—and a veteran of much bad television viewing—I thought my likeliest reaction would be a fifty-minute cringe. Really happy to be wrong on that one; despite some weaker vocal performances, the songs were fun and right in character, from Buffy's Disney-infused "I want" number that opened the episode ("Going Through the Motions"), to the beautifully performed and timed ensemble piece "Walk Through the Fire." (The firetrucks passing the group as they sing "Let It Burn" was excellently choreographed.) What's more, it made great use of the act structure that both theater and television drama share, as when Act Three concludes with Buffy storming the Bronze and Sweet (Hinton Battle) giving a small smile and saying "Showtime" just before the episode cuts to commercial. While it wasn't the first musical episode in a non-musical show, it set the standard for musical episodes moving forward, and, for better or worse, implied that it could work on any show. (Spoiler alert: It doesn't.)

NOTES

Introduction

1 Millie Taylor and Dominic Symonds, *Studying Musical Theatre: Theory and Practice* (London: Bloomsbury, 2017), 3.

2 "The Birth of Magazine Concept Television Advertising," The Historical Archive, January 23, 2007, https://www.thehistoricalarchive.com/happenings/50/the-birth-of-magazine-concept-television-advertising/

3 Sally Bedell, *Up the Tube: Primetime TV in the Silverman Years*. New York: Viking, 1981.

4 *Friends*, season 8, episode 9, "The One with the Rumor," directed by Gary Halvorson, written by Shana Goldberg-Meehan, featuring Jennifer Aniston, David Schwimmer, Courteney Cox, Matthew Perry, and Matt LeBlanc, aired November 22, 2001, on NBC, Warner Home Video, 2012, DVD.

5 *The Brady Bunch*, season 3, episode 16, "Dough Re Mi," directed by Allen Baron, written by Ben Starr, featuring Robert Reed, Florence Henderson, Barry Williams, and Christopher Knight, aired January 14, 1972, on ABC, Paramount, 2007, DVD.

6 *Moonlighting*, season 3, episode 7, "Atomic Shakespeare," directed by Will MacKenzie, written by Ron Osborn and Jeff Reno, featuring Cybill Shepherd, Bruce Willis, Curtis Armstrong, and Allyce Beasley, aired November 25, 1986, on ABC, Lionsgate, 2007, DVD; *Moonlighting*, season 3, episode 6, "Big Man on Mulberry Street," directed by Christian Nyby, written by Karen Hall, featuring Cybill Shepherd, Bruce Willis, Curtis Armstrong, and Allyce Beasley, aired November 18, 1986, on ABC, Lionsgate, 2007, DVD; *Moonlighting*, season 2, episode 4, "The Dream Sequence Always Rings Twice," directed by Peter Werner, written by Debra Frank and Carl Sautter, featuring Cybill Shepherd, Bruce Willis, Curtis Armstrong, and Allyce Beasley, aired October 15, 1985, on ABC, Lionsgate, 2007, DVD.

7 *How I Met Your Mother*, season 5, episode 12, "Girls vs. Suits," directed by Pamela Fryman, written by Carter Bays and Craig Thomas, featuring Neil Patrick Harris, Jason Segal, Alyson Hannigan, Cobie Smolders, and Josh Radnor, aired January 11, 2010, on CBS, 20th Century Fox, 2010, DVD.

Chapter 1

1 *Poltergeist*, directed by Tobe Hooper (1982; Culver City, CA: MGM Home Entertainment, 1997), DVD.

2 Carina Jaramillo, "An Annotated History of the Vaudeville Theater," *Theater Seat Store Blog*, March 27, 2025, https://www.theaterseatstore.com/blog/vaudeville-theater?srsltid=AfmBOopUvqQIYpjTV9E47Rlbca8LghXtkAyTsZRXevLaM3O5ajZXmY7y#early-entertainment Linda

3 Armond Field, *Tony Pastor, Father of Vaudeville* (Jefferson, NC: McFarland, 2007).

4 Jaramillo, "An Annotated History"; Nicholas Sammond, *Birth of an Industry: Blackface Minstrelsy and the Rise of American Animation* (Durham, NC: Duke University Press, 2015).

5 Jaramillo, "An Annotated History."

6 Robert Lloyd, "What Made Betty White the Most Beloved TV Star of Her (or Maybe Any) Generation," *Los Angeles Times*, January 1, 2022, https://www.latimes.com/entertainment-arts/tv/story/2022-01-01/betty-white-death-mary-tyler-moore-golden-girls-hot-in-cleveland-appreciation

7 Gillian Brockell, "'Live with It': Betty White Defied Racist Demands in 1954," *Washington Post*, December 31, 2021, https://www.washingtonpost.com/history/2021/12/31/betty-white-arthur-duncan-racism/

8 *The Red Skelton Show*, season 13, episode 1, "Passion in Pasadena, or Love Is a Many-Splintered Thing," directed by Seymour Berns, written by Mort Greene, Dave O'Brien, and Arthur Phillips, featuring Red Skelton, Frankie Darro, and Douglas Fowley, aired September 24, 1963, on CBS.

9 *The Brady Bunch*, season 3, episode 16, "Dough Re Mi," directed by Allen Baron, written by Ben Starr, featuring Robert Reed, Florence Henderson, Barry Williams, and Christopher Knight, aired January 14, 1972, on ABC, Paramount, 2007, DVD; *The Brady Bunch*, season 5, episode 1, "Adios, Johnny Bravo," directed by Jerry London, written by Joanna Lee, featuring Robert Reed, Florence Henderson, Barry Williams, and Christopher Knight, aired September 14, 1973, on ABC, Paramount, 2007, DVD.

10 Steve Cohen, "American Bandstand's Untold Story," *The Cultural Critic*, https://theculturalcritic.com/american-bandstands-untold-story/

11 Jack Doyle, "American Bandstand, 1956–2007," *PopHistoryDig.com*, March 25, 2008.

12 *Hairspray*, directed by John Waters (1988; Los Angeles, CA: New Line Home Entertainment, 2002), DVD.

13 John Waters, "Ladies and Gentleman . . . the Nicest Kids in Town! Keeping the Memory of the Buddy Deane Show Alive," *Baltimore Magazine*, April 1995, https://

www.baltimoremagazine.com/section/artsentertainment/john-waters-on-keeping-the-memory-of-the-buddy-deane-show-alive/

14 *Hairspray*, 1988.

15 *American Dreams*, season 1, episode 1, "Pilot," directed by David Semel, written by Jonathan Prince and Josh Goldstein, featuring Brittany Snow, Will Estes, Jonathan Adams, and Arlen Escarpeta, aired September 29, 2002, on NBC.

16 *American Dreams*, season 1, episode 7, "Cold Snap," directed by Michael W. Watkins, written by Rama Laurie Stanger, featuring Brittany Snow, Will Estes, Jonathan Adams, and Arlen Escarpeta, aired November 10, 2002, on NBC; *American Dreams*, season 1, episode 23, "Down the Shore," directed by Leslie Libman, written by Jon Cowan and Richard L. Rovner, featuring Brittany Snow, Will Estes, Jonathan Adams, and Arlen Escarpeta, aired May 4, 2003, on NBC; *American Dreams*, season 2, episode 4, "Crossing the Line," directed by Craig Zisk, written by Josh Reims, featuring Brittany Snow, Will Estes, Jonathan Adams, and Arlen Escarpeta, aired October 19, 2003, on NBC; *American Dreams*, season 2, episode 10, "The 7–10 Split," directed by Mark Piznarski, written by Becky Hartman Edwards, featuring Brittany Snow, Will Estes, Jonathan Adams, and Arlen Escarpeta, aired January 4, 2004, on NBC; *American Dreams*, season 3, episode 15, "California Dreamin'," directed by Jim Chory, written by Liz Tagelaar, featuring Brittany Snow, Will Estes, Jonathan Adams, and Arlen Escarpeta, aired March 16, 2005, on NBC.

17 Dorian Lynskey, "'An Ad for Blackness': How Soul Train Made America Do the Hustle," *The Guardian*, February 20, 2019, https://www.theguardian.com/music/2019/feb/20/american-soul-train-don-cornelius

18 Ibid.

19 Sam Sanders, Anjuli Sastry Krbechek, Liam McBain, and Jordana Hochman, "There Was Nothing Like 'Soul Train' on TV: There's Never Been Anything Like It Since," *NPR*, September 28, 2021, https://www.npr.org/2021/09/14/1037118049/soul-train-hanif-abdurraqib

20 Lynskey, "'An Ad for Blackness'"; Jake Austen, *TV-a-Go-Go: Rock on TV from American Bandstand to American Idol* (Chicago, IL: Chicago Review Press, 2005), 100–1.

21 A fairly recent example occurred in season two of *Crazy Ex-Girlfriend* (see chapter 6), in which Rebecca and Josh duet on "We'll Never Have Problems Again" on a *Soul Train*-inspired set, including the *Soul Train* Line ("Will Scarsdale Like Josh's Shayna Punim?" 2.10).

22 Gretchen Smail, "*American Soul* Has More of Don Cornelius' Legacy to Explore," *Bustle*, July 15, 2020, https://www.bustle.com/entertainment/american-soul-season-3-renewed-canceled; *American Soul*, season 1, episode 3, "Lost and Found," directed by Robert Townsend, written by Annmarie Morais, featuring Sinqua Wells, Christopher Jefferson, Kelly Price, and Iantha Richardson, aired February 12, 2019, on BET; *American Soul*, season 1, episode 4, "Just Us," directed by Robert Townsend, written by A. Zell Williams, featuring Sinqua Wells, Christopher Jefferson, Kelly Price, and Iantha Richardson, aired February 19, 2019, on BET; *American Soul*, season 2, episode 5, "Say You Love Me," directed by Crystle Roberson Dorsey, written by Norman Vance Jr, featuring Sinqua Wells, Christopher Jefferson, Kelly Price, and Iantha Richardson, aired June 24, 2020, on BET.

23 Erik Barnouw, *Tube of Plenty: The Evolution of American Television* (Oxford: Oxford University Press, 1990), 117–21.

Chapter 2

1 Dan Maloney, "Never Twice the Same Color: Why NTSC Is So Weird," *Hackaday*, October 6, 2016, https://hackaday.com/2016/10/06/never-twice-the-same-color-why-ntsc-is-so-weird/

2 Paul Saettler, *The Evolution of American Educational Technology* (Charlotte, NC: Information Age Publishing, 2004), 376.

3 *NET Playhouse*, season 1, episode 21, "The World of Kurt Weill," directed by David M. Davis, written by George Tabori, featuring Lotte Lenya and George Voskovec, aired February 24, 1967, on NET; *NET Playhouse*, season 1, episode 24, "Satire," directed by Francis Coleman, written by Peter Ustinov, featuring Peter Ustinov, Dudley Moore, Anthony Hopkins, and Bernard Keeffe, aired February 17, 1967, on NET; *NET Playhouse*, season 4, episode 17, "Jesus, A Passion Play for Americans," directed by Timothy Mayer, written by Timothy Mayer, featuring Laura Esterman, Stephan Mo Hanan, and Asha Puthii, aired May 26, 1970, on NET.

4 Nik Popli, "What the Corporation for Public Broadcasting Shutting Down Means for PBS and NPR," *Time*, August 1, 2025, https://time.com/7307069/corporation-for-public-broadcasting-pbs-npr/

5 *Great Performances*, season 44, episode 4, "Hamilton's America," directed by Alex Horowitz, featuring Lin-Manuel Miranda, Christopher Jackson, Leslie Odom Jr, and Barack Obama, aired October 21, 2016, on PBS; *Great Performances*, season 13, episode 14, "Einstein on the Beach: The Changing Image of Opera," directed by Mark Obenhaus, written by Robert Wilson, featuring Lucinda Childs, Philip Glass, and Will Lyman, aired January 31, 1986, on PBS; *Great Performances*, season 21, episode 2, "Jammin': Jelly Roll Morton on Broadway," written by Tom Bywaters, featuring Denzel Washington, Gregory Hines, and Keith David, aired November 2, 1992, on PBS.

6 Julia Antopol Hirsch, *The Sound of Music: The Making of America's Favorite Movie* (Chicago, IL: Chicago Review Press, 2018), 209.

7 *Gypsy*, directed by Emile Ardolino (1993; Golden Valley, MN: Mill Creek Entertainment, 2013), DVD.

8 Tony Sloman, "Obituary: Emile Ardolino," *The Independent*, December 4, 1993, https://www.independent.co.uk/news/people/obituary-emile-ardolino-1465147.html

9 *Cinderella*, directed by Ralph Nelson (1957; Los Angeles, CA: Image Entertainment, 2004), DVD.

10 *Cinderella*, directed by Charles S. Dubin (1965; Culver City, CA: Samuel Goldwyn Films, 2023), DVD.

11 *Cinderella*, directed by Roger Iscove (1997; Los Angeles, CA: Sony Pictures Home Entertainment, 2002), DVD.

12 AJ Marechal, "Greenblatt Discusses 'Sound of Music,' 'Revolution' in journo-chat," *Variety*, November 20, 2012, https://variety.com/2012/tv/news/greenblatt-discusses-sound-of-music-revolution-in-journo-chat-9023/

13 Mikey O'Connell, "TV Ratings: NBC's 'Sound of Music Live' Nears 22 Million Viewers with DVR," *The Hollywood Reporter*, December 23, 2013, https://www.hollywoodreporter.com/tv/tv-news/tv-ratings-nbcs-sound-music-667543

14 Maureen Lee Lenker, "Every Live TV Musical, Ranked: See Where Your Favorite Landed in Our Rankings," *Entertainment Weekly*, December 15, 2022, https://ew.com/tv/every-live-tv-musical-ranked/

15 *Annie*, directed by John Huston (1982; Los Angeles, CA: Sony Pictures Home Entertainment, 2004), DVD.

16 Jackie Mansky, "Seventy-Five Years Ago, the Television Musical Made Its Debut: 'Rent: Live' Meet 'The Boys from Boise,'" *Smithsonian Magazine*, January 25, 2019, https://www.smithsonianmag.com/arts-culture/television-musical-actually-debuted-75-years-ago-180971342/

17 Eric Grundhauser, "Whatever Happened to Captain Video and the DuMont Programming Library? One of the Original Television Networks Has All but Disappeared," Atlas Obscura, June 30, 2017, https://www.atlasobscura.com/articles/dumont-network-gleason-lost-kinescope

18 *NBC Opera Theater*, season 3, episode 3, "Amahl and the Night Visitors," directed by Kirk Browning, written by Gian Carlo Menotti, featuring Chet Allen, Rosemary Kuhlmann, and Andrew McKinley, aired December 24, 1951, on NBC.

19 *NBC Opera Theater*, season 6, episode 1, "The Abduction from the Seraglio," directed by Kirk Browning, written by Christoph Friedrich Bretzner and Stephanie Gottlieb Jr, featuring Davis Cunningham, Virginia Haskins, Nadja Witkowska, and David Lloyd, aired October 31, 1954, on NBC.

20 Mitchell Hadley, "The Life and Death of 'NBC Opera Theater,'" *It's About TV!* June 12, 2019, https://www.itsabouttv.com/2019/06/the-life-and-death-of-nbc-opera-theatre.html

21 *The Motorola Television Hour*, season 1, episode 5, "The Thirteen Clocks," directed by Don Richardson, written by James Thurber, John Crilley, and Fred Sadoff, featuring Basil Rathbone, John Raitt, and Roberta Peters, aired December 29, 1953, on ABC.

22 *Satins and Spurs*, directed by Max Liebman and Charles O'Curran (1954; Brooklyn, NY: NBC Studios), TV.

23 *Sunday Spectacular: The Bachelor*, directed by Joseph Cates (1956; New York: NBC Studios), TV.

24 *The United States Steel Hour*, season 4, episode 6, "Tom Sawyer," directed by John Haggott, written by Frank Luther and Mark Twain, featuring John Sharpe, Jimmy Boyd, and Bennye Gatteys, aired November 21, 1956, on CBS.

25 *The United States Steel Hour*, season 5, episode 6, "The Adventures of Huckleberry Finn," directed by Elliot Silverstein, written by Anne Pearson Crosswell, Lee Pockriss, and Mark Twain, featuring Jimmy Boyd, Earle Hyman, Basil Rathbone, and Florence Henderson, aired November 20, 1957, on CBS.

26 *The Stingiest Man in Town*, directed by Daniel Petrie (1954; Pleasantville, NY: Video Artists International, 2011), DVD; *The Stingiest Man in Town*, directed by Jules Bass and Arthur Rankin Jr. (1978; Los Angeles, CA: Universal Pictures Home Entertainment, 2022), DVD.

27 *Hallmark Hall of Fame*, season 7, episode 4, "Hans Brinker and the Silver Skates," directed by Sidney Lumet, written by Sally Benson and Frederick Knott, featuring Tab Hunter, Basil Rathbone, Peggy King, and Dick Button, aired February 9, 1958, on NBC.

28 *The Dangerous Christmas of Red Riding Hood*, directed by Sid Smith (1965; New York: Eritas Productions), TV.

29 *The Great Man's Whiskers*, directed by Philip Leacock (1973; Universal City, CA: Universal Television), TV; *Dr. Jekyll and Mr. Hyde*, directed by David Winters (1973; New York: NBC Studios), TV.

30 *Three for the Girls*, directed by Bob LaHendro (1973; New York: UGO Productions), TV.

31 *Queen of the Stardust Ballroom*, directed by Sam O'Steen (1975; New York: Tomorrow Entertainment), TV.

32 *Minstrel Man*, directed by William A. Graham (1977; New York: Tomorrow Entertainment), TV.

33 *Happy Days*, season 8, episode 22, "American Musical," directed by Jerry Paris, written by James P. Dunne and Elizabeth Bradley, featuring Henry Winkler, Marion Ross, Anson Williams, and Erin Moran, aired May 26, 1981, on ABC; *The Love Boat*, season 5, episode 22, "The Musical/My Aunt, the Warrior/The Show Must Go On/ The Pest/My Ex-Mom," directed by Roger Duchowny, written by Ray Jessel, Tony Webster, Bel Joelson, and Art Baer, featuring Gavin McLeod, Bernie Kopell, Ted Lange, and Fred Grandy, aired February 27, 1982, on ABC.

34 *Alice at the Palace*, directed by Emile Ardolino (1982; New York: New York Shakespeare Festival), TV.

35 *The Magical World of Disney*, season 34, episode 6, "Polly," directed by Debbie Allen, written by William Blin and Eleanor H. Porter, featuring Keshia Knight Pulliam, Phylicia Rashad, and Dorian Horewood, aired November 12, 1989, on NBC.

36 *The Magical World of Disney*, season 35, episode 1, "Polly: Comin' Home," directed by Debbie Allen, written by William Blin and Eleanor H. Porter, featuring Keshia Knight Pulliam, Phylicia Rashad, and Dorian Horewood, aired November 18, 1990, on NBC.

37 *Copacabana*, directed by Waris Hussein (1985; Beverly Hills, CA: Dick Clark Productions), TV.

38 John O'Connor, "TV Review; Barry Manilow Stars in 'Copacabana' on CBS," *The New York Times*, December 3, 1985, https://www.nytimes.com/1985/12/03/arts/tv-review-barry-manilow-stars-in-copacabana-on-cbs.html

39 *Xena: Warrior Princess*, season 3, episode 12, "The Bitter Suite," directed by Oley Sassone, written by Steven L. Sears and Chris Manheim, featuring Lucy Lawless, Renee O'Connor, and Ted Raimi, aired February 14, 1998, in First-run syndication, Universal Home Video, 2024, DVD; *Daria*, season 3, episode 1, "Daria!," directed by Karen Disher, written by Glenn Eichler and Peter Elwell, featuring Tracy Grandstaff, Wendy Hoopes, and Julián Rebolledo, aired February 17, 1999, on MTV, Paramount Home Entertainment, 2010, DVD.

40 *Mrs. Santa Claus*, directed by Terry Hughes (1996; Los Angeles, CA: Hallmark Entertainment), TV.

41 *Geppetto*, directed by Tom Moore (2000; Burbank, CA: Walt Disney Television), TV.

42 Scott Weinberg, "High School Musical: Remix," *DVD Talk*, December 5, 2006, https://www.dvdtalk.com/reviews/25544/high-school-musical-remix/; Gary Graff, "'High School Musical' Kids Soaking Up Success," *Billboard*, August 21, 2007, https://www.billboard.com/music/music-news/high-school-musical-kids-soaking-up-success-1049761/

43 *The Passion: New Orleans*, directed by David Grifhorst (2016; Beverly Hills, CA: Dick Clark Productions), TV.

Chapter 3

1 Alan Hanson, "Elvis on The Ed Sullivan Show . . . A View Out of the Ordinary," Elvis History Blog, November 2011, http://www.elvis-history-blog.com/elvis-sullivan.html

2 Katrina Jesick Quinn, "The 1950s: Decade of Economic Prosperity, Rock 'n' Roll, and a Red Scare," *Butler Eagle*, January 14, 2025, https://www.butlereagle.com/20250114/the-1950s-decade-of-economic-prosperity-rocknroll-and-a-red-scare/

3 *The Monkees*, season 1, episode 18, "I Was a Teenage Monster," directed by Sidney Miller, written by Gerald Gardner, Dee Caruso, and Dave Evans, featuring Davy Jones, Mickey Dolenz, Mike Nesmith, and Peter Tork, aired January 16, 1967, on NBC, Rhino Entertainment Company, 2003, DVD.

4 *The Monkees*, season 1, episode 32, "Monkees on Tour," directed by Robert Rafelson, written by Robert Rafelson, featuring Davy Jones, Mickey Dolenz, Mike Nesmith, and Peter Tork, aired January 24, 1967, on NBC, Rhino Entertainment Company, 2003, DVD.

5 Andy Greene, "Exclusive: Michael Nesmith Remembers Davy Jones," *Rolling Stone*, March 8, 2012, https://www.rollingstone.com/music/music-news/exclusive-michael-nesmith-remembers-davy-jones-102258/#ixzz1v8CRGRDd

6 *The Brady Bunch*, season 3, episode 16, "Dough Re Mi," directed by Allen Baron, written by Ben Starr, featuring Robert Reed, Florence Henderson, Barry Williams, and Christopher Knight, aired January 14, 1972, on ABC, Paramount, 2007, DVD.

7 *Dream a Little Dream*, directed by Marc Rocco (1989; Los Angeles, CA: Lionsgate Pictures Entertainment, 2003), DVD.

8 *Buffy the Vampire Slayer*, season 6, episode 7, "Once More, With Feeling," directed by Joss Whedon, written by Joss Whedon, featuring Sarah Michelle Gellar, Alyson Hannigan, Nicholas Brendan, and James Marsters, aired November 6, 2001, on the WB, 20th Century Fox Home Entertainment, 2005, DVD; *Angel*, season 2, episode 18, "Dead End," directed by James A. Contner, written by David Greenwalt, featuring David Boreanaz, Charisma Carpenter, J. August Richards, and Alexis Denisof, aired April 24, 2001, on the WB, 20th Century Fox Home Entertainment, 2007, DVD; *Supernatural*, season 15, episode 7, "Last Call," directed by Amyn Kaderali, written by Jeremy Adams, featuring Jensen Ackles, Jared Padalecki, Misha Collins, and Alexander Calvert, aired December 5, 2019, on the CW, Warner Home Entertainment, 2021, DVD.

9 *Scrubs*, season 4, episode 17, "My Life in Four Cameras," directed by Adam Bernstein, written by Debra Fordham, featuring Zach Braff, Donald Faison, Judy Reyes, and Sarah Chalke, aired February 15, 2005, on NBC, Buena Vista Home Entertainment, 2006, DVD.

10 *The Brady Bunch*, season 3, episode 12, "Getting Davy Jones," directed by Oscar Rudolph, written by Phil Leslie and Al Schwartz, featuring Robert Reed, Florence Henderson, Barry Williams, and Christopher Knight, aired December 10, 1971, on ABC, Paramount, 2007, DVD.

11 *21 Jump Street*, season 3, episode 13, "A.W.O.L.," directed by Michael Robinson, written by Glen Morgan and James Wong, featuring Johnny Depp, Peter DeLuise, Holly Robinson, and Dustin Nguyen, aired March 19, 1989, on Fox, Visual Entertainment, 2022, DVD.

12 *Parker Lewis Can't Lose*, season 1, episode 14, "Rent-a-Kube," directed by Andy Tennant, written by Tom Straw, featuring Corin Nemec, Billy Jayne, and Troy Slaten,

aired December 16, 1990, on Fox, Shout! Factory, 2009, DVD; *Parker Lewis Can't Lose*, season 1, episode 18, "The Human Grace," directed by Max Tash, written by Tom Straw, featuring Corin Nemec, Billy Jayne, and Troy Slaten, aired February 17, 1991, on Fox, Shout! Factory, 2009, DVD; *Parker Lewis Can't Lose*, season 1, episode 19, "Citizen Kube," directed by Max Tash, written by Alan Cross and Tom Spezialy, featuring Corin Nemec, Billy Jayne, and Troy Slaten, aired February 17, 1991, on Fox, Shout! Factory, 2009, DVD.

13 *Buffy the Vampire Slayer*, season 2, episode 1, "When She Was Bad," directed by Joss Whedon, written by Joss Whedon, featuring Sarah Michelle Gellar, Alyson Hannigan, Nicholas Brendan, and Anthony Stewart Head, aired September 15, 1997, on the WB, 20th Century Fox Home Entertainment, 2005, DVD; *Buffy the Vampire Slayer*, season 7, episode 8, "Sleeper," directed by Alan J. Levi, written by David Fury and Jane Espenson, featuring Sarah Michelle Gellar, Alyson Hannigan, Nicholas Brendan, and James Marsters, aired November 19, 2002, on UPN, 20th Century Fox Home Entertainment, 2005, DVD; *Buffy the Vampire Slayer*, season 7, episode 6, "Him," directed by Michael Gershman, written by Drew Z. Greenberg, featuring Sarah Michelle Gellar, Alyson Hannigan, Nicholas Brendan, and Michelle Trachtenberg, aired November 5, 2002, on UPN, 20th Century Fox Home Entertainment, 2005, DVD.

14 *Supernatural*, season 3, episode 16, "No Rest for the Wicked," directed by Kim Manners, written by Eric Kripke, featuring Jensen Ackles, Jared Padalecki, and Jim Beaver, aired May 15, 2008, on the CW, Warner Home Entertainment, 2008, DVD.

15 Liana Bekakos, "Supernatural Creator Eric Kripke Answers Fan Questions—Part 1," *Eclipse Magazine*, April 23, 2008, https://eclipsemagazine.com/supernatural-creator-eric-kripke-answers-fan-questions-%E2%80%93-part-i/

16 *Supernatural*, season 12, episode 13, "Family Feud," directed by P. J. Pesce, written by Brad Buckner and Eugenie Ross-Leming, featuring Jensen Ackles, Jared Padalecki, and Misha Collins, aired February 23, 2017, on the CW, Warner Home Entertainment, 2017, DVD.

Chapter 4

1 Richard Dyer, *Only Entertainment* (London: Routledge, 2002), 27.

2 Peter Royston, "Kiss Me, Kate: The Love Connection," *Center Stage Magazine*, Winter/Spring 2002, https://www.portwashington.com/moveweb/Guidewrite/kissmekate.html

3 Ed Gross, "Buffy the Vampire Slayer Turns 20: Joss Whedon Looks Back," *Empire*, March 9, 2017, https://www.empireonline.com/movies/features/buffy-vampire-slayer-turns-20-joss-whedon-looks-back/

4 *Uncle Buck*, season 1, episode 1, "Pilot," directed by John Tracy, written by Tim O'Donnell, featuring Kevin Meaney, Dah-ve Chodan, Audrey Meadows, and Lacey Chabert, aired September 10, 1990, on CBS.

5 *Fame*, directed by Alan Parker (1980; Burbank, CA: Warner Home Video, 2003), DVD.

6 *Fame*, season 1, episode 3, "Tomorrow's Farewell," directed by Thomas Carter, written by William Blinn, featuring Debbie Allen, Erica Gimpel, Gene Anthony Ray, and Cynthia Gibb, aired January 21, 1982, on NBC, Fox/MGM Television, 2010, DVD; *Fame*, season 4, episode 2, "Czech-Mate," directed by William F. Claxton, written by Patricia Jones, Donald Reiker, and Ira Steven Behr, featuring Debbie Allen, Erica Gimpel, Gene Anthony Ray, and Carlo Imperato, aired October 6, 1984, in First-run syndication, TV; *Fame*, season 4, episode 1, "Indian Summer," directed by William F. Claxton, written by Patricia Jones, Donald Reiker, and Ira Steven Behr, featuring Debbie Allen, Erica Gimpel, Gene Anthony Ray, and Carlo Imperato, aired September 29, 1984, in First-run syndication, TV; *Fame*, season 6, episode 11, "Go Softly into Morning," directed by Win Phelps, written by Renee Schonfeld Longstreet, featuring Debbie Allen, Erica Gimpel, Gene Anthony Ray, and Carlo Imperato, aired January 5, 1987, in First-run syndication, TV.

7 *Fame*, season 5, episode 10, "Choices," directed by Donald Reiker, written by Patricia Jones and Donald Reiker, featuring Debbie Allen, Gene Anthony Ray, and Carlo Imperato, aired January 4, 1986, in First-run syndication, TV; *Fame*, season 1, episode 9, "But Seriously, Folks," directed by Alan J. Levi, written by Parke Perine, featuring Debbie Allen, Erica Gimpel, Gene Anthony Ray, and Cynthia Gibb, aired March 4, 1982, on NBC, Fox/MGM Television, 2010, DVD; *Fame*, season 5, episode 17, "The Comedian," directed by Reza Badiyi, written by Adam Leslie, featuring Debbie Allen, Gene Anthony Ray, and Carlo Imperato, aired March 22, 1986, in First-run syndication, TV.

8 *Fame*, season 1, episode 2, "Passing Grade," directed by Nicholas Sgarro, written by Lee H. Grant and William Blinn, featuring Debbie Allen, Erica Gimpel, Gene Anthony Ray, and Cynthia Gibb, aired January 14, 1982, on NBC, Fox/MGM Television, 2010, DVD; *Fame*, season 1, episode 10, "Come One, Come All," directed by Robert Scheerer, written by Hindi Brooks, featuring Debbie Allen, Erica Gimpel, Gene Anthony Ray, and Cynthia Gibb, aired March 11, 1982, on NBC, Fox/MGM Television, 2010, DVD.

9 *Fame*, season 2, episode 20, "The Kids from 'Fame' in Concert," directed by Terry Sanders, written by Draper Lewis, featuring Debbie Allen, Erica Gimpel, Gene Anthony Ray, and Cynthia Gibb, aired March 3, 1983, on NBC, TV.

10 *Fame*, season 3, episode 4, "The Kids from 'Fame' in Israel," directed by Yossi Zemach, written by Christopher Gore, featuring Debbie Allen, Erica Gimpel, Gene

Anthony Ray, and Cynthia Gibb, aired November 5, 1983, in First-run syndication, TV; *Fame*, season 3, episode 11, "Fame Looks at Music '83," directed by Walter C. Miller, written by Ken Ehrlich, featuring Debbie Allen, Erica Gimpel, Gene Anthony Ray, and Cynthia Gibb, aired January 28, 1984, in First-run syndication, TV.

11 *Fame*, season 4, episode 5, "The Heart of Rock 'n' Roll," directed by Walter C. Miller, written by Ken Ehrlich, featuring Debbie Allen, Erica Gimpel, Gene Anthony Ray, and Cynthia Gibb, aired October 27, 1984, in First-run syndication, TV; *Fame*, season 4, episode 5, "The Heart of Rock 'n' Roll II," directed by Walter C. Miller, written by Ken Ehrlich, featuring Debbie Allen, Erica Gimpel, Gene Anthony Ray, and Cynthia Gibb, aired January 26, 1985, in First-run syndication, TV.

12 *Crazy Ex-Girlfriend*, season 4, episode 18, "Yes, It's Really Us Singing: The Crazy Ex-Girlfriend Concert Special!," directed by Martin Pasetta Jr, written by Rachel Bloom, Adam Schlesinger, and Jack Dolgen, featuring Rachel Bloom, Donna Lynne Champlin, Vincent Rodriguez III, Vella Lovell, and Scott Michael Foster, aired April 5, 2019, on the CW, Warner Home Video, 2009, DVD.

13 *Fame*, season 4, episode 19, "Coco Returns," directed by Debbie Allen, written by Carol Mendelsohn, featuring Debbie Allen, Erica Gimpel, Gene Anthony Ray, and Cynthia Gibb, aired March 2, 1985, in First-run syndication, TV; *Fame*, season 4, episode 13, "Tomorrow's Children," directed by Debbie Allen, written by Patricia Jones and Donald Reiker, featuring Debbie Allen, Erica Gimpel, Gene Anthony Ray, and Cynthia Gibb, aired January 12, 1985, in First-run syndication, TV; *Fame*, season 1, episode 10, "Come One, Come All," aired March 11, 1982; *Fame*, season 2, episode 22, "Ending on a High Note," directed by Jack Bender, written by Christopher Beaumont, featuring Debbie Allen, Erica Gimpel, Gene Anthony Ray, and Cynthia Gibb, aired March 31, 1983, on NBC, Fox/MGM Television, 2010, DVD; *Fame*, season 1, episode 1, "Metamorphosis," directed by Bob Kelljan, written by Christopher Gore, featuring Debbie Allen, Erica Gimpel, Gene Anthony Ray, and Cynthia Gibb, aired January 7, 1982, on NBC, Fox/MGM Television, 2010, DVD; *Fame*, season 5, episode 10, "Choices," aired January 4, 1986.

14 *Ferris Bueller*, season 1, episode 1, "Pilot," directed by Jonathan Lynn, written by John Masius, featuring Charlie Schlatter, Richard Riehle, Jennifer Aniston, Ami Dolenz, and Brandon Douglas, aired August 23, 1990, on NBC, TV.

15 *Parker Lewis Can't Lose*, season 1, episode 26, "Parker Lewis Can't Win," directed by Bryan Spicer, written by Tom Straw, featuring Corin Nemec, Billy Jayne, and Troy Slaten, aired May 19, 1991, on Fox, Fox/MGM Television, 2010, DVD.

16 Stacey Abbott and Lorna Jowett, *TV Horror: The Dark Side of the Small Screen* (London: IB Tauris, 2013), 25.

17 Bill Carter, "NBC Spends Millions on the Buildup to 'Smash,'" *New York Times*, February 5, 2012. https://www.nytimes.com/2012/02/06/business/media/nbc-spends-millions-on-the-buildup-to-smash.html

18 Maureen Ryan, "'Smash' Exclusive First Look: Is This the Show That Will Save NBC?" *Huffington Post*, November 21, 2011, https://web.archive.org/web/20120126070044/http://www.aoltv.com/2011/11/21/smash-nbc-exclusive-first-look-katharine-mcphee/; Tim Goodman, "Smash: TV Review," *The Hollywood Reporter*, February 1, 2012, https://www.hollywoodreporter.com/tv/tv-reviews/smash-tv-review-katharine-mcphee-debra-messing-286296/; David Weigand, "'Smash' Review: NBC Series Lives up the Hype," *San Francisco Chronicle*, March 27, 2012.

19 Kevin Fallon, "The TV Musical Is Dead," *The Atlantic*, April 10, 2012, https://www.theatlantic.com/entertainment/archive/2012/04/the-tv-musical-is-dead/255643/

20 Lesley Goldberg, "'Smash' Creator Steps Down as Showrunner," *The Hollywood Reporter*, March 22, 2012, https://www.hollywoodreporter.com/tv/tv-news/smash-creator-theresa-rebeck-step-down-showrunner-303451/

21 Fallon, "The TV Musical Is Dead."

22 Kate Arthur, "How 'Smash' Became TV's Biggest Train Wreck," *Buzzfeed*, January 30, 2013, https://www.buzzfeed.com/kateaurthur/how-smash-became-tvs-biggest-train-wreck

23 *Smash*, season 2, episode 1, "On Broadway," directed by Michael Morris, written by Josh Safran, featuring Debra Messing, Jack Davenport, and Anjelica Huston, aired February 5, 2013, on NBC, Universal Pictures Home Entertainment, 2013, DVD.

24 Adam Gold, "Inside the Music of 'Nashville': Stars and Producers Strive for Authenticity, and It's Paying Off," *Rolling Stone*, November 7, 2012, https://www.rollingstone.com/music/music-news/inside-the-music-of-nashville-177944/

25 Ibid.

26 *Nashville*, season 1, episode 21, "I'll Never Get Out of This World Alive," directed by Callie Khouri, written by Callie Khouri, featuring Connie Britton, Hayden Panettiere, Clare Bowen, and Eric Close, aired May 22, 2013, on ABC, Walt Disney Studios Home Entertainment, 2013, DVD; *Nashville*, season 2, episode 10, "Tomorrow Never Comes," directed by Patrick Norris, written by Meredith Lavender and Marcie Ulin, featuring Connie Britton, Hayden Panettiere, Clare Bowen, and Eric Close, aired December 11, 2013, on ABC, Walt Disney Studios Home Entertainment, 2013, DVD; *Nashville*, season 4, episode 6, "Please Help Me, I'm Fallin," directed by Callie Khouri, written by Taylor Hamra, featuring Connie Britton, Hayden Panettiere, Clare Bowen, and Eric Close, aired October 28, 2015, on ABC, Walt Disney Studios Home Entertainment, 2016, DVD.

27 Chris Willman, "T Bone Burnett on Quitting Wife Callie Khouri's 'Nashville': It Was a 'Drag-Out Fight,'" *The Hollywood Reporter*, October 30, 2013, https://www.hollywoodreporter.com/news/general-news/t-bone-burnett-quitting-wife-651400/

28 Brittany Hodak, "The Real-Life Impact of ABC's 'Nashville,'" *Forbes*, October 28, 2015, https://www.forbes.com/sites/brittanyhodak/2015/10/28/the-real-life-impact-of-abcs-nashville/

29 *Nashville*, season 5, episode 9, "If Tomorrow Never Comes," directed by Callie Khouri, written by Geoffrey Nauffts, featuring Connie Britton, Hayden Panettiere, Clare Bowen, and Eric Close, aired February 23, 2017, on CMT, Walt Disney Studios Home Entertainment, 2017, DVD.

30 Hodak, "The Real-Life Impact of ABC's 'Nashville.'"

31 Kyle Herrera, Travis Gonzales, Joseph Buck, and Christian Naranjo, "How Has Breaking Bad Affected New Mexico's Economy?", *New Mexico News Port*, March 23, 2015, https://newmexiconewsport.com/how-has-breaking-bad-affected-new-mexicos-economy/

32 Diane Werts, "Review: CBS' 'Viva Laughlin' a Train Wreck," *Newsday*, October 18, 2007, https://web.archive.org/web/20071020034800/http://www.newsday.com/entertainment/tv/ny-ettell5415699oct18,0,5351094.story; Alessandro Stanley, "Singing in the Casino? That's a Gamble," *New York Times*, October 18, 2007, https://www.nytimes.com/2007/10/18/arts/television/18stan.html

33 *Fame*, season 1, episode 1, "Metamorphosis," aired January 7, 1982.

Chapter 5

1 *Daria*, season 3, episode 1, "Daria!," directed by Karen Disher, written by Glenn Eichler and Peter Elwell, featuring Tracy Grandstaff, Wendy Hoopes, and Julián Rebolledo, aired February 17, 1999, on MTV, Paramount Home Entertainment, 2010, DVD; *Ally McBeal*, season 3, episode 21, "Ally McBeal: The Musical, Almost," directed by Bill D'Elia, written by David E. Kelley, featuring Calista Flockhart, Greg Germann, Lisa Nicole Carson, and Gil Bellows, aired May 22, 2000, on Fox, 20th Century Fox Home Entertainment, 2009, DVD.

2 *Ally McBeal*, season 1, episode 12, "Cro-Magnon," directed by Allan Arkush, written by David E. Kelley, featuring Calista Flockhart, Greg Germann, Lisa Nicole Carson, and Gil Bellows, aired January 5, 1998, on Fox, 20th Century Fox Home Entertainment, 2009, DVD.

3 *Northern Exposure*, season 4, episode 25, "Old Tree," directed by Michael Fresco, written by Diane Frolov and Robin Green, featuring Rob Morrow, Janine Turner, John Corbett, and Darren E. Burrows, aired May 24, 1993, on CBS, Universal Home Entertainment, 2007, DVD.

4 *Xena: Warrior Princess*, season 3, episode 12, "The Bitter Suite," directed by Oley Sassone, written by Steven L. Sears and Chris Manheim, featuring Lucy Lawless, Renee O'Connor, and Ted Raimi, aired February 14, 1998, in First-run syndication, Universal Home Video, 2024, DVD.

5 *Dawson's Creek*, season 1, episode 12, "Beauty Contest," directed by Arvin Brown, written by Dana Baratta, featuring James Van Der Beek, Katie Holmes, Michelle Williams, and Joshua Jackson, aired May 12, 1998, on the WB, Sony Pictures Home Entertainment, 2009, DVD; *Roswell*, season 3, episode 8, "Behind the Music," directed by Jonathan Frakes, written by Russel Friend and Garrett Lerner, featuring Shiri Appleby, Jason Behr, Brendan Fehr, Katherine Heigl, and Majandra Delfino, aired November 27, 2001, on UPN, Paramount, 2005, DVD.

6 *Riverdale*, season 3, episode 16, "Chapter Fifty-One: Big Fun," directed by Maggie Kiley, written by Tessa Leigh Williams, featuring KJ Apa, Lili Reinhart, Camila Mendes, and Cole Sprouse, aired March 20, 2019, on the CW, Warner Home Entertainment, 2023, DVD; *Riverdale*, season 4, episode 17, "Chapter Seventy-Four: Wicked Little Town," directed by Antonio Negret, written by Tessa Leigh Williams, featuring KJ Apa, Lili Reinhart, Camila Mendes, and Cole Sprouse, aired April 15, 2020, on the CW, Warner Home Entertainment, 2023, DVD.

7 *Buffy the Vampire Slayer*, season 5, episode 4, "Out of My Mind," directed by David Grossman, written by Rebecca Rand Kirshner, featuring Sarah Michelle Gellar, Alyson Hannigan, Nicholas Brendan, Anthony Stewart Head, and James Marsters, aired October 17, 2000, on the WB, 20th Century Fox, 2005, DVD.

8 *Buffy the Vampire Slayer*, season 1, episode 12, "Prophesy Girl," directed by Joss Whedon, written by Joss Whedon, featuring Sarah Michelle Gellar, Alyson Hannigan, Nicholas Brendan, Anthony Stewart Head, and David Boreanaz, aired June 2, 1997, on the WB, 20th Century Fox, 2005, DVD; *Buffy the Vampire Slayer*, season 5, episode 22, "The Gift," directed by Joss Whedon, written by Joss Whedon, featuring Sarah Michelle Gellar, Alyson Hannigan, Nicholas Brendan, Anthony Stewart Head, and James Marsters, aired May 22, 2001, on the WB, 20th Century Fox, 2005, DVD; *Buffy the Vampire Slayer*, season 6, episode 2, "Bargaining, Part 2," directed by David Grossman, written by David Fury, featuring Sarah Michelle Gellar, Alyson Hannigan, Nicholas Brendan, Anthony Stewart Head, and James Marsters, aired October 2, 2001, on UPN, 20th Century Fox, 2005, DVD.

9 *Buffy the Vampire Slayer*, season 2, episode 22, "Becoming (Part 2)," directed by Joss Whedon, written by Joss Whedon, featuring Sarah Michelle Gellar, Alyson Hannigan, Nicholas Brendan, Anthony Stewart Head, and David Boreanaz, aired May 19, 1998, on the WB, 20th Century Fox, 2005, DVD.

10 *Buffy the Vampire Slayer*, season 6, episode 3, "After Life," directed by David Solomon, written by Jane Espenson, featuring Sarah Michelle Gellar, Alyson Hannigan, Nicholas Brendan, and James Marsters, aired October 9, 2001, on UPN, 20th Century Fox, 2005, DVD.

11 *Buffy the Vampire Slayer*, season 6, episode 7, "Once More, With Feeling," directed by Joss Whedon, written by Joss Whedon, featuring Sarah Michelle Gellar, Alyson Hannigan, Nicholas Brendan, Anthony Stewart Head, and James Marsters, aired November 6, 2001, on UPN, 20th Century Fox, 2005, DVD.

12 Ibid.

13 Rhonda Wilcox, *Why Buffy Matters: The Art of Buffy the Vampire Slayer* (London: IB Tauris, 2005), 201.

14 *Buffy the Vampire Slayer*, season 6, episode 7, "Once More, With Feeling," aired November 6, 2001.

15 Erin Giannini, *Supernatural: A History of Television's Unearthly Road Trip* (Lanham, MD: Rowman & Littlefield, 2021), 53–70.

16 *Supernatural*, season 4, episode 18, "The Monster at the End of This Book," directed by Mike Rohl, written by Julie Siege, featuring Jensen Ackles, Jared Padalecki, and Misha Collins, aired April 2, 2009, on the CW, Warner Home Video, 2009, DVD.

17 *Supernatural*, season 6, episode 15, "The French Mistake," directed by Charles Beeson, written by Ben Edlund, featuring Jensen Ackles, Jared Padalecki, and Misha Collins, aired February 25, 2011, on the CW, Warner Home Video, 2011, DVD.

18 *Supernatural*, season 10, episode 5, "Fan Fiction," directed by Phil Sgriccia, written by Robbie Thompson, featuring Jensen Ackles, Jared Padalecki, and Misha Collins, aired November 11, 2014, on the CW, Warner Home Video, 2015, DVD.

19 *Supernatural*, season 2, episode 17, "Heart," directed by Kim Manners, written by Sera Gamble, featuring Jensen Ackles and Jared Padalecki, aired March 22, 2007, on the CW, Warner Home Video, 2007, DVD.

20 *Supernatural*, season 4, episode 18, "The Monster at the End of This Book," aired April 2, 2009.

21 *Supernatural*, season 7, episode 8, "Season 7, Time for a Wedding!" directed by Tim Andrew, written by Andrew Dabb and Daniel Loflin, featuring Jensen Ackles, Jared Padalecki, and Misha Collins, aired November 11, 2011, on the CW, Warner Home Video, 2012, DVD.

22 *Supernatural*, season 15, episode 4, "Atomic Monsters," directed by Jensen Ackles, written by Davy Perez, featuring Jensen Ackles, Jared Padalecki, and Misha Collins, aired November 7, 2019, on the CW, Warner Home Video, 2020, DVD.

23 *Supernatural*, season 10, episode 5, "Fan Fiction," aired November 11, 2014.

24 *Once Upon a Time*, season 1, episode 22, "A Land Without Magic," directed by Dean White, written by Edward Kitsis and Adam Horowitz, featuring Jennifer Morrison, Ginnifer Goodwin, Lana Parrilla, and Josh Dallas, aired May 13, 2012, on ABC, Walt Disney Video, 2012, DVD.

25 Carlo Collodi, *The Adventures of Pinocchio*, trans. John Hooper (New York: Penguin Random House, 2021).

26 *Zootopia*, directed by Bryon Howard and Rich Moore (2016; Burbank, CA: Walt DisneyStudios Home Entertainment, 2016), DVD.

27 *Once Upon a Time*, season 1, episode 1, "Pilot," directed by Mark Mylod, written by Edward Kitsis and Adam Horowitz, featuring Jennifer Morrison, Ginnifer Goodwin, Lana Parrilla, and Josh Dallas, aired October 23, 2011, on ABC, Walt Disney Video, 2012, DVD.

28 *Once Upon a Time*, season 6, episode 20, "The Song in Your Heart," directed by Ron Underwood, written by David H. Goodman and Andrew Chambliss, featuring Jennifer Morrison, Ginnifer Goodwin, Lana Parrilla, and Josh Dallas, aired May 7, 2017, on ABC, Walt Disney Video, 2017, DVD.

29 *Scrubs*, season 1, episode 23, "My Hero," directed by Michael Spiller, written by Neil Goldman and Garrett Donovan, featuring Zach Braff, Donald Faison, Judy Reyes, and Sarah Chalke, aired May 14, 2002, on NBC, Buena Vista Home Entertainment, 2005, DVD.

30 *Scrubs*, season 2, episode 2, "My Nightingale," directed by Craig Zisk, written by Eric Weinberg, featuring Zach Braff, Donald Faison, Judy Reyes, and Sarah Chalke, aired October 3, 2002, on NBC, Buena Vista Home Entertainment, 2005, DVD.

31 *Scrubs*, season 2, episode 13, "My Philosophy," directed by Chris Koch, written by Matt Tarses and Tim Hobert, featuring Zach Braff, Donald Faison, Judy Reyes, and Sarah Chalke, aired January 16, 2003, on NBC, Buena Vista Home Entertainment, 2005, DVD.

32 *Scrubs*, season 3, episode 19, "My Choosiest Choice of All," directed by Adam Bernstein, written by Mike Schwartz, featuring Zach Braff, Donald Faison, Judy Reyes, and Sarah Chalke, aired April 20, 2004, on NBC, Buena Vista Home Entertainment, 2006, DVD.

33 Dustin Rowles, "The Internet Is Toxic. Zach Braff and Donald Faison's Live Rendition of 'Guy Love' Is Not," *Pajiba*, June 3, 2014, https://www.pajiba.com/videos/the-internet-is-toxic-zach-braff-and-donald-faisons-live-rendition-of-guy-love-is-not.php

34 *Scrubs*, season 6, episode 6, "My Musical," directed by Will Mackenzie, written by Debra Fordham, featuring Zach Braff, Donald Faison, Judy Reyes, and Sarah Chalke, aired January 18, 2007, on NBC, Buena Vista Home Entertainment, 2007, DVD.

35 *Scrubs*, season 3, episode 3, "My White Whale," directed by Michael Spiller, written by Eric Weinberg, featuring Zach Braff, Donald Faison, Judy Reyes, and Sarah Chalke, aired October 23, 2003, on NBC, Buena Vista Home Entertainment, 2006, DVD.

36 Feras A. Al-Awad, "The Phenomenon of Musical Hallucinations: An Updated Review," *Electronic Journal of General Medicine* 20, no. 6 (2023): em533.

Chapter 6

1 *Amadeus*, directed by Miloš Forman (1984; Los Angeles, CA: Warner Home Video, 2009), DVD.

2 Rowen Smith, "The Beggar's Opera Review—the Original Jukebox Musical Reimagined," *The Guardian*, August 17, 2018, https://www.theguardian.com/music/2018/aug/17/the-beggars-opera-review-kings-theatre-edinburgh-international-festival

3 *Singin' in the Rain*, directed by Stanley Donen and Gene Kelly (1952; Los Angeles, CA: Warner Home Video, 2002), DVD.

4 *Rock Rock Rock!*, directed by Will Price (1956; Wayne, PA: Alpha Video, 2022), DVD; *An American in Paris*, directed by Vincente Minnelli (1951; Los Angeles, CA: Warner Home Video, 2000), DVD.

5 Michael D. Dwyer, *Back to the Fifties: Nostalgia, Hollywood Film, and Popular Music of the Seventies and Eighties* (London: Oxford University Press, 2015).

6 *Yesterday*, directed by Danny Boyle (2019; Los Angeles, CA: Universal Pictures Home Entertainment, 2019), DVD.

7 *Walking on Sunshine*, directed by Max Giwa and Dania Pasquini (2014; Los Angeles, CA: Sony Pictures Home Entertainment, 2016), DVD.

8 *Mamma Mia!*, directed by Phyllida Lloyd (2008; Los Angeles, CA: Universal Pictures Home Entertainment, 2011), DVD.

9 Stagedoor Editors, "The Longest-Running West End Shows: Here Are the 5 Longest-Running Musicals in London History," *Stagedoor*, October 11, 2024, https://stagedoor.com/theatre-guide/stagedoor-editors/the-longest-running-west-end-shows?ia=1820; Dee McCourt, "Facts and Figures: Mamma Mia! Stage Show," *Judy Cramer*, https://www.judycraymer.com/press-centre/facts-and-figures.php

10 *Grey's Anatomy*, season 7, episode 18, "Song Beneath the Song," directed by Tony Phelan, written by Shonda Rhimes, featuring Ellen Pompeo, Sandra Oh, Sara Ramirez, and Jesse Williams, aired March 31, 2011, on ABC, Buena Vista Home Entertainment, 2011, DVD.

11 *The Flash*, season 3, episode 17, "Duet," directed by Dermont Daniel Downs, written by Aaron Helbing and Todd Helbing, featuring Grant Gustin, Melissa Benoist, and Darren Criss, aired March 21, 2017, on the CW, Warner Home Video, 2017, DVD.

12 *House*, season 6, episode 20, "The Choice," directed by Juan J. Campanella, written by David Hoselton, featuring Hugh Laurie, Robert Sean Leonard, and Lisa Edelstein, aired May 3, 2010, on Fox, Universal Pictures Home Entertainment, 2010, DVD.

13 *Bones*, season 5, episode 19, "The Rocker in the Rinse Cycle," directed by Jeff Woolnough, written by Karine Rosenthal, featuring David Boreanaz, Emily Deschanel, and Tamara Taylor, aired April 29, 2010, on Fox, 20th Century Fox, 2010, DVD; Michael Schneider, "'Fox Rocks' Week Misses Catchy Spelling Opportunity," *Variety*, April 7, 2010, https://variety.com/2010/tv/news/fox-rocks-week-misses-catchy-spelling-opportunity-16335/

14 *Fringe*, season 2, episode 20, "Brown Betty," directed by Seith Mann, written by Jeff Pinkner, J. H. Wyman, and Akiva Goldsman, featuring John Noble, Joshua Jackson, and Anna Torv, aired April 29, 2010, on Fox, Warner Home Video, 2010, DVD.

15 Lauren Herstick, "Interview: Lev Grossman on The Magician's Land," *Nerdist*, August 7, 2014, https://web.archive.org/web/20180616075004/https://nerdist.com/interview-lev-grossman-on-the-magicians-land/

16 *The Magicians*, season 2, episode 9, "Lesser Evils," directed by Rebecca Johnson, written by Elle Lipson and John McNamara, featuring Jason Ralph, Stella Maeve, Hale Appleman, and Arjun Gupta, aired March 22, 2017, on SyFy, Universal Pictures Home Entertainment, 2020, DVD.

17 *The Magicians*, season 4, episode 10, "All That Hard, Glossy Armor," directed by Shannon Kohli, written by John McNamara and Mike Moore, featuring Jason Ralph, Stella Maeve, Hale Appleman, and Arjun Gupta, aired March 27, 2019, on SyFy, Universal Pictures Home Entertainment, 2020, DVD.

18 *The Magicians*, season 3, episode 9, "All That Josh," directed by James L. Conway, written by John McNamara, Jay Gard, and Alex Raiman, featuring Jason Ralph, Stella Maeve, Hale Appleman, and Arjun Gupta, aired March 7, 2018, on SyFy, Universal Pictures Home Entertainment, 2020, DVD.

19 *The Magicians*, season 5, episode 12, "The Balls," directed by Meera Menon, written by Elle Lipson, John McNamara, and Joseph Mireles, featuring Stella Maeve, Hale Appleman, and Arjun Gupta, aired March 25, 2020, on SyFy, Universal Pictures Home Entertainment, 2020, DVD.

20 *Lucifer*, season 1, episode 1, "Pilot," directed by Len Wiseman, written by Tom Kapinos, featuring Tom Ellis, Lauren German, D.B. Woodside, and Lesley-Ann Brandt, aired January 25, 2016, on Fox, Warner Home Video, 2022, DVD.

21 *Lucifer*, season 1, episode 6, "Favorite Son," directed by David Paymer, written by Jason Ning, featuring Tom Ellis, Lauren German, D.B. Woodside, and Lesley-Ann Brandt, aired February 29, 2016, on Fox, Warner Home Video, 2022, DVD; *Lucifer*, season 2, episode 1, "Everything's Coming Up Lucifer," directed by Nathan Hope, written by Joe Henderson, featuring Tom Ellis, Lauren German, D.B. Woodside, and Lesley-Ann Brandt, aired September 19, 2016, on Fox, Warner Home Video, 2022, DVD; *Lucifer*, season 3, episode 7, "Off the Record," directed by Eduardo Sánchez, written by Chris Rafferty and Mike Costa, featuring Tom Ellis, Lauren German, D.B. Woodside, and Lesley-Ann Brandt, aired November 13, 2017, on Fox, Warner

Home Video, 2022, DVD; *Lucifer*, season 4, episode 1, "Everything's Okay," directed by Sherwin Shilati, written by Joe Henderson, featuring Tom Ellis, Lauren German, D.B. Woodside, and Lesley-Ann Brandt, aired May 8, 2019, on Netflix, Warner Home Video, 2022, DVD.

22 *Lucifer* was one of the earlier series that found a second life on streaming, and did pull high viewership number for Netflix (Hersko 2021). The episode times ran longer on streaming (50–58 minutes, rather than the standard 40–45 for broadcast) and some of the content restrictions were eased.

23 *Lucifer*, season 5, episode 8, "Spoiler Alert," directed by Kevin Alejandro, written by Chris Rafferty, featuring Tom Ellis, Lauren German, D.B. Woodside, and Lesley-Ann Brandt, aired August 21, 2020, on Netflix, Warner Home Video, 2022, DVD.

24 Wanna Thompson, "TLC's 'No Scrubs' Is Still on Top 20 Years Later: The Trio's Hit Single Continues to Resonate with Young Women Across the Globe," *Vibe*, February 2, 2019, https://www.vibe.com/features/editorial/tlc-no-scrubs-anniversary-633169/

25 Austin Williams, "Will Smith's 'Just the Two of Us,' and the Protection That Comes With His Love," *Vibe*, March 31, 2022, https://www.vibe.com/features/opinion/will-smith-just-the-two-of-us-yellow-diamonds-lyric-break-down-1234654616/

26 *Lucifer*, season 5, episode 10, "Bloody Celestial Karaoke Jam," directed by Sherwin Shilati, written by Ildy Modrovich, featuring Tom Ellis, Lauren German, D.B. Woodside, and Lesley-Ann Brandt, aired May 28, 2021, on Netflix, Warner Home Video, 2022, DVD.

Chapter 7

1 Newton N. Minow, "Television and the Public Interest," address to the National Association of Broadcasters, Washington, DC, May 9, 1961, https://www.americanrhetoric.com/speeches/newtonminow.htm

2 Brent Staples, "Just a Toaster with Pictures," *The New York Times*, February 8, 1987, https://www.nytimes.com/1987/02/08/books/just-a-toaster-with-pictures.html

3 Peter J. Boyer, "Under Fowler, F. C. C. Treated TV as Commerce," *The New York Times*, January 19, 1987, https://www.nytimes.com/1987/01/19/arts/under-fowler-fcc-treated-tv-as-commerce.html

4 Jackie Mansky, "An Early Run-In with Censors Led Rod Serling to 'The Twilight Zone': His Failed Attempts to Bring the Emmett Till Tragedy to Television Forced Him to Get Creative," *Smithsonian Magazine*, April 1, 2019, https://www.smithsonianmag.com/arts-culture/early-run-censors-led-rod-serling-twilight-zone-180971837/

5 Michaela Finley, "Lucy and Desi Return to Newburgh," *Poughkeepsie Journal*, May 15, 2014, https://www.poughkeepsiejournal.com/story/entertainment/theater/2014/05/15/lucy-desi-arnaz-newburgh/9132425/

6 Ryan Parker, "Barbara Bush's Letter to Marge Simpson Revealed by Series Showrunner," *The Hollywood Reporter*, April 18, 2018, https://www.hollywoodreporter.com/tv/tv-news/barbara-bushs-letter-marge-simpson-revealed-by-series-showrunner-1103722/; William Hughes, "George H. W. Bush Has Died, but Pop Culture's Impression of Him Lives On," *The AV Club*, December 1, 2018, https://www.avclub.com/george-h-w-bush-has-died-but-pop-cultures-impression-1830789538

7 Mark Ehrman, "Cliques: The Importance of Hating Brenda," *Los Angeles Times*, February 7, 1993, https://www.latimes.com/archives/la-xpm-1993-02-07-tm-1357-story.html

8 *LA Law*, season 5, episode 16, "Good to the Last Drop," directed by Menachem Binetski, written by David E. Kelley, Patricia Green, and Alan Brennert, featuring Harry Hamlin, Corbin Bernsen, Richard Dysart, Blair Underwood, and Susan Ruttan, aired March 21, 1991, on NBC, Revelation Films, 2013, DVD.

9 Bill Kelley, "The Best and Brightest ABC's Hooperman—the Hands-Down Winner of Best New Show of the Year—Introduces a New Format, 'Dramedy,' While Slap Maxwell Reintroduces Dabney Coleman," *South Florida Sun Sentinel*, September 23, 1987, https://web.archive.org/web/20170924095527/http://articles.sun-sentinel.com/1987-09-23/features/8703150300_1_hooperman-lewis-erlicht-brandon-stoddard

10 Diane Haithman, "Steven Bochco, the $10-Million Man: Industry Ponders Whether His Exclusive Deal with ABC Will Pay Off for Network," *Los Angeles Times*, November 24, 1987, https://www.latimes.com/archives/la-xpm-1987-11-24-ca-24479-story.html

11 Will Harris, "An Oral History of *Cop Rock*, TV's First and Last Musical Police Drama," *AV Club*, May 26, 2016, https://www.avclub.com/an-oral-history-of-cop-rock-tv-s-first-and-last-musica-1798248164

12 Sam Adams, "The '90s Police Musical Cop Rock, Just Released on DVD, Was a Terrible Show That Could've Been Great," *Slate*, May 19, 2016, https://slate.com/culture/2016/05/the-90s-police-musical-cop-rock-just-released-on-dvd-was-a-terrible-show-that-could-ve-been-great.html

13 *Cop Rock*, season 1, episode 1, "Pilot," directed by Gregory Hoblit, written by Steven Bochco and William M. Finkelstein, featuring Anne Bobby, Barbara Bosson, Peter Onorati, and Vondie Curtis-Hall, aired September 26, 1990, on ABC, Shout! Factory, 2016, DVD.

14 *Cop Rock*, season 1, episode 9, "Marital Blitz," directed by Gilbert Shilton, written by Steven Bochco, William M. Finkelstein, Toni Graphia, and John Romano,

featuring Anne Bobby, Barbara Bosson, Peter Onorati, and Vondie Curtis-Hall, aired December 5, 1990, on ABC, Shout! Factory, 2016, DVD.

15 Emily Maeser, "The Syntax of Television, Part 3: Making a Show," *Movie Jawn*, June 1, 2023, https://www.moviejawn.com/home/2023/6/1/the-syntax-of-television-part-3-making-a-show?srsltid=AfmBOorJJEx2INB6fo5tc-Md0A55DTLhqioCcLPmyx82zcnd3_X88Uw3

16 The *Buffy* episode took several weeks to put together; see Nikki Stafford, *Bite Me! The Unofficial Guide to Buffy the Vampire Slayer* (Toronto: ECW Press, 2007).

17 Katharine Coldiron, "Something to Sing About: Why *Cop Rock* Fails," *Bright Lights Film Journal*, May 9, 2021, https://brightlightsfilm.com/something-to-sing-about-why-cop-rock-fails/

18 *Cop Rock*, season 1, episode 4, "A Three-Corpse Meal," directed by Fred Gerber, written by William M. Finkelstein, Toni Graphia, and John Romano, featuring Anne Bobby, Barbara Bosson, Peter Onorati, and Vondie Curtis-Hall, aired October 17, 1990, on ABC, Shout! Factory, 2016, DVD.

19 Coldiron, "Something to Sing About"; *Cop Rock*, season 1, episode 10, "No Noose Is Good Noose," directed by Michael M. Robin, written by Steven Bochco, William M. Finkelstein, Toni Graphia, and John Romano, featuring Anne Bobby, Barbara Bosson, Peter Onorati, and Vondie Curtis-Hall, aired December 12, 1990, on ABC, Shout! Factory, 2016, DVD.

20 *Cop Rock*, season 1, episode 1, "Pilot," aired September 26, 1990; *Cop Rock*, season 1, episode 3, "Happy Mudder's Day," directed by Charles Haid, written by Steven Bochco, William M. Finkelstein, and John Romano, featuring Anne Bobby, Barbara Bosson, Peter Onorati, and Vondie Curtis-Hall, aired October 10, 1990, on ABC, Shout! Factory, 2016, DVD.

21 *Cop Rock*, season 1, episode 11, "Bang the Potts Slowly," directed by Fred Gerber, written by William M. Finkelstein and John Romano, featuring Anne Bobby, Barbara Bosson, Peter Onorati, and Vondie Curtis-Hall, aired December 26, 1990, on ABC, Shout! Factory, 2016, DVD.

22 Coldiron, "Something to Sing About."

23 *Cop Rock*, season 1, episode 1, "Pilot," aired September 26, 1990.

24 *Hull High*, season 1, episode 1, "Episode One," directed by Kenny Ortega, written by Gil Grant, featuring Will Lyman, Nancy Valen, Kristin Dattalio, and Carl Anthony Payne II, aired August 20, 1990, on NBC.

25 Ibid.

26 Harris, "An Oral History of *Cop Rock*, TV's First and Last Musical Police Drama."

Chapter 8

1 Chris Morgan, "Remember TV's Rural Purge," *Medium*, May 19, 2017, https://medium.com/@ChrisXMorgan/remember-tvs-rural-purge-b0a115c2a2b2

2 Susan Faludi, *Backlash: The Undeclared War Against American Women: 15th Anniversary Edition* (New York: Three Rivers Press, 2006 [1991]), 174.

3 *Community*, season 2, episode 21, "Paradigms of Human Memory," directed by Tristram Shapeero, written by Chris McKenna, featuring Joel McHale, Donald Glover, Alison Brie, Yvette Nicole Brown, and Chevy Chase, aired April 21, 2011, on NBC, Mill Creek Entertainment, 2019, DVD.

4 *Invasion of the Body Snatchers*, directed by Philip Kauffman (1978; Los Angeles, CA: Universal Pictures Home Entertainment, 2020), DVD.

5 *Community*, season 3, episode 10, "Regional Holiday Music," directed by Tristram Shapeero, written by Steve Basilone and Annie Mebane, featuring Joel McHale, Donald Glover, Alison Brie, Yvette Nicole Brown, and Chevy Chase, aired December 8, 2011, on NBC, Mill Creek Entertainment, 2019, DVD.

6 Taylor Diamond, "How Dan Harmon Used Community to Show His Hatred for Glee," *Screen Rant*, October 15, 2022, https://screenrant.com/community-dan-harmon-glee-show-dislike/

7 *Glee*, season 1, episode 1, "Pilot," directed by Ryan Murphy, written by Ryan Murphy, Brad Falchuk, and Ian Brennan, featuring Matthew Morrison, Lea Michele, Cory Monteith, Jane Lynch, and Chris Colfer, aired May 19, 2009, on Fox, Sony Pictures Home Entertainment, 2018, DVD.

8 *Glee*, season 1, episode 5, "The Rhodes Not Taken," directed by John Scott, written by Ian Brennan, featuring Matthew Morrison, Lea Michele, Cory Monteith, Jane Lynch, and Chris Colfer, aired September 30, 2009, on Fox, Sony Pictures Home Entertainment, 2018, DVD; *Glee*, season 1, episode 7, "Throwdown," directed by Ryan Murphy, written by Brad Falchuk, featuring Matthew Morrison, Lea Michele, Cory Monteith, Jane Lynch, and Chris Colfer, aired October 14, 2009, on Fox, Sony Pictures Home Entertainment, 2018, DVD; *Glee*, season 1, episode 4, "Preggers," directed by Brad Falchuk, written by Brad Falchuk, featuring Matthew Morrison, Lea Michele, Cory Monteith, Jane Lynch, and Chris Colfer, aired September 23, 2009, on Fox, Sony Pictures Home Entertainment, 2018, DVD; *Glee*, season 1, episode 12, "Mattress," directed by Elodie Keene, written by Ryan Murphy, featuring Matthew Morrison, Lea Michele, Cory Monteith, Jane Lynch, and Chris Colfer, aired December 2, 2009, on Fox, Sony Pictures Home Entertainment, 2018, DVD.

9 EW Staff, "26 Best Cult Shows Ever," *Entertainment Weekly*, June 1, 2022, https://ew.com/gallery/26-best-cult-tv-shows-ever/#380657

10 Kaitlin Reilly, "Hollywood Is Ryan Murphy's Response to Years of the Industry's Homophobia," *Refinery 29*, May 1, 2020, https://www.refinery29.com/en-us/2020/05/9756058/ryan-murphy-hollywood-homophobia-story

11 *Glee*, season 3, episode 16, "Saturday Night Glee-ver," directed by Bradley Buecker, written by Matthew Hodgson, featuring Matthew Morrison, Lea Michele, Cory Monteith, Jane Lynch, and Chris Colfer, aired April 17, 2012, on Fox, Sony Pictures Home Entertainment, 2018, DVD; *Glee*, season 1, episode 4, "Preggers," aired September 23, 2009.

12 *Glee*, season 2, episode 12, "Silly Love Songs," directed by Tate Donovan, written by Ryan Murphy, featuring Matthew Morrison, Lea Michele, Cory Monteith, Jane Lynch, and Chris Colfer, aired February 8, 2011, on Fox, Sony Pictures Home Entertainment, 2018, DVD.

13 *Glee*, season 2, episode 15, "Sexy," directed by Ryan Murphy, written by Brad Falchuk, featuring Matthew Morrison, Lea Michele, Cory Monteith, Jane Lynch, and Chris Colfer, aired March 8, 2011, on Fox, Sony Pictures Home Entertainment, 2018, DVD.

14 "Glitter Jailed over Child Porn," *BBC News*, November 12, 1999, http://news.bbc.co.uk/2/hi/uk_news/517604.stm; Ashley Cullins, "'Glee' Actor Mark Salling Indicted for Possessing Child Pornography: If Convicted, the Actor Faces a Mandatory Minimum of Five Years in Prison," *The Hollywood Reporter*, May 27, 2016, https://www.hollywoodreporter.com/business/business-news/glee-actor-mark-salling-indicted-897996/?facebook_20160527; Nancy Dillon and Rachel Desantis, "'Glee' Star Mark Salling Dead at 35 in Suspected Suicide," *New York Daily News*, April 7, 2018, https://www.nydailynews.com/2018/01/30/glee-star-mark-salling-dead-at-35-in-suspected-suicide-by-hanging/

15 *Glee*, season 3, episode 11, "Michael," directed by Alfonso Gomez-Rejon, written by Ryan Murphy, featuring Matthew Morrison, Lea Michele, Cory Monteith, Jane Lynch, and Chris Colfer, aired January 31, 2012, on Fox, Sony Pictures Home Entertainment, 2018, DVD.

16 Richard Lawson, "'Glee' Was Bad, Really Really Bad," *The Atlantic*, February 1, 2012, https://www.theatlantic.com/culture/archive/2012/02/glee-was-bad-really-really-bad/332381/

17 *Glee*, season 5, episode 12, "100," directed by Paris Barclay, written by Ryan Murphy, Brad Falchuk, and Ian Brennan, featuring Matthew Morrison, Lea Michele, Jane Lynch, and Chris Colfer, aired March 10, 2014, on Fox, Sony Pictures Home Entertainment, 2018, DVD.

18 *Glee*, season 6, episode 13, "Dreams Come True," directed by Bradley Buecker, written by Ryan Murphy, Brad Falchuk, and Ian Brennan, featuring Matthew Morrison, Lea Michele, Jane Lynch, and Chris Colfer, aired March 20, 2015, on Fox, Sony Pictures Home Entertainment, 2018, DVD.

19 *Glee*, season 1, episode 7, "Throwdown," aired October 14, 2009; *Community*, season 3, episode 10, "Regional Holiday Music," aired December 8, 2011.

20 Maxine Sibihwana, "'You're All Minorities. You're in the Glee Club': Neoliberalism, and the Disappearing Black People in the Ryan Murphy Cinematic Universe," *Medium*, April 25, 2025, https://medium.com/@maxinesibihwana/youre-all-minorities-you-re-in-the-glee-club-4301d932383f; Abbey White, "Lea Michele Responds to Racism, On-Set Bullying Accusations Ahead of 'Funny Girl' Debut," *The Hollywood Reporter*, September 1, 2022, www.hollywoodreporter.com/lifestyle/arts/lea-michele-racism-bullying-allegations-funny-girl-1235210209/

21 *Glee*, season 3, episode 12, "The Spanish Teacher," directed by Paris Barclay, written by Ian Brennan, featuring Matthew Morrison, Lea Michele, Cory Monteith, Jane Lynch, and Chris Colfer, aired February 7, 2012, on Fox, Sony Pictures Home Entertainment, 2018, DVD; *Glee*, season 1, episode 9, "Wheels," directed by Paris Barclay, written by Ryan Murphy, featuring Matthew Morrison, Lea Michele, Cory Monteith, Jane Lynch, and Chris Colfer, aired November 11, 2009, on Fox, Sony Pictures Home Entertainment, 2018, DVD.

22 Dustin Petty, "Glee: Best of Intentions, Problematic Messages," *Medium*, April 17, 2018, https://medium.com/@pettydus/glee-best-of-intentions-problematic-messages-52b15ddca221; Maureen Ryan, "Perfect Pitch? Not Quite, but There's Much to Enjoy as 'Glee' Returns," *Chicago Tribune*, November 10, 2009, https://web.archive.org/web/20091114080253/http://featuresblogs.chicagotribune.com/entertainment_tv/2009/11/glee-fox-music.html

23 *Zoey's Extraordinary Playlist*, season 1, episode 1, "Zoey's Extraordinary Power," directed by Richard Shepard, written by Austin Winsberg, featuring Jane Levy, Skylar Astin, Alex Newell, and Mary Steenburgen, aired January 7, 2020, on NBC, TV.

24 Ibid.

25 Ibid; *Zoey's Extraordinary Playlist*, season 1, episode 3, "Zoey's Extraordinary Boss," directed by Daisy von Scherler Mayer, written by Sam Laybourne, featuring Jane Levy, Skylar Astin, Alex Newell, and Mary Steenburgen, aired February 23, 2020, on NBC, TV.

26 Ibid.

27 *Zoey's Extraordinary Playlist*, season 1, episode 2, "Zoey's Extraordinary Best Friend," directed by Adam Davidson, written by Austin Winsberg, featuring Jane Levy, Skylar Astin, Alex Newell, and Mary Steenburgen, aired February 23, 2020, on NBC, TV; *Zoey's Extraordinary Playlist*, season 1, episode 5, "Zoey's Extraordinary Failure," directed by Darnell Martin, written by Jack Kenny and Austin Winsberg, featuring Jane Levy, Skylar Astin, Alex Newell, and Mary Steenburgen, aired March 8, 2020, on NBC, TV.

28 *Zoey's Extraordinary Playlist*, season 1, episode 12, "Zoey's Extraordinary Dad," directed by John Turteltaub and Adam Davidson, written by Austin Winsberg, featuring Jane Levy, Skylar Astin, Alex Newell, and Mary Steenburgen, aired May 3, 2020, on NBC, TV.

29 *Donnie Darko*, directed by Richard Kelly (2001; Los Angeles, CA: 20th Century Fox Pictures Home Entertainment, 2002), DVD.

30 *Zoey's Extraordinary Playlist*, season 1, episode 1, "Zoey's Extraordinary Power," aired January 7, 2020.

31 *Zoey's Extraordinary Playlist*, season 2, episode 8, "Zoey's Extraordinary Birthday," directed by Shasta Spahn, written by Lindsay Rosin, featuring Jane Levy, Skylar Astin, Alex Newell, and Mary Steenburgen, aired April 4, 2021, on NBC, TV.

32 Amal Awad, "Zoey's Extraordinary Playlist: Yes, the Musical Series Is Cheesy. But It's Also a Glorious Lockdown Escape," *The Guardian*, April 28, 2020, https://www.theguardian.com/culture/2020/apr/29/zoeys-extraordinary-playlist-yes-the-musical-series-is-cheesy-but-its-also-a-glorious-lockdown-escape

33 *Zoey's Extraordinary Playlist*, season 1, episode 4, "Zoey's Extraordinary Neighbor," directed by Adam Davidson, written by Gretchen J. Berg and Aaron Harberts, featuring Jane Levy, Skylar Astin, Alex Newell, and Mary Steenburgen, aired March 1, 2020, on NBC, TV.

34 *Zoey's Extraordinary Playlist*, season 1, episode 5, "Zoey's Extraordinary Failure," aired March 8, 2020; *Zoey's Extraordinary Playlist*, season 1, episode 7, "Zoey's Extraordinary Confession," directed by Richie Keen, written by Davah Avena, featuring Jane Levy, Skylar Astin, Alex Newell, and Mary Steenburgen, aired March 22, 2020, on NBC, TV.

35 *Zoey's Extraordinary Playlist*, season 2, episode 13, "Zoey's Extraordinary Goodbye," directed by John Terlesky, written by Austin Winsberg, featuring Jane Levy, Skylar Astin, Alex Newell, and Mary Steenburgen, aired May 16, 2021, on NBC, TV.

36 *Zoey's Extraordinary Christmas*, directed by Richard Shepard (2021; San Jose, CA: Roku Channel, 2021), streaming.

37 *Glee*, season 3, episode 16, "Saturday Night Glee-ver," aired April 17, 2012.

38 *Zoey's Extraordinary Playlist*, season 2, episode 10, "Zoey's Extraordinary Girls' Night," directed by Richard Lewis, written by Alicia Carroll, featuring Jane Levy, Skylar Astin, Alex Newell, and Mary Steenburgen, aired April 18, 2021, on NBC, TV; *Zoey's Extraordinary Playlist*, season 2, episode 2, "Zoey's Extraordinary Distraction," directed by Anya Adams, written by Sam Laybourne, featuring Jane Levy, Skylar Astin, Alex Newell, and Mary Steenburgen, aired January 12, 2021, on NBC, TV.

39 *Zoey's Extraordinary Playlist*, season 1, episode 9, "Zoey's Extraordinary Silence," directed by Charles Stone III, written by Matthew Irving Epstein, featuring Jane Levy, Skylar Astin, Alex Newell, and Mary Steenburgen, aired April 5, 2020, on NBC, TV.

Chapter 9

1 *Grey's Anatomy*, season 7, episode 18, "Song Beneath the Song," directed by Tony Phelan, written by Shonda Rhimes, featuring Ellen Pompeo, Sandra Oh, Sara Ramirez, and Jesse Williams, aired March 31, 2011, on ABC, Buena Vista Home Entertainment, 2011, DVD; *7th Heaven*, season 9, episode 15, "Red Socks," directed by Michael Preece, written by Martha Plimpton, featuring Stephen Collins, Catherine Hicks, Beverley Mitchell, and David Gallagher, aired February 14, 2005, on the WB, Paramount Home Entertainment, 2017, DVD.

2 *Legends of Tomorrow*, season 4, episode 11, "Seance and Sensibility," directed by Alexandra La Roche, written by Grainne Godfree and Jackie Canino, featuring Caity Lotz, Nick Zano, Brandon Routh, Tala Ashe, and Matt Ryan, aired April 15, 2019, on the CW, Warner Home Video, 2022, DVD.

3 *Legends of Tomorrow*, season 6, episode 1, "Ground Control to Sara Lance," directed by Kevin Mock, written by James Eagan and Mark Bruner, featuring Caity Lotz, Nick Zano, Tala Ashe, and Matt Ryan, aired May 2, 2021, on the CW, Warner Home Video, 2022, DVD; *Legends of Tomorrow*, season 5, episode 13, "The One Where We're Trapped on TV," directed by Marc Guggenheim, written by Grainne Godfree and James Eagan, featuring Caity Lotz, Nick Zano, Tala Ashe, and Matt Ryan, aired May 26, 2020, on the CW, Warner Home Video, 2022, DVD.

4 *Galavant*, season 1, episode 1, "Pilot," directed by Chris Koch, written by Dan Fogelman, featuring Joshua Sasse, Karen David, Luke Youngblood, Mallory Jansen, and Timothy Omundsen, aired January 4, 2015, on ABC, Disney Home Video, 2017, DVD.

5 Ibid.

6 *Robin Hood*, directed by Wolfgang Reitherman (1973; Los Angeles, CA: Walt Disney Home Video, 2000), DVD.

7 *Galavant*, season 1, episode 2, "Joust Friends," directed by Chris Koch, written by Dan Fogelman, featuring Joshua Sasse, Karen David, Luke Youngblood, Mallory Jansen, and Timothy Omundsen, aired January 4, 2015, on ABC, Disney Home Video, 2017, DVD.

8 *Galavant*, season 1, episode 8, "It's All in the Executions," directed by Chris Koch, written by Kristin Newman, featuring Joshua Sasse, Karen David, Luke Youngblood, Mallory Jansen, and Timothy Omundsen, aired January 25, 2015, on ABC, Disney Home Video, 2017, DVD; *Galavant*, season 2, episode 2, "World's Best Kiss," directed by John Fortenberry, written by Dan Fogelman, featuring Joshua Sasse, Karen David, Luke Youngblood, Mallory Jansen, and Timothy Omundsen, aired January 3, 2016, on ABC, Disney Home Video, 2017, DVD.

9 *Galavant*, season 1, episode 1, "Pilot," aired January 4, 2015.

10 *Galavant*, season 2, episode 8, "Do the D'DEW," directed by Chris Koch, written by Jeremy Hall, featuring Joshua Sasse, Karen David, Luke Youngblood, Mallory Jansen, and Timothy Omundsen, aired January 24, 2016, on ABC, Disney Home Video, 2017, DVD; *Galavant*, season 2, episode 5, "Giants vs. Dwarves," directed by Declan Lowney, written by Dan Kopelman, featuring Joshua Sasse, Karen David, Luke Youngblood, Mallory Jansen, and Timothy Omundsen, aired January 17, 2016, on ABC, Disney Home Video, 2017, DVD.

11 *Galavant*, season 2, episode 6, "About Last Knight," directed by Paul Murphy, written by Scott Weinger, featuring Joshua Sasse, Karen David, Luke Youngblood, Mallory Jansen, and Timothy Omundsen, aired January 17, 2016, on ABC, Disney Home Video, 2017, DVD.

12 *Galavant*, season 2, episode 1, "A New Season aka Suck It Cancellation Bear," directed by John Fortenberry, written by Dan Fogelman, featuring Joshua Sasse, Karen David, Luke Youngblood, Mallory Jansen, and Timothy Omundsen, aired January 3, 2016, on ABC, Disney Home Video, 2017, DVD.

13 *Galavant*, season 1, episode 8, "It's All in the Executions," aired January 25, 2015; *Galavant*, season 2, episode 9, "Battle of the Three Armies," directed by John Fortenberry, written by Rick Wiener and Kenny Schwartz, featuring Joshua Sasse, Karen David, Luke Youngblood, Mallory Jansen, and Timothy Omundsen, aired January 31, 2016, on ABC, Disney Home Video, 2017, DVD; *Galavant*, season 2, episode 1, "A New Season aka Suck It Cancellation Bear," aired January 3, 2016; *Galavant*, season 2, episode 7, "Love and Death," directed by Paul Murphy, written by Robin Shorr, featuring Joshua Sasse, Karen David, Luke Youngblood, Mallory Jansen, and Timothy Omundsen, aired January 24, 2016, on ABC, Disney Home Video, 2017, DVD.

14 *Galavant*, season 2, episode 10, "The One True King (to Unite Them All)," directed by John Fortenberry, written by Rick Wiener and Kenny Schwartz, featuring Joshua Sasse, Karen David, Luke Youngblood, Mallory Jansen, and Timothy Omundsen, aired January 31, 2016, on ABC, Disney Home Video, 2017, DVD.

15 *Galavant*, season 2, episode 1, "A New Season aka Suck It Cancellation Bear," aired January 3, 2016.

16 Leo Barraclough, "ABC Studios to Shoot 'Galavant' in the U.K., Benefitting from New Tax Credit," *Variety*, December 20, 2013, https://variety.com/2013/tv/global/abc-studios-to-shoot-galavant-in-the-u-k-benefiting-from-new-tv-tax-credit-1200975804/

17 James Hibberd, "Galavant Canceled by ABC After Two Seasons," *Entertainment Weekly*, May 12, 2016, https://web.archive.org/web/20160516025458/http://www.ew.com/article/2016/05/12/galavant-canceled

18 Rob Gordon, "Supernatural Creator in Fight over Unpaid Profits," *Screen Rant*, November 21, 2017, https://screenrant.com/supernatural-warner-bros-profits-lawsuit/

19 Lesley Goldberg, "Mad About the CW Cancellations? Blame Streaming, But Also Its Unusual Corporate Structure," *The Hollywood Reporter*, May 13, 2022, https://www.hollywoodreporter.com/tv/tv-news/the-cw-cancellations-blame-streaming-but-also-its-unusual-corporate-structure-1235146038/

20 *Crazy Ex-Girlfriend*, season 3, episode 12, "Trent?!," directed by Stuart McDonald, written by Dan Gregor and Doug Mand, featuring Rachel Bloom, Vincent Rodriguez III, Donna Lynne Champlin, Gabrielle Ruiz, and Vella Lovell, aired February 9, 2018, on the CW, Warner Home Video, 2018, DVD.

21 *My Best Friend's Wedding*, directed by P. J. Hogan (1997; Burbank, CA: Columbia Tri-Star Home Entertainment, 2001), DVD; *Felicity*, season 1, episode 1, "Pilot," directed by Matt Reeves, written by JJ Abrams, featuring Keri Russell, Scott Speedman, Scott Foley, and Amy Jo Johnson, aired September 29, 1998, on the WB, ABC Studios, 2009, DVD.

22 *Crazy Ex-Girlfriend*, season 1, episode 1, "Josh Just Happens to Live Here!," directed by Marc Webb, written by Rachel Bloom and Aline Brosh McKenna, featuring Rachel Bloom, Vincent Rodriguez III, Donna Lynne Champlin, Gabrielle Ruiz, and Vella Lovell, aired October 12, 2015, on the CW, Warner Home Video, 2016, DVD.

23 *Crazy Ex-Girlfriend*, season 1, episode 6, "My First Thanksgiving with Josh!," directed by Joanna Kerns, written by Rene Gube, featuring Rachel Bloom, Vincent Rodriguez III, Donna Lynne Champlin, Gabrielle Ruiz, and Vella Lovell, aired November 16, 2015, on the CW, Warner Home Video, 2016, DVD.

24 *Crazy Ex-Girlfriend*, season 2, episode 9, "When Do I Get to Spend Time with Josh?," directed by Kabir Akhtar, written by Rachel Bloom and Aline Brosh McKenna, featuring Rachel Bloom, Vincent Rodriguez III, Donna Lynne Champlin, Gabrielle Ruiz, and Vella Lovell, aired January 6, 2017, on the CW, Warner Home Video, 2017, DVD.

25 *Crazy Ex-Girlfriend*, season 1, episode 1, "Josh Just Happens to Live Here!," aired October 12, 2015.

26 *Crazy Ex-Girlfriend*, season 3, episode 3, "Josh Is a Liar," directed by Stuart McDonald, written by Michael Hitchcock, featuring Rachel Bloom, Vincent Rodriguez III, Donna Lynne Champlin, Gabrielle Ruiz, and Vella Lovell, aired October 27, 2017, on the CW, Warner Home Video, 2018, DVD; *Crazy Ex-Girlfriend*, season 3, episode 4, "Josh's Ex-Girlfriend Is Crazy," directed by Joseph Kahn, written by Rachel Bloom and Aline Brosh McKenna, featuring Rachel Bloom, Vincent Rodriguez III, Donna Lynne Champlin, Gabrielle Ruiz, and Vella Lovell, aired November 3, 2017, on the CW, Warner Home Video, 2018, DVD.

27 *Crazy Ex-Girlfriend*, season 3, episode 5, "I Never Want to See Josh Again," directed by Stuart McDonald, written by Jack Dolgen, featuring Rachel Bloom, Vincent Rodriguez III, Donna Lynne Champlin, Gabrielle Ruiz, and Vella Lovell, aired November 10, 2017, on the CW, Warner Home Video, 2018, DVD.

28 *Crazy Ex-Girlfriend*, season 3, episode 6, "Josh Is Irrelevant," directed by Stuart McDonald, written by Rachel Bloom, Aline Brosh McKenna, and Ilana Peña, featuring Rachel Bloom, Vincent Rodriguez III, Donna Lynne Champlin, Gabrielle Ruiz, and Vella Lovell, aired November 17, 2017, on the CW, Warner Home Video, 2018, DVD.

29 *Crazy Ex-Girlfriend*, season 1, episode 18, "Paula Needs to Get over Josh!," directed by Aline Brosh McKenna, written by Rene Gube, featuring Rachel Bloom, Vincent Rodriguez III, Donna Lynne Champlin, Gabrielle Ruiz, and Vella Lovell, aired April 18, 2016, on the CW, Warner Home Video, 2016, DVD.

30 *Crazy Ex-Girlfriend*, season 1, episode 14, "Josh Is Going to Hawaii!," directed by Erin Ehrlich, written by Sono Patel, featuring Rachel Bloom, Vincent Rodriguez III, Donna Lynne Champlin, Gabrielle Ruiz, and Vella Lovell, aired March 7, 2016, on the CW, Warner Home Video, 2016, DVD.

31 *Crazy Ex-Girlfriend*, season 2, episode 11, "Josh Is the Man of My Dreams, Right?," directed by Michael Patrick Jann, written by Elisabeth Kiernan Averick, featuring Rachel Bloom, Vincent Rodriguez III, Donna Lynne Champlin, Gabrielle Ruiz, and Vella Lovell, aired January 20, 2017, on the CW, Warner Home Video, 2017, DVD.

32 *Crazy Ex-Girlfriend*, season 1, episode 6, "My First Thanksgiving With Josh!," aired November 16, 2015.

33 *Crazy Ex-Girlfriend*, season 1, episode 16, "Josh's Sister Is Getting Married!," directed by Alex Hardcastle, written by Rachel Specter and Audrey Wauchope, featuring Rachel Bloom, Vincent Rodriguez III, Donna Lynne Champlin, Gabrielle Ruiz, and Vella Lovell, aired March 28, 2016, on the CW, Warner Home Video, 2016, DVD.

34 *Crazy Ex-Girlfriend*, season 1, episode 13, "Josh and I Go to Los Angeles!," directed by Michael Patrick Jann, written by Aline Brosh McKenna, featuring Rachel Bloom, Vincent Rodriguez III, Donna Lynne Champlin, Gabrielle Ruiz, and Vella Lovell, aired February 29, 2016, on the CW, Warner Home Video, 2016, DVD.

35 *Crazy Ex-Girlfriend*, season 1, episode 18, "Paula Needs to Get over Josh!," aired April 18, 2016.

36 *Crazy Ex-Girlfriend*, season 1, episode 9, "I'm Going to the Beach with Josh's Friends!," directed by Kenny Ortega, written by Dan Gregor and Doug Mand, featuring Rachel Bloom, Vincent Rodriguez III, Donna Lynne Champlin, Gabrielle Ruiz, and Vella Lovell, aired January 25, 2016, on the CW, Warner Home Video, 2016, DVD; *Crazy Ex-Girlfriend*, season 2, episode 6, "Who Needs Josh When You Have a Girl Group?," directed by Stuart McDonald, written by Jack Dolgen, featuring Rachel Bloom, Vincent Rodriguez III, Donna Lynne Champlin, Gabrielle Ruiz, and Vella Lovell, aired December 2, 2016, on the CW, Warner Home Video, 2017, DVD.

37 *Crazy Ex-Girlfriend*, season 2, episode 2, "When Will Josh See How Cool I Am?," directed by Jay Chandrasekhar, written by Rene Gube, featuring Rachel Bloom, Vincent Rodriguez III, Donna Lynne Champlin, Gabrielle Ruiz, and Vella Lovell,

aired October 28, 2016, on the CW, Warner Home Video, 2017, DVD; *Crazy Ex-Girlfriend*, season 3, episode 7, "Getting over Jeff," directed by Stuart McDonald, written by Erin Ehrlich, featuring Rachel Bloom, Vincent Rodriguez III, Donna Lynne Champlin, Gabrielle Ruiz, and Vella Lovell, aired December 8, 2017, on the CW, Warner Home Video, 2018, DVD.

38 *Crazy Ex-Girlfriend*, season 4, episode 5, "I'm So Happy for You," directed by Erin Ehrlich, written by Ilana Peña, featuring Rachel Bloom, Vincent Rodriguez III, Donna Lynne Champlin, Gabrielle Ruiz, and Vella Lovell, aired November 8, 2018, on the CW, Warner Home Video, 2019, DVD.

39 *Crazy Ex-Girlfriend*, season 4, episode 16, "I Have a Date Tonight," directed by Dan Gregor, written by Erin Ehrlich, featuring Rachel Bloom, Vincent Rodriguez III, Donna Lynne Champlin, Gabrielle Ruiz, and Vella Lovell, aired March 29, 2019, on the CW, Warner Home Video, 2019, DVD.

40 *Crazy Ex-Girlfriend*, season 4, episode 17, "I'm in Love," directed by Aline Brosh McKenna, written by Aline Brosh McKenna and Rachel Bloom, featuring Rachel Bloom, Vincent Rodriguez III, Donna Lynne Champlin, Gabrielle Ruiz, and Vella Lovell, aired April 5, 2019, on the CW, Warner Home Video, 2019, DVD.

Chapter 10

1 Frederic Delano, "How the Parisian Enjoys Opera at Home," *Scientific American*, September 1925, 174.

2 Joe Hindy, "Streaming Has Overtaken Traditional TV for the First Time Ever," *CNET*, June 17, 2025, https://www.cnet.com/culture/entertainment/streaming-has-overtaken-traditional-tv-for-the-first-time-ever/

3 "NBC Aligning Brands with A-list Talent—Online," *Advertising Age*, October 9, 2008, https://adage.com/article/madisonvine-news/nbc-aligning-brands-a-list-talent-online/131605/

4 Ibid.

5 Josef Adalain, "Viral Vid Bug Bites Bochco: Producer Enters Pact with Metacafed," *Variety*, November 14, 2006, http://www.variety.com/article/VR1117953949.html?categoryid=14&cs=1

6 "Joss Whedon on Those WGA Popinjays," *Variety*, November 6, 2007, https://variety.com/2007/biz/news/joss-whedon-on-those-wga-popinjays-25900/

7 Rich Drees, "Harlan Ellison Speaks Up on the Writers' Strike Settlement," *FilmBuffOnline*, February 15, 2008, https://www.filmbuffonline.com/FBOLNewsreel/wordpress/2008/02/15/harlan-ellison-speaks-up-on-the-writers-strike-settlement/

8 Laura Sydell, "'Buffy' Creator Proves Doogie Can Sing," *NPR*, July 18, 2008, http://www.npr.org/templates/story/story.php?storyId=92678153

9 *Dr. Horrible's Sing-Along Blog*, directed by Joss Whedon (2008; New York: New Video Group, 2009), DVD.

10 Amanda D. Lotz, *The Television Will Be Revolutionized* (New York: New York University Press, 2007), 37.

11 Los Angeles Times Staff, "Writers' Strike: What Happened, How It Ended and Its Impact on Hollywood," *Los Angeles Times*, May 1, 2023, https://www.latimes.com/entertainment-arts/business/story/2023-05-01/writers-strike-what-to-know-wga-guild-hollywood-productions

12 *Schmigadoon!*, season 1, episode 1, "Schmigadoon!," directed by Barry Sonnenfeld, written by Cinco Paul and Ken Daurio, featuring Cecily Strong, Keegan-Michael Key, Alan Cumming, Kristin Chenoweth, and Ariana DeBose, aired July 16, 2021, on AppleTV+, Streaming.

13 *The Lorax*, directed by Chris Renaud (2012; Los Angeles, CA: Universal Home Entertainment, 2012), DVD.

14 Terry Gross, "'Schmigadoon!' Co-Creator Says Series Was Inspired by a 'Love Affair' with Musicals," *NPR*, August 23, 2021, https://www.npr.org/2021/08/23/1030268798/schmigadoon-co-creator-says-series-was-inspired-by-a-love-affair-with-musicals

15 *Schmigadoon!*, season 1, episode 4, "Suddenly," directed by Barry Sonnenfeld, written by Cinco Paul, Ken Daurio, and Kate Gersten, featuring Cecily Strong, Keegan-Michael Key, Alan Cumming, Kristin Chenoweth, and Ariana DeBose, aired July 30, 2021, on AppleTV+, Streaming.

16 *Schmigadoon!*, season 1, episode 5, "Tribulation," directed by Barry Sonnenfeld, written by Alison Silverman, featuring Cecily Strong, Keegan-Michael Key, Alan Cumming, Kristin Chenoweth, and Ariana DeBose, aired August 6, 2021, on AppleTV+, Streaming.

17 Chris Murphy, "From Leprechauns to Corn Puddin': All the Musical References in *Schmigadoon!*" *Vanity Fair*, July 19, 2021, https://www.vanityfair.com/hollywood/2021/07/from-leprechauns-to-corn-puddin-all-the-musical-references-in-schmigadoon

18 *Schmigadoon!*, season 2, episode 3, "Bells and Whistles," directed by Alice Mathias, written by Julie Klausner, featuring Cecily Strong, Keegan-Michael Key, Alan Cumming, Kristin Chenoweth, and Ariana DeBose, aired April 12, 2023, on AppleTV+, Streaming.

19 *Schmigadoon!*, season 2, episode 4, "Something Real," directed by Alice Mathias, written by Raina Morris, featuring Cecily Strong, Keegan-Michael Key, Alan Cumming, Kristin Chenoweth, and Ariana DeBose, aired April 19, 2023, on AppleTV+, Streaming.

20 *Schmigadoon!*, season 2, episode 3, "Bells and Whistles," aired April 12, 2023.

21 *Schmigadoon!*, season 2, episode 4, "Something Real," aired April 19, 2023.

22 *Schmigadoon!*, season 2, episode 3, "Bells and Whistles," aired April 12, 2023.

23 *Schmigadoon!*, season 1, episode 6, "How We Change," directed by Barry Sonnenfeld, written by Cinco Paul and Ken Daurio, featuring Cecily Strong, Keegan-Michael Key, Alan Cumming, Kristin Chenoweth, and Ariana DeBose, aired August 13, 2021, on AppleTV+, Streaming.

24 *Schmigadoon!*, season 2, episode 6, "Over and Done," directed by Robert Luketic, written by Cinco Paul, featuring Cecily Strong, Keegan-Michael Key, Alan Cumming, Kristin Chenoweth, and Ariana DeBose, aired May 3, 2023, on AppleTV+, Streaming.

25 Lesley Goldberg, "'Schmigadoon' Cancelled at Apple: The Musical Comedy Staring Cecily Strong Ran for Two Seasons on the Streamer," *The Hollywood Reporter*, January 18, 2024, https://www.hollywoodreporter.com/tv/tv-news/schmigadoon-canceled-apple-1235791955/

26 Keith Loria, "Review: 'Schmigadoon!' Finds New Life as Part of the Kenendy Center's Broadway Center Stage Series," *TheaterMania*, February 3, 2025, https://www.theatermania.com/news/review-schmigadoon-finds-new-life-as-part-of-kennedy-centers-broadway-center-stage-series_1762764/; Logan Culwell-Black, "Is Schmigadoon! Destined to Become a Stage Musical Trilogy?" *Playbill*, January 29, 2025, https://playbill.com/article/is-schmigadoon-destined-to-become-a-stage-musical-trilogy

BIBLIOGRAPHY

Abbott, Stacey, and Lorna Jowett. *TV Horror: The Dark Side of the Small Screen*. London: IB Tauris, 2013.

Abrams, JJ, writer. *Felicity*. Season 1, episode 1, "Pilot." Directed by Matt Reeves, featuring Keri Russell, Scott Speedman, Scott Foley, and Amy Jo Johnson. Aired September 29, 1998, on the WB, ABC Studios, 2009, DVD.

Adalain, Josef. "Viral Vid Bug Bites Bochco: Producer Enters Pact with Metacafe." *Variety*. November 14, 2006, http://www.variety.com/article/VR1117953949.html?categoryid=14&cs=1

Adams, Jeremy, writer. *Supernatural*. Season 15, episode 7, "Last Call." Directed by Amyn Kaderali, featuring Jensen Ackles, Jared Padalecki, Misha Collins, and Alexander Calvert. Aired December 5, 2019, on the CW, Warner Home Entertainment, 2021, DVD.

Adams, Sam. "The '90s Police Musical Cop Rock, Just Released on DVD, Was a Terrible Show That Could've Been Great." *Slate*. May 19, 2016, https://slate.com/culture/2016/05/the-90s-police-musical-cop-rock-just-released-on-dvd-was-a-terrible-show-that-could-ve-been-great.html

Al-Awad, Feras A. "The Phenomenon of Musical Hallucinations: An Updated Review." *Electronic Journal of General Medicine* 20, no. 6 (2023): em533.

Ardolino, Emile, dir. *Alice at the Palace*. 1982; New York: New York Shakespeare Festival. TV.

Ardolino, Emile, dir. *Gypsy*. 1993; Golden Valley, MN: Mill Creek Entertainment, 2013. DVD.

Arthur, Kate. "How 'Smash' Became TV's Biggest Train Wreck." *Buzzfeed*. January 30, 2013, https://www.buzzfeed.com/kateaurthur/how-smash-became-tvs-biggest-train-wreck

Austen, Jake. *TV-a-Go-Go: Rock on TV from American Bandstand to American Idol*. Chicago, IL: Chicago Review Press, 2005.

Avena, Davah, writer. *Zoey's Extraordinary Playlist*. Season 1, episode 7, "Zoey's Extraordinary Confession." Directed by Richie Keen, featuring Jane Levy, Skylar Astin, Alex Newell, and Mary Steenburgen. Aired March 22, 2020, on NBC, TV.

Averick, Elisabeth Kiernan, writer. *Crazy Ex-Girlfriend*. Season 2, episode 11, "Josh Is the Man of My Dreams, Right?" Directed by Michael Patrick Jann, featuring Rachel Bloom, Vincent Rodriguez III, Donna Lynne Champlin, Gabrielle Ruiz, and Vella Lovell. Aired January 20, 2017, on the CW, Warner Home Video, 2017, DVD.

Awad, Amal. "Zoey's Extraordinary Playlist: Yes, the Musical Series Is Cheesy. But It's Also a Glorious Lockdown Escape." *The Guardian*. April 28, 2020, https://www.theguardian.com/culture/2020/apr/29/zoeys-extraordinary-playlist-yes-the-musical-series-is-cheesy-but-its-also-a-glorious-lockdown-escape

Baratta, Dana, writer. *Dawson's Creek*. Season 1, episode 12, "Beauty Contest." Directed by Arvin Brown, featuring James Van Der Beek, Katie Holmes, Michelle Williams, and Joshua Jackson. Aired May 12, 1998, on the WB, Sony Pictures Home Entertainment, 2009, DVD.

Barnouw, Erik. *Tube of Plenty: The Evolution of American Television*. Oxford: Oxford University Press, 1990.

Barraclough, Leo. "ABC Studios to Shoot 'Galavant' in the U.K., Benefitting from New Tax Credit." *Variety*. December 20, 2013, https://variety.com/2013/tv/global/abc-studios-to-shoot-galavant-in-the-u-k-benefiting-from-new-tv-tax-credit-1200975804/

Basilone, Steve, and Annie Mebane, writers. *Community*. Season 3, episode 10, "Regional Holiday Music." Directed by Tristram Shapeero, featuring Joel McHale, Donald Glover, Alison Brie, Yvette Nicole Brown, and Chevy Chase. Aired December 8, 2011, on NBC, Mill Creek Entertainment, 2019, DVD.

Bass, Jules, and Arthur Rankin Jr., dirs. *The Stingiest Man in Town*. 1978; Los Angeles, CA: Universal Pictures Home Entertainment, 2022. DVD.

Bays, Carter, and Craig Thomas, writers. *How I Met Your Mother*. Season 5, episode 12, "Girls vs. Suits." Directed by Pamela Fryman, featuring Neil Patrick Harris, Jason Segal, Alyson Hannigan, Cobie Smulders, and Josh Radnor. Aired January 11, 2010, on CBS, 20th Century Fox, 2010, DVD.

Beaumont, Christopher, writer. *Fame*. Season 2, episode 22, "Ending on a High Note." Directed by Jack Bender, featuring Debbie Allen, Erica Gimpel, Gene Anthony Ray, and Cynthia Gibb. Aired March 31, 1983, on NBC, Fox/MGM Television, 2010, DVD.

Bedell, Sally. *Up the Tube: Primetime TV in the Silverman Years*. New York: Viking, 1981.

Bekakos, Liana. "Supernatural Creator Eric Kripke Answers Fan Questions—Part 1." *Eclipse Magazine*. April 23, 2008, https://eclipsemagazine.com/supernatural-creator-eric-kripke-answers-fan-questions-%E2%80%93-part-i/

Benson, Sally, and Frederick Knott, writers. *Hallmark Hall of Fame*. Season 7, episode 4, "Hans Brinker and the Silver Skates." Directed by Sidney Lumet, featuring Tab Hunter, Basil Rathbone, Peggy King, and Dick Button. Aired February 9, 1958, on NBC.

Berg, Gretchen J., and Aaron Harberts, writers. *Zoey's Extraordinary Playlist*. Season 1, episode 4, "Zoey's Extraordinary Neighbor." Directed by Adam Davidson, featuring Jane Levy, Skylar Astin, Alex Newell, and Mary Steenburgen. Aired March 1, 2020, on NBC, TV.

"The Birth of Magazine Concept Television Advertising." The Historical Archive. January 23, 2007, https://www.thehistoricalarchive.com/happenings/50/the-birth-of-magazine-concept-television-advertising/

Blin, William, and Eleanor H. Porter, writers. *The Magical World of Disney*. Season 34, episode 6. "Polly." Directed by Debbie Allen, featuring Keshia Knight Pulliam, Phylicia Rashad, and Dorian Harewood. Aired November 12, 1989, on NBC.

Blin, William, and Eleanor H. Porter, writers. *The Magical World of Disney*. Season 35, episode 1, "Polly: Comin' Home." Directed by Debbie Allen, featuring Keshia Knight Pulliam, Phylicia Rashad, and Dorian Horewood. Aired November 18, 1990, on NBC.

Blinn, William, writer. *Fame*. Season 1, episode 3, "Tomorrow's Farewell." Directed by Thomas Carter, featuring Debbie Allen, Erica Gimpel, Gene Anthony Ray, and Cynthia Gibb. Aired January 21, 1982, on NBC, Fox/MGM Television, 2010, DVD.

Bloom, Rachel, and Aline Brosh McKenna, writers. *Crazy Ex-Girlfriend*. Season 1, episode 1, "Josh Just Happens to Live Here!" Directed by Marc Webb, featuring Rachel Bloom, Vincent Rodriguez III, Donna Lynne Champlin, Gabrielle Ruiz, and Vella Lovell. Aired October 12, 2015, on the CW, Warner Home Video, 2016, DVD.

Bloom, Rachel, and Aline Brosh McKenna, writers. *Crazy Ex-Girlfriend*. Season 2, episode 9, "When Do I Get to Spend Time with Josh?" Directed by Kabir Akhtar, featuring Rachel Bloom, Vincent Rodriguez III, Donna Lynne Champlin, Gabrielle Ruiz, and Vella Lovell. Aired January 6, 2017, on the CW, Warner Home Video, 2017, DVD.

Bloom, Rachel, and Aline Brosh McKenna, writers. *Crazy Ex-Girlfriend*. Season 3, episode 4, "Josh's Ex-Girlfriend Is Crazy." Directed by Joseph Kahn, featuring Rachel Bloom, Vincent, Rodriguez III, Donna Lynne Champlin, Gabrielle Ruiz, and Vella Lovell. Aired November 3, 2017, on the CW, Warner Home Video, 2018, DVD.

Bloom, Rachel, Adam, Schlesinger, and Jack Dolgen, writers. *Crazy Ex-Girlfriend*. Season 4, episode 18, "Yes, It's Really Us Singing: The Crazy Ex-Girlfriend Concert Special!" Directed by Martin, Pasetta Jr, featuring Rachel Bloom, Donna Lynne Champlin, Vincent Rodriguez III, Vella Lovell, and Scott Michael Foster. Aired April 5, 2019, on the CW, Warner Home Video, 2009, DVD.

Bloom, Rachel, Aline, Brosh McKenna, and Ilana Peña, writers. *Crazy Ex-Girlfriend*. Season 3, episode 6, "Josh Is Irrelevant." Directed by Stuart McDonald, featuring Rachel Bloom, Vincent Rodriguez III, Donna Lynne Champlin, Gabrielle Ruiz, and Vella Lovell. Aired November 17, 2017, on the CW, Warner Home Video, 2018, DVD.

Bochco, Steven, and William M. Finkelstein, writers. *Cop Rock*. Season 1, episode 1, "Pilot." Directed by Gregory Hoblit, featuring Anne Bobby, Barbara Bosson, Peter Onorati, and Vondie Curtis-Hall. Aired September 26, 1990, on ABC, Shout! Factory, 2016, DVD.

Bochco, Steven, William M. Finkelstein, and John Romano, writers. *Cop Rock*. Season 1, episode 3, "Happy Mudder's Day." Directed by Charles Haid, featuring Anne Bobby, Barbara Bosson, Peter Onorati, and Vondie Curtis-Hall. Aired October 10, 1990, on ABC, Shout! Factory, 2016, DVD.

Bochco, Steven, William M. Finkelstein, Toni Graphia, and John Romano, writers. *Cop Rock*. Season 1, episode 9, "Marital Blitz." Directed by Gilbert Shilton, featuring Anne Bobby, Barbara Bosson, Peter Onorati, and Vondie Curtis-Hall. Aired December 5, 1990, on ABC, Shout! Factory, 2016, DVD.

Bochco, Steven, William M. Finkelstein, Toni Graphia, and John Romano, writers. *Cop Rock*. Season 1, episode 10, "No Noose Is Good Noose." Directed by Michael M. Robin, featuring Anne Bobby, Barbara Bosson, Peter Onorati, and Vondie Curtis-Hall. Aired December 12, 1990, on ABC, Shout! Factory, 2016, DVD.

Boyer, Peter J. "Under Fowler, F. C. C. Treated TV as Commerce." *The New York Times*. January 19, 1987, https://www.nytimes.com/1987/01/19/arts/under-fowler-fcc-treated-tv-as-commerce.html

Boyle, Danny, dir. *Yesterday*. 2019; Los Angeles, CA: Universal Pictures Home Entertainment, 2019. DVD.

Brennan, Ian, writer. *Glee*. Season 1, episode 5, "The Rhodes Not Taken." Directed by John Scott, featuring Matthew Morrison, Lea Michele, Cory Monteith, Jane Lynch, and

Chris Colfer. Aired September 30, 2009, on Fox, Sony Pictures Home Entertainment, 2018, DVD.

Brennan, Ian, writer. *Glee*. Season 3, episode 12, "The Spanish Teacher." Directed by Paris Barclay, featuring Matthew Morrison, Lea Michele, Cory Monteith, Jane Lynch, and Chris Colfer. Aired February 7, 2012, on Fox, Sony Pictures Home Entertainment, 2018, DVD.

Bretzner, Christoph Friedrich, and Stephanie Gottlieb, Jr, writers. *NBC Opera Theater*. Season 6, episode 1, "The Abduction from the Seraglio." Directed by Kirk Browning, featuring Davis Cunningham, Virginia Haskins, Nadja Witkowska, and David Lloyd. Aired October 31, 1954, on NBC.

Brockell, Gillian. "'Live with It': Betty White Defied Racist Demands in 1954." *Washington Post*. December 31, 2021, https://www.washingtonpost.com/history/2021/12/31/betty-white-arthur-duncan-racism/

Brooks, Hindi, writer. *Fame*. Season 1, episode 10, "Come One, Come All." Directed by Robert Scheerer, featuring Debbie Allen, Erica Gimpel, Gene Anthony Ray, and Cynthia Gibb. Aired March 11, 1982, on NBC, Fox/MGM Television, 2010, DVD.

Buckner, Brad, and Eugenie Ross-Leming, writers. *Supernatural*. Season 12, episode 13, "Family Feud." Directed by P. J. Pesce, featuring Jensen Ackles, Jared Padalecki, and Misha Collins. Aired February 23, 2017, on the CW, Warner Home Entertainment, 2017, DVD.

Bywaters, Tom, writer. *Great Performances*. Season 21, episode 2, "Jammin': Jelly Roll Morton on Broadway." Featuring Denzel Washington, Gregory Hines, and Keith David. Aired November 2, 1992, on PBS.

Carroll, Alicia, writer. *Zoey's Extraordinary Playlist*. Season 2, episode 10, "Zoey's Extraordinary Girls' Night." Directed by Richard Lewis, featuring Jane Levy, Skylar Astin, Alex Newell, and Mary Steenburgen. Aired April 18, 2021, on NBC, TV.

Carter, Bill. "NBC Spends Millions on the Buildup to 'Smash.'" *New York Times*. February 5, 2012, https://www.nytimes.com/2012/02/06/business/media/nbc-spends-millions-on-the-buildup-to-smash.html

Cates, Joseph, dir. *Sunday Spectacular: The Bachelor*. 1956; New York: NBC Studios. TV.

Cohen, Steve. "American Bandstand's untold story." *The Cultural Critic*. https://theculturalcritic.com/american-bandstands-Untold-Story/

Cohn, Angel. "Why You Must 'Tune' In to Tonight's Scrubs Musical!" *TV Guide*. January 18, 2007, https://www.tvguide.com/news/tune-tonights-scrubs-35612/

Coldiron, Katharine. "Something to Sing About: Why *Cop Rock* Fails." *Bright Lights Film Journal*. May 9, 2021, https://brightlightsfilm.com/something-to-sing-about-why-cop-rock-fails/

Collodi, Carlo. *The Adventures of Pinocchio*. Translated by John Hooper. New York: Penguin Random House, 2021.

Cowan, Jon, and Richard L. Royner, writers. *American Dreams*. Season 1, episode 23, "Down the Shore." Directed by Leslie Libman, featuring Brittany Snow, Will Estes, Jonathan Adams, and Arlen Escarpeta. Aired May 4, 2003, on NBC.

Cross, Alan, and Tom Spezialy, writers. *Parker Lewis Can't Lose*. Season 1, episode 19, "Citizen Kube." Directed by Max Tash, featuring Corin Nemec, Billy Jayne, and Troy Slaten. Aired February 17, 1991, on Fox, Shout! Factory, 2009, DVD.

Croswell, Anne Pearson, Lee Pockriss, and Mark Twain, writers. *The United States Steel Hour*. Season 5, episode 6, "The Adventures of Huckleberry Finn." Directed by Elliot Silverstein, featuring Jimmy Boyd, Earle Hyman, Basil Rathbone, and Florence Henderson. Aired November 20, 1957, on CBS.

Cullins, Ashley. "'Glee' Actor Mark Salling Indicted for Possessing Child Pornography: If Convicted, the Actor Faces a Mandatory Minimum of Five Years in Prison." *The Hollywood Reporter*. May 27, 2016, https://www.hollywoodreporter.com/business/business-news/glee-actor-mark-salling-indicted-897996/?facebook_20160527

Culwell-Black, Logan. "Is Schmigadoon! Destined to Become a Stage Musical Trilogy?" *Playbill*. January 29, 2025, https://playbill.com/article/is-schmigadoon-destined-to-become-a-stage-musical-trilogy

Dabb, Andrew, and Daniel Loflin, writers. *Supernatural*. Season 7, episode 8, "Season 7, Time for a Wedding!" Directed by Tim Andrew, featuring Jensen Ackles, Jared Padalecki, and Misha Collins. Aired November 11, 2011, on the CW, Warner Home Video, 2012, DVD.

Delano, Frederic. "How the Parisian Enjoys Opera at Home." *Scientific American*. September 1925.

Diamond, Taylor. "How Dan Harmon Used Community to Show His Hatred for Glee." *Screen Rant*. October 15, 2022, https://screenrant.com/community-dan-harmon-glee-show-dislike/

Dillon, Nancy, and Rachel Desantis. "'Glee' Star Mark Salling Dead at 35 in Suspected Suicide." *New York Daily News*. April 7, 2018, https://www.nydailynews.com/2018/01/30/glee-star-mark-salling-dead-at-35-in-suspected-suicide-by-hanging/

Dolgen, Jack, writer. *Crazy Ex-Girlfriend*. Season 2, episode 6, "Who Needs Josh When You Have a Girl Group?" Directed by Stuart McDonald, featuring Rachel Bloom, Vincent Rodriguez III, Donna Lynne Champlin, Gabrielle Ruiz, and Vella Lovell. Aired December 2, 2016, on the CW, Warner Home Video, 2017, DVD.

Dolgen, Jack, writer. *Crazy Ex-Girlfriend*. Season 3, episode 5, "I Never Want to See Josh Again." Directed by Stuart McDonald, featuring Rachel Bloom, Vincent Rodriguez III, Donna Lynne Champlin, Gabrielle Ruiz, and Vella Lovell. Aired November 10, 2017, on the CW, Warner Home Video, 2018, DVD.

Donen, Stanley, and Gene Kelly, dirs. *Singin' in the Rain*. 1952; Los Angeles, CA: Warner Home Video, 2002. DVD.

Doyle, Jack. "American Bandstand, 1956–2007." *PopHistoryDig.com*. March 25, 2008.

Drees, Rich. "Harlan Ellison Speaks Up on the Writers' Strike Settlement," *FilmBuffOnline*. February 15, 2008, https://www.filmbuffonline.com/FBOLNewsreel/wordpress/2008/02/15/harlan-ellison-speaks-up-on-the-writers-strike-settlement/

Dubin, Charles S., dir. *Cinderella*. 1965; Culver City, CA: Samuel Goldwyn Films, 2023. DVD.

Dunne, James P., and Elizabeth Bradley, writers. *Happy Days*. Season 8, episode 22, "American Musical." Directed by Jerry Paris, featuring Henry Winkler, Marion Ross, Anson Williams, and Erin Moran. Aired May 26, 1981, on ABC.

Dwyer, Michael D. *Back to the Fifties: Nostalgia, Hollywood Film, and Popular Music of the Seventies and Eighties*. London: Oxford University Press, 2015.

Dyer, Richard. *Only Entertainment*. London: Routledge, 2002.

Eagen, James, and Mark Bruner, writers. *Legends of Tomorrow*. Season 6, episode 1, "Ground Control to Sara Lance." Directed by Kevin Mock, featuring Caity Lotz, Nick Zano, Tala Ashe, and Matt Ryan. Aired May 2, 2021, on the CW, Warner Home Video, 2022, DVD.

Edlund, Ben, writer. *Supernatural*. Season 6, episode 15, "The French Mistake." Directed by Charles Beeson, featuring Jensen Ackles, Jared Padalecki, and Misha Collins. Aired February 25, 2011, on the CW, Warner Home Video, 2011, DVD.

Edwards, Becky Hartman, writer. *American Dreams*. Season 2, episode 10, "The 7–10 Split." Directed by Mark Piznarski, featuring Brittany Snow, Will Estes, Jonathan Adams, and Arlen Escarpeta. Aired January 4, 2004, on NBC.

Ehrlich, Erin, writer. *Crazy Ex-Girlfriend*. Season 3, episode 7, "Getting over Jeff." Directed by Stuart McDonald, featuring Rachel Bloom, Vincent Rodriguez III, Donna Lynne Champlin, Gabrielle Ruiz, and Vella Lovell. Aired December 8, 2017, on the CW, Warner Home Video, 2018, DVD.

Ehrlich, Erin, writer. *Crazy Ex-Girlfriend*. Season 4, episode 16, "I Have a Date Tonight." Directed by Dan Gregor, featuring Rachel Bloom, Vincent Rodriguez III, Donna Lynne Champlin, Gabrielle Ruiz, and Vella Lovell. Aired March 29, 2019, on the CW, Warner Home Video, 2019, DVD.

Ehrlich, Ken, writer. *Fame*. Season 3, episode 11, "Fame Looks at Music '83." Directed by Walter C. Miller, featuring Debbie Allen, Erica Gimpel, Gene Anthony Ray, and Cynthia Gibb. Aired January 28, 1984, in first-run syndication, TV.

Ehrlich, Ken, writer. *Fame*. Season 4, episode 5, "The Heart of Rock 'n' Roll." Directed by Walter C. Miller, featuring Debbie Allen, Erica Gimpel, Gene Anthony Ray, and Cynthia Gibb. Aired October 27, 1984, in First-run syndication, TV.

Ehrlich, Ken, writer. *Fame*. Season 4, episode 5, "The Heart of Rock 'n' Roll II." Directed by Walter C. Miller, featuring Debbie Allen, Erica Gimpel, Gene Anthony Ray, and Cynthia Gibb. Aired January 26, 1985, in First-run syndication, TV.

Ehrman, Mark. "Cliques: The Importance of Hating Brenda." *Los Angeles Times*. February 7, 1993, https://www.latimes.com/archives/la-xpm-1993-02-07-tm-1357-story.html

Eichler, Glenn, and Peter Elwell, writer. *Daria*. Season 3, episode 1, "Daria!" Directed by Karen Disher, featuring Tracy Grandstaff, Wendy Hoopes, and Julián Rebolledo. Aired February 17, 1999, on MTV, Paramount Home Entertainment, 2010, DVD.

Epstein, Matthew Irving, writers. *Zoey's Extraordinary Playlist*. Season 1, episode 9, "Zoey's Extraordinary Silence." Directed by Charles Stone III, featuring Jane Levy, Skylar Astin, Alex Newell, and Mary Steenburgen. Aired April 5, 2020, on NBC, TV.

Espenson, Jane, writer. *Buffy the Vampire Slayer*. Season 6, episode 3, "After Life." Directed by David Solomon, featuring Sarah Michelle Gellar, Alyson Hannigan, Nicholas Brendan, and James Marsters. Aired October 9, 2001, on UPN, 20th Century Fox, 2005, DVD.

EW Staff. "26 Best Cult Shows Ever." *Entertainment Weekly*. June 1, 2022, https://ew.com/gallery/26-best-cult-tv-shows-ever/#380657

Falchuk, Brad, writer. *Glee*. Season 1, episode 4, "Preggers." Directed by Brad Falchuk, featuring Matthew Morrison, Lea Michele, Cory Monteith, Jane Lynch, and Chris

Colfer. Aired September 23, 2009, on Fox, Sony Pictures Home Entertainment, 2018, DVD.

Falchuk, Brad, writer. *Glee*. Season 1, episode 7, "Throwdown." Directed by Ryan Murphy, featuring Matthew Morrison, Lea Michele, Cory Monteith, Jane Lynch, and Chris Colfer. Aired October 14, 2009, on Fox, Sony Pictures Home Entertainment, 2018, DVD.

Falchuk, Brad, writer. *Glee*. Season 2, episode 15, "Sexy." Directed by Ryan Murphy, featuring Matthew Morrison, Lea Michele, Cory Monteith, Jane Lynch, and Chris Colfer. Aired March 8, 2011, on Fox, Sony Pictures Home Entertainment, 2018, DVD.

Fallon, Kevin. "The TV Musical Is Dead." *The Atlantic*. April 10, 2012, https://www.theatlantic.com/entertainment/archive/2012/04/the-tv-musical-is-dead/255643/

Faludi, Susan. *Backlash: The Undeclared War Against American Women: 15th Anniversary Edition*. New York: Three Rivers Press, 2006 [1991].

Field, Armond. *Tony Pastor, Father of Vaudeville*. Jefferson, NC: McFarland, 2007.

Finkelstein, William M., and John Romano, writers. *Cop Rock*. Season 1, episode 11, "Bang the Potts Slowly." Directed by Fred Gerber, featuring Anne Bobby, Barbara Bosson, Peter Onorati, and Vondie Curtis-Hall. Aired December 26, 1990, on ABC, Shout! Factory, 2016, DVD.

Finkelstein, William M., Toni Graphia, and John Romano, writers. *Cop Rock*. Season 1, episode 4, "A Three-Corpse Meal." Directed by Fred Gerber, featuring Anne Bobby, Barbara Bosson, Peter Onorati, and Vondie Curtis-Hall. Aired October 17, 1990, on ABC, Shout! Factory, 2016, DVD.

Finley, Michaela. "Lucy and Desi Return to Newburgh." *Poughkeepsie Journal*. May 15, 2014, https://www.poughkeepsiejournal.com/story/entertainment/theater/2014/05/15/lucy-desi-arnaz-newburgh/9132425/

Fogelman, Dan, writer. *Galavant*. Season 1, episode 1, "Pilot." Directed by Chris Koch, featuring Joshua Sasse, Karen David, Luke Youngblood, Mallory Jansen, and Timothy Omundsen. Aired January 4, 2015, on ABC, Disney Home Video, 2017, DVD.

Fogelman, Dan, writer. *Galavant*. Season 1, episode 2, "Joust Friends." Directed by Chris Koch, featuring Joshua Sasse, Karen David, Luke Youngblood, Mallory Jansen, and Timothy Omundsen. Aired January 4, 2015, on ABC, Disney Home Video, 2017, DVD.

Fogelman, Dan, writer. *Galavant*. Season 2, episode 1, "A New Season aka Suck It Cancellation Bear." Directed by John Fortenberry, featuring Joshua Sasse, Karen David, Luke Youngblood, Mallory Jansen, and Timothy Omundsen. Aired January 3, 2016, on ABC, Disney Home Video, 2017, DVD.

Fogelman, Dan, writer. *Galavant*. Season 2, episode 2, "World's Best Kiss." Directed by John Fortenberry, featuring Joshua Sasse, Karen David, Luke Youngblood, Mallory Jansen, and Timothy Omundsen. Aired January 3, 2016, on ABC, Disney Home Video, 2017, DVD.

Fordham, Debra, writer. *Scrubs*. Season 4, episode 17, "My Life in Four Cameras." Directed by Adam Bernstein, featuring Zach Braff, Donald Faison, Judy Reyes, and Sarah Chalke. Aired February 15, 2005, on NBC, Buena Vista Home Entertainment, 2006, DVD.

Fordham, Debra, writer. *Scrubs*. Season 6, episode 6, "My Musical." Directed by Will Mackenzie, featuring Zach Braff, Donald Faison, Judy Reyes, and Sarah Chalke. Aired January 18, 2007, on NBC, Buena Vista Home Entertainment, 2007, DVD.

Forman, Miloš, dir. *Amadeus*. 1984; Los Angeles, CA: Warner Home Video, 2009. DVD.

Frank, Debra, and Carl Sautter, writers. *Moonlighting*. Season 2, episode 4, "The Dream Sequence Always Rings Twice." Directed by Peter Werner, featuring Cybill Shepherd, Bruce Willis, Curtis Armstrong, and Allyce Beasley. Aired October 15, 1985, on ABC, Lionsgate, 2007, DVD.

Friend, Russel, and Garrett Lerner, writers. *Roswell*. Season 3, episode 8, "Behind the Music." Directed by Jonathan Frakes, featuring Shiri Appleby, Jason Behr, Brendan Fehr, Katherine Heigl, and Majandra Delfino. Aired November 27, 2001, on UPN, Paramount, 2005, DVD.

Frolov, Diane, and Robin Green, writers. *Northern Exposure*. Season 4, episode 25, "Old Tree." Directed by Michael Fresco, featuring Rob Morrow, Janine Turner, John Corbett, and Darren E. Burrows. Aired May 24, 1993, on CBS, Universal Home Entertainment, 2007, DVD.

Fury, David, writer. *Buffy the Vampire Slayer*. Season 6, episode 2, "Bargaining, Part 2." Directed by David Grossman, featuring Sarah Michelle Gellar, Alyson Hannigan, Nicholas Brendan, Anthony Stewart Head, and James Marsters. Aired October 2, 2001, on UPN, 20th Century Fox, 2005, DVD.

Fury, David, and Jane Espenson, writers. *Buffy the Vampire Slayer*. Season 7, episode 8, "Sleeper." Directed by Alan J. Levi, featuring Sarah Michelle Gellar, Alyson Hannigan, Nicholas Brendan, and James Marsters. Aired November 19, 2002, on UPN, 20th Century Fox Home Entertainment, 2005, DVD.

Gamble, Sera, writer. *Supernatural*. Season 2, episode 17, "Heart." Directed by Kim Manners, featuring Jensen Ackles and Jared Padalecki. Aired March 22, 2007, on the CW, Warner Home Video, 2007, DVD.

Gardner, Gerald, Dee Caruso, and Dave Evans, writers. *The Monkees*. Season 1, episode 18, "I Was a Teenage Monster." Directed by Sidney Miller, featuring Davy Jones, Mickey Dolenz, Mike Nesmith, and Peter Tork. Aired January 16, 1967, on NBC, Rhino Entertainment Company, 2003, DVD.

Giannini, Erin. *Supernatural: A History of Television's Unearthly Road Trip*. Lanham, MD: Rowman & Littlefield, 2021.

Giwa, Max, and Dania Pasquini, dirs. *Walking on Sunshine*. 2014; Los Angeles, CA: Sony Pictures Home Entertainment, 2016. DVD.

"Glitter Jailed over Child Porn." *BBC News*. November 12, 1999, http://news.bbc.co.uk/2/hi/uk_news/517604.stm

Godfree, Grainne, and Jackie Canino, writers. *Legends of Tomorrow*. Season 4, episode 11, "Séance and Sensibility." Directed by Alexandra La Roche, featuring Caity Lotz, Nick Zano, Brandon Routh, Tala Ashe, and Matt Ryan. Aired April 15, 2019, on the CW, Warner Home Video, 2022, DVD.

Godfree, Grainne, and James Eagan, writers. *Legends of Tomorrow*. Season 5, episode 13, "The One Where We're Trapped on TV." Directed by Marc Guggenheim, featuring

Caity Lotz, Nick Zano, Tala Ashe, and Matt Ryan. Aired May 26, 2020, on the CW, Warner Home Video, 2022, DVD.

Gold, Adam. "Inside the Music of 'Nashville': Stars and Producers Strive for Authenticity, and It's Paying Off." *Rolling Stone*. November 7, 2012, https://www.rollingstone.com/music/music-news/inside-the-music-of-nashville-177944/

Goldberg, Lesley. "Mad About the CW Cancellations? Blame Streaming, But Also Its Unusual Corporate Structure." *The Hollywood Reporter*. May 13, 2022, https://www.hollywoodreporter.com/tv/tv-news/the-cw-cancellations-blame-streaming-but-also-its-unusual-corporate-structure-1235146038/

Goldberg, Lesley. "'Schmigadoon Cancelled at Apple: The Musical Comedy Starring Cecily Strong Ran for Two Seasons on the Streamer." *The Hollywood Reporter*. January 18, 2024, https://www.hollywoodreporter.com/tv/tv-news/schmigadoon-canceled-apple-1235791955/

Goldberg, Lesley. "'Smash' Creator Steps Down as Showrunner." *The Hollywood Reporter*. March 22, 2012, https://www.hollywoodreporter.com/tv/tv-news/smash-creator-theresa-rebeck-step-down-showrunner-303451/

Goldberg-Meehan, Shana, writer. *Friends*. Season 8, episode 9, "The One with the Rumor." Directed by Gary Halvorson, featuring Jennifer Aniston, David Schwimmer, Courteney Cox, Matthew Perry, and Matt LeBlanc, aired November 22, 2001, on NBC, Warner Home Video, 2012, DVD.

Goldman, Neil, and Garrett Donovan, writers. *Scrubs*. Season 1, episode 23, "My Hero." Directed by Michael Spiller, featuring Zach Braff, Donald Faison, Judy Reyes, and Sarah Chalke. Aired May 14, 2002, on NBC, Buena Vista Home Entertainment, 2005, DVD.

Goodman, David H., and Andrew Chambliss, writers. *Once Upon a Time*. Season 6, episode 20, "The Song in Your Heart." Directed by Ron Underwood, featuring Jennifer Morrison, Ginnifer Goodwin, Lana Parrilla, and Josh Dallas. Aired May 7, 2017, on ABC, Walt Disney Video, 2017, DVD.

Goodman, Tim. "Smash: TV Review." *The Hollywood Reporter*. February 1, 2012, https://www.hollywoodreporter.com/tv/tv-reviews/smash-tv-review-katharine-mcphee-debra-messing-286296/

Gordon, Rob. "Supernatural Creator in Fight over Unpaid Profits." *Screen Rant*. November 21, 2017, https://screenrant.com/supernatural-warner-bros-profits-lawsuit/

Gore, Christopher, writer. *Fame*. Season 1, episode 1, "Metamorphosis." Directed by Bob Kelljan, featuring Debbie Allen, Erica Gimpel, Gene Anthony Ray, and Cynthia Gibb. Aired January 7, 1982, on NBC, Fox/MGM Television, 2010, DVD.

Gore, Christopher, writer. *Fame*. Season 3, episode 4, "The Kids from 'Fame' in Israel." Directed by Yossi Zemach, featuring Debbie Allen, Erica Gimpel, Gene Anthony Ray, and Cynthia Gibb. Aired November 5, 1983, in First-run syndication, TV.

Graff, Gary. "'High School Musical' Kids Soaking Up Success." *Billboard*. August 21, 2007, https://www.billboard.com/music/music-news/high-school-musical-kids-soaking-up-success-1049761/

Graham, William A., dir. *Minstrel Man*. 1977; New York: Tomorrow Entertainment. TV.

Grant, Gil, writer. *Hull High*. Season 1, episode 1, "Episode One." Directed by Kenny Ortega, featuring Will Lyman, Nancy Valen, Kristin Dattalio, and Carl Anthony, Payne II. Aired August 20, 1990, on NBC.

Grant, Lee H., and William Blinn, writers. *Fame*. Season 1, episode 2, "Passing Grade." Directed by Nicholas Sgarro, featuring Debbie Allen, Erica Gimpel, Gene Anthony Ray, and Cynthia Gibb. Aired January 14, 1982, on NBC, Fox/MGM Television, 2010, DVD.

Greenberg, Drew Z., writer. *Buffy the Vampire Slayer*. Season 7, episode 6, "Him." Directed by Michael Gershman, featuring Sarah Michelle Gellar, Alyson Hannigan, Nicholas Brendan, and Michelle Trachtenberg. Aired November 5, 2002, on UPN, 20th Century Fox Home Entertainment, 2005, DVD.

Greene, Andy. "Exclusive: Michael Nesmith Remembers Davy Jones." *Rolling Stone*. March 8, 2012, https://www.rollingstone.com/music/music-news/exclusive-michael-nesmith-remembers-davy-jones-102258/#ixzz1v8CRGRDd

Greene, Mort, Dave O'Brien, and Arthur Phillips, writers. *The Red Skelton Show*. Season 13, episode 1, "Passion in Pasadena, or Love Is a Many-Splintered Thing." Directed by Seymour Berns, featuring Red Skelton, Frankie Darro, and Douglas Fowley. Aired September 24, 1963, on CBS.

Greenwalt, David, writer. *Angel*. Season 2, episode 18, "Dead End." Directed by James A. Contner, featuring David Boreanaz, Charisma Carpenter, J. August Richards, and Alexis Denisof. Aired April 24, 2001, on the WB, 20th Century Fox Home Entertainment, 2007, DVD.

Gregor, Dan, and Doug Mand, writers. *Crazy Ex-Girlfriend*. Season 1, episode 9, "I'm Going to the Beach with Josh's Friends!" Directed by Kenny Ortega, featuring Rachel Bloom, Vincent Rodriguez III, Donna Lynne Champlin, Gabrielle Ruiz, and Vella Lovell. Aired January 25, 2016, on the CW, Warner Home Video, 2016, DVD.

Gregor, Dan, and Doug Mand, writers. *Crazy Ex-Girlfriend*. Season 2, episode 10 "Will Scarsdale Like Josh's Shayna Punim?" Directed by Alex Hardcastle, featuring Rachel Bloom, Vincent Rodriguez III, Tovah Feldshuh, and Patti LuPone. Aired January 13, 2017, on the CW, Warner Home Video, 2017, DVD.

Gregor, Dan, and Doug Mand, writers. *Crazy Ex-Girlfriend*. Season 3, episode 12, "Trent?!" Directed by Stuart McDonald, featuring Rachel Bloom, Vincent Rodriguez III, Donna Lynne Champlin, Gabrielle Ruiz, and Vella Lovell. Aired February 9, 2018, on the CW, Warner Home Video, 2018, DVD.

Grifhorst, David, dir. *The Passion: New Orleans*. 2016; Beverly Hills, CA: Dick Clark Productions. TV.

Gross, Ed. "Buffy the Vampire Slayer Turns 20: Joss Whedon Looks Back." *Empire*. March 9, 2017, https://www.empireonline.com/movies/features/buffy-vampire-slayer-turns-20-joss-whedon-looks-back/

Gross, Terry. "'Schmigadoon!' Co-Creator Says Series Was Inspired by a 'Love Affair' with Musicals." *NPR*. August 23, 2021, https://www.npr.org/2021/08/23/1030268798/schmigadoon-co-creator-says-series-was-inspired-by-a-love-affair-with-musicals

Grundhauser, Eric. "Whatever Happened to Captain Video and the DuMont Programming Library? One of the Original Television Networks Has All but

Disappeared." Atlas Obscura. June 30, 2017, https://www.atlasobscura.com/articles/dumont-network-gleason-lost-kinescope

Gube, Rene, writer. *Crazy Ex-Girlfriend*. Season 1, episode 6, "My First Thanksgiving with Josh!" Directed by Joanna Kerns, featuring Rachel Bloom, Vincent Rodriguez III, Donna Lynne Champlin, Gabrielle Ruiz, and Vella Lovell. Aired November 16, 2015, on the CW, Warner Home Video, 2016, DVD.

Gube, Rene, writer. *Crazy Ex-Girlfriend*. Season 1, episode 18, "Paula Needs to Get over Josh!" Directed by Aline Brosh McKenna, featuring Rachel Bloom, Vincent Rodriguez III, Donna Lynne Champlin, Gabrielle Ruiz, and Vella Lovell. Aired April 18, 2016, on the CW, Warner Home Video, 2016, DVD.

Gube, Rene, writer. *Crazy Ex-Girlfriend*. Season 2, episode 2, "When Will Josh See How Cool I Am?" Directed by Jay Chandrasekhar, featuring Rachel Bloom, Vincent Rodriguez III, Donna Lynne Champlin, Gabrielle Ruiz, and Vella Lovell. Aired October 28, 2016, on the CW, Warner Home Video, 2017, DVD.

Hadley, Mitchell. "The Life and Death of 'NBC Opera Theater.'" *It's About TV!* June 12, 2019, https://www.itsabouttv.com/2019/06/the-life-and-death-of-nbc-opera-theatre.html

Haithman, Diane. "Steven Bochco, the $10-Million Man: Industry Ponders Whether His Exclusive Deal with ABC Will Pay Off for Network." *Los Angeles Times*. November 24, 1987, https://www.latimes.com/archives/la-xpm-1987-11-24-ca-24479-story.html

Hall, Jeremy, writer. *Galavant*. Season 2, episode 8, "Do the D'DEW." Directed by Chris Koch, featuring Joshua Sasse, Karen David, Luke Youngblood, Mallory Jansen, and Timothy Omundsen. Aired January 24, 2016, on ABC, Disney Home Video, 2017, DVD.

Hall, Karen, writer. *Moonlighting*. Season 3, episode 6, "Big Man on Mulberry Street." Directed by Christian Nyby, featuring Cybill Shepherd, Bruce Willis, Curtis Armstrong, and Allyce Beasley. Aired November 18, 1986, on ABC, Lionsgate, 2007, DVD.

Hamra, Taylor, writer. *Nashville*. Season 4, episode 6, "Please Help Me, I'm Fallin.'" Directed by Callie Khouri, featuring Connie Britton, Hayden Panettiere, Clare Bowen, and Eric Close. Aired October 28, 2015, on ABC, Walt Disney Studios Home Entertainment, 2016, DVD.

Hanson, Alan. "Elvis on the Ed Sullivan Show . . . A View Out of the Ordinary." Elvis History Blog. November 2011, http://www.elvis-history-blog.com/elvis-sullivan.html

Harris, Will. "An Oral History of *Cop Rock*, TV's First and Last Musical Police Drama." *AV Club*. May 26, 2016, https://www.avclub.com/an-oral-history-of-cop-rock-tv-s-first-and-last-musica-1798248164

Helbing, Aaron, and Todd Helbing, writers. *The Flash*. Season 3, episode 17, "Duet." Directed by Dermont Daniel Downs, featuring Grant Gustin, Melissa Benoist, and Darren Criss. Aired March 21, 2017, on the CW, Warner Home Video, 2017, DVD.

Henderson, Joe, writer. *Lucifer*. Season 2, episode 1, "Everything's Coming Up Lucifer." Directed by Nathan Hope, featuring Tom Ellis, Lauren German, D.B. Woodside, and Lesley-Ann Brandt. Aired September 19, 2016, on Fox, Warner Home Video, 2022, DVD.

Henderson, Joe, writer. *Lucifer*. Season 4, episode 1, "Everything's Okay." Directed by Sherwin Shilati, featuring Tom Ellis, Lauren German, D.B. Woodside, and Lesley-Ann Brandt. Aired May 8, 2019, on Netflix, Warner Home Video, 2022, DVD.

Herrera, Kyle, Travis Gonzales, Joseph Buck, and Christian Naranjo. "How Has Breaking Bad Affected New Mexico's Economy?" *New Mexico News Port*. March 23, 2015, https://newmexiconewsport.com/how-has-breaking-bad-affected-new-mexicos-economy/

Hersko, Tyler. "'Lucifer' Reclaims Viewership Throne in Nielsen's Latest Streaming Report." *Indiewire*. October 15, 2021, https://www.indiewire.com/features/general/lucifer-viewership-nielsen-streaming-rankings-1234671768/

Herstick, Lauren. "Interview: Lev Grossman on the Magician's Land." *Nerdist*. August 7, 2014, https://web.archive.org/web/20180616075004/https://nerdist.com/interview-lev-grossman-on-the-magicians-land/

Hibberd, James. "Galavant Canceled by ABC After Two Seasons." *Entertainment Weekly*. May 12, 2016, https://web.archive.org/web/20160516025458/http://www.ew.com/article/2016/05/12/galavant-canceled

Hindy, Joe. "Streaming Has Overtaken Traditional TV for the First Time Ever." *CNET*. June 17, 2025, https://www.cnet.com/culture/entertainment/streaming-has-overtaken-traditional-tv-for-the-first-time-ever/

Hirsch, Julia Antopol. *The Sound of Music: The Making of America's Favorite Movie*. Chicago, IL: Chicago Review Press, 2018.

Hitchcock, Michael, writer. *Crazy Ex-Girlfriend*. Season 3, episode 3, "Josh Is a Liar." Directed by Stuart McDonald, featuring Rachel Bloom, Vincent Rodriguez III, Donna Lynne Champlin, Gabrielle Ruiz, and Vella Lovell. Aired October 27, 2017, on the CW, Warner Home Video, 2018, DVD.

Hodak, Brittany. "The Real-Life Impact of ABC's 'Nashville.'" *Forbes*. October 28, 2015, https://www.forbes.com/sites/brittanyhodak/2015/10/28/the-real-life-impact-of-abcs-nashville/

Hodgson, Matthew, writer. *Glee*. Season 3, episode 16, "Saturday Night Glee-ver." Directed by Bradley Buecker, featuring Matthew Morrison, Lea Michele, Cory Monteith, Jane Lynch, and Chris Colfer. Aired April 17, 2012, on Fox, Sony Pictures Home Entertainment, 2018, DVD.

Hogan, PJ, dir. *My Best Friend's Wedding*. 1997; Burbank, CA: Columbia Tri-Star Home Entertainment, 2001. DVD.

Hooper, Tobe, dir. *Poltergeist*. 1982; Culver City, CA: MGM Home Entertainment, 1997. DVD.

Horowitz, Alex, dir. *Great Performances*. Season 44, episode 4, "Hamilton's America." Featuring Lin-Manuel Miranda, Christopher Jackson, Leslie Odom, Jr, and Barack Obama. Aired October 21, 2016, on PBS.

Hoselton, David, writer. *House*. Season 6, episode 20, "The Choice." Directed by Juan J. Campanella, featuring Hugh Laurie, Robert Sean Leonard, and Lisa Edelstein. Aired May 3, 2010, on Fox, Universal Pictures Home Entertainment, 2010, DVD.

Howard, Bryon, and Rich Moore, dirs. *Zootopia*. 2016; Burbank, CA: Walt Disney Studios Home Entertainment, 2016. DVD.

Hughes, Terry, dir. *Mrs. Santa Claus*. 1996; Los Angeles, CA: Hallmark Entertainment. TV.

Hughes, William. "George H. W. Bush Has Died, but Pop Culture's Impression of Him Lives On." *The AV Club*. December 1, 2018, https://www.avclub.com/george-h-w-bush-has-died-but-pop-cultures-impression-1830789538

Hussein, Waris, dir. *Copacabana*. 1985; Beverly Hills, CA: Dick Clark Productions. TV.

Huston John, dir. *Annie*. 1982; Los Angeles, CA: Sony Pictures Home Entertainment, 2004. DVD.

Iscove, Roger, dir. *Cinderella*. 1997; Los Angeles, CA: Sony Pictures Home Entertainment, 2002. DVD.

Jaramillo, Carina. "An Annotated History of the Vaudeville Theater." *Theater Seat Store Blog*. March 27, 2025, https://www.theaterseatstore.com/blog/vaudeville-theater?srsltid=AfmBOopUvqQIYpjTV9E47Rlbca8LghXtkAyTsZRXevLaM3O5ajZXmY7y#early-entertainment

Jessel, Ray, Tony Webster, Bel Joelson, and Art Baer, writers. *The Love Boat*. Season 5, episode 22, "The Musical/My Aunt, the Warrior/The Show Must Go On/The Pest/My Ex-Mom." Directed by Roger Duchowny, featuring Gavin McLeod, Bernie Kopell, Ted Lange, and Fred Grandy. Aired February 27, 1982, on ABC.

Jones, Patricia, and Donald Reiker, writers. *Fame*. Season 4, episode 13, "Tomorrow's Children." Directed by Debbie Allen, featuring Debbie Allen, Erica Gimpel, Gene Anthony Ray, and Cynthia Gibb. Aired January 12, 1985, in First-run syndication, TV.

Jones, Patricia, and Donald Reiker, writers. *Fame*. Season 5, episode 10, "Choices." Directed by Donald Reiker, featuring Debbie Allen, Gene Anthony Ray, and Carlo Imperato. Aired January 4, 1986, in First-run syndication, TV.

Jones, Patricia, Donald, Reiker, and Ira Steven Behr, writers. *Fame*. Season 4, episode 1, "Indian Summer." Directed by William F. Claxton, featuring Debbie Allen, Erica Gimpel, Gene Anthony Ray, and Carlo Imperato. Aired September 29, 1984, in First-run syndication, TV.

Jones, Patricia, Donald, Reiker, and Ira Steven Behr, writers. *Fame*. Season 4, episode 2, "Czech-Mate." Directed by William F. Claxton, featuring Debbie Allen, Erica Gimpel, Gene Anthony Ray, and Carlo Imperato. Aired October 6, 1984, in First-run syndication, TV.

"Joss Whedon on Those WGA Popinjays." *Variety*. November 6, 2007, https://variety.com/2007/biz/news/joss-whedon-on-those-wga-popinjays-25900/

Kapinos, Tom, writer. *Lucifer*. Season 1, episode 1, "Pilot." Directed by Len Wiseman, featuring Tom Ellis, Lauren German, D.B. Woodside, and Lesley-Ann Brandt. Aired January 25, 2016, on Fox, Warner Home Video, 2022, DVD.

Kauffman, Philip, dir. *Invasion of the Body Snatchers*. 1978; Los Angeles, CA: Universal Pictures Home Entertainment, 2020. DVD.

Kelley, Bill. "The Best and Brightest ABC's Hooperman—the Hands-Down Winner of Best New Show of the Year—Introduces a New Format, 'Dramedy,' While Slap Maxwell Reintroduces Dabney Coleman." *South Florida Sun Sentinel*. September 23, 1987, https://web.archive.org/web/20170924095527/http://articles.sun-sentinel.com/1987-09-23/features/8703150300_1_hooperman-lewis-erlicht-brandon-stoddard

Kelley, David E., writer. *Ally McBeal*. Season 1, episode 12, "Cro-Magnon." Directed by Allan Arkush, featuring Calista Flockhart, Greg Germann, Lisa Nicole Carson, and Gil

Bellows. Aired January 5, 1998, on Fox, 20th Century Fox Home Entertainment, 2009, DVD.

Kelley, David E., writer. *Ally McBeal*. Season 3, episode 21, "Ally McBeal: The Musical, Almost." Directed by Bill D'Elia, featuring Calista Flockhart, Greg Germann, Lisa Nicole Carson, and Gil Bellows. Aired May 22, 2000, on Fox, 20th Century Fox Home Entertainment, 2009, DVD.

Kelley, David E., Patricia Green, and Alan Brennert, writers. *LA Law*. Season 5, episode 16, "Good to the Last Drop." Directed by Menachem Binetski, featuring Harry Hamlin, Corbin Bernsen, Richard Dysart, Blair Underwood, and Susan Ruttan. Aired March 21, 1991, on NBC, Revelation Films, 2013, DVD.

Kelly, Richard, dir. *Donnie Darko*. 2001; Los Angeles, CA: 20th Century Fox Pictures Home Entertainment, 2002. DVD.

Kenny, Jack, and Austin Winsberg, writers. *Zoey's Extraordinary Playlist*. Season 1, episode 5, "Zoey's Extraordinary Failure." Directed by Darnell Martin, featuring Jane Levy, Skylar Astin, Alex Newell, and Mary Steenburgen. Aired March 8, 2020, on NBC, TV.

Khouri, Callie, writer. *Nashville*. Season 1, episode 21, "I'll Never Get Out of This World Alive." Directed by Callie Khouri, featuring Connie Britton, Hayden Panettiere, Clare Bowen, and Eric Close. Aired May 22, 2013, on ABC, Walt Disney Studios Home Entertainment, 2013, DVD.

Kirshner, Rebecca Rand, writer. *Buffy the Vampire Slayer*. Season 5, episode 4, "Out of My Mind." Directed by David Grossman, featuring Sarah Michelle Gellar, Alyson Hannigan, Nicholas Brendan, Anthony Stewart Head, and James Marsters. Aired October 17, 2000, on the WB, 20th Century Fox, 2005, DVD.

Kitsis, Edward, and Adam Horowitz, writers. *Once Upon a Time*. Season 1, episode 1, "Pilot." Directed by Mark Mylod, featuring Jennifer Morrison, Ginnifer Goodwin, Lana Parrilla, and Josh Dallas. Aired October 23, 2011, on ABC, Walt Disney Video, 2012, DVD.

Kitsis, Edward, and Adam Horowitz, writers. *Once Upon a Time*. Season 1, episode 22, "A Land Without Magic." Directed by Dean White, featuring Jennifer Morrison, Ginnifer Goodwin, Lana Parrilla, and Josh Dallas. Aired May 13, 2012, on ABC, Walt Disney Video, 2012, DVD.

Klausner, Julie, writer. *Schmigadoon!* Season 2, episode 3, "Bells and Whistles." Directed by Alice Mathias, featuring Cecily Strong, Keegan-Michael Key, Alan Cumming, Kristin Chenoweth, and Ariana DeBose. Aired April 12, 2023, on AppleTV+, Streaming.

Kopelman, Dan, writer. *Galavant*. Season 2, episode 5, "Giants vs. Dwarves." Directed by Declan Lowney, featuring Joshua Sasse, Karen David, Luke Youngblood, Mallory Jansen, and Timothy Omundsen. Aired January 17, 2016, on ABC, Disney Home Video, 2017, DVD.

Kripke, Eric, writer. *Supernatural*. Season 3, episode 16, "No Rest for the Wicked." Directed by Kim Manners, featuring Jensen Ackles, Jared Padalecki, and Jim Beaver. Aired May 15, 2008, on the CW, Warner Home Entertainment, 2008, DVD.

LaHendro, Bob, dir. *Three for the Girls*. 1973; New York: UGO Productions. TV.

Lavender, Meredith, and Marcie Ulin, writers. *Nashville*. Season 2, episode 10, "Tomorrow Never Comes." Directed by Patrick Norris, featuring Connie Britton, Hayden

Panettiere, Clare Bowen, and Eric Close. Aired December 11, 2013, on ABC, Walt Disney Studios Home Entertainment, 2013, DVD.

Lawson, Richard. "'Glee' Was Bad, Really Really Bad." *The Atlantic*. February 1, 2012, https://www.theatlantic.com/culture/archive/2012/02/glee-was-bad-really-really-bad/332381/

Laybourne, Sam, writer. *Zoey's Extraordinary Playlist*. Season 1, episode 3, "Zoey's Extraordinary Boss." Directed by Daisy von Scherler Mayer, featuring Jane Levy, Skylar Astin, Alex Newell, and Mary Steenburgen. Aired February 23, 2020, on NBC, TV.

Laybourne, Sam, writer. *Zoey's Extraordinary Playlist*. Season 2, episode 2, "Zoey's Extraordinary Distraction." Directed by Anya Adams, featuring Jane Levy, Skylar Astin, Alex Newell, and Mary Steenburgen. Aired January 12, 2021, on NBC, TV.

Leacock, Philip, dir. *The Great Man's Whiskers*. 1973; Universal City, CA: Universal Television. TV.

Lee, Joanna, writer. *The Brady Bunch*. Season 5, episode 1, "Adios, Johnny Bravo." Directed by Jerry London, featuring Robert Reed, Florence Henderson, Barry Williams, and Christopher Knight. Aired September 14, 1973, on ABC, Paramount, 2007, DVD.

Lenker, Maureen Lee. "Every Live TV Musical, Ranked: See Where Your Favorite Landed in Our Rankings." *Entertainment Weekly*. December 15, 2022, https://ew.com/tv/every-live-tv-musical-ranked/

Leslie, Adam, writer. *Fame*. Season 5, episode 17, "The Comedian." Directed by Reza Badiyi, featuring Debbie Allen, Gene Anthony Ray, and Carlo Imperato. Aired March 22, 1986, in First-run syndication, TV.

Leslie, Phil, and Al Schwartz, writers. *The Brady Bunch*. Season 3, episode 12, "Getting Davy Jones." Directed by Oscar Rudolph, featuring Robert Reed, Florence Henderson, Barry Williams, and Christopher Knight. Aired December 10, 1971, on ABC, Paramount, 2007, DVD.

Lewis, Draper, writer. *Fame*. Season 2, episode 20, "The Kids from 'Fame' in Concert." Directed by Terry Sanders, featuring Debbie Allen, Erica Gimpel, Gene Anthony Ray, and Cynthia Gibb. Aired March 3, 1983, on NBC, TV.

Liebman, Max, and Charles O'Curran, dirs. *Satins and Spurs*. 1954; Brooklyn, NY: NBC Studios. TV.

Lipson, Elle, and John McNamara, writers. *The Magicians*. Season 2, episode 9, "Lesser Evils." Directed by Rebecca Johnson, featuring Jason Ralph, Stella Maeve, Hale Appleman, and Arjun Gupta. Aired March 22, 2017, on SyFy, Universal Pictures Home Entertainment, 2020, DVD.

Lipson, Elle, John McNamara, and Joseph Mireles, writers. *The Magicians*. Season 5, episode 12, "The Balls." Directed by Meera Menon, featuring Stella Maeve, Hale Appleman, and Arjun Gupta. Aired March 25, 2020, on SyFy, Universal Pictures Home Entertainment, 2020, DVD.

Lloyd, Phyllida, dir. *Mamma Mia*. 2008; Los Angeles, CA: Universal Pictures Home Entertainment, 2011. DVD.

Lloyd, Robert. "What Made Betty White the Most Beloved TV Star of Her (or Maybe Any) Generation." *Los Angeles Times*. January 1, 2022, https://www.latimes.com/

entertainment-arts/tv/story/2022-01-01/betty-white-death-mary-tyler-moore-golden-girls-hot-in-cleveland-appreciation

Loria, Keith. "Review: 'Schmigadoon!' Finds New Life as Part of the Kenendy Center's Broadway Center Stage Series." *TheaterMania*. February 3, 2025, https://www.theatermania.com/news/review-schmigadoon-finds-new-life-as-part-of-kennedy-centers-broadway-center-stage-series_1762764/

Los Angeles Times Staff. "Writers' Strike: What Happened, How It Ended and Its Impact on Hollywood." *Los Angeles Times*. May 1, 2023, https://www.latimes.com/entertainment-arts/business/story/2023-05-01/writers-strike-what-to-know-wga-guild-hollywood-productions

Lotz, Amanda D. *The Television Will Be Revolutionized*. New York: New York University Press, 2007.

Luther, Frank, and Mark Twain, writers. *The United States Steel Hour*. Season 4, episode 6, "Tom Sawyer." Directed by John Haggott, featuring John Sharpe, Jimmy Boyd, and Bennye Gatteys. Aired November 21, 1956, on CBS.

Lynskey, Dorian. "'An Ad for Blackness': How Soul Train Made America Do the Hustle." *The Guardian*. February 20, 2019, https://www.theguardian.com/music/2019/feb/20/american-soul-train-don-cornelius

Maeser, Emily. "The Syntax of Television, Part 3: Making a Show." *Movie Jawn*. June 1, 2023, https://www.moviejawn.com/home/2023/6/1/the-syntax-of-television-part-3-making-a-show?srsltid=AfmBOorJJEx2INB6fo5tc-Md0A55DTLhqioCcLPmyx82zcnd3_X88Uw3

Maloney, Dan. "Never Twice the Same Color: Why NTSC Is So Weird." *Hackaday*. October 6, 2016, https://hackaday.com/2016/10/06/never-twice-the-same-color-why-ntsc-is-so-weird/

Mansky, Jackie. "An Early Run-In with Censors Led Rod Serling to 'The Twilight Zone': His Failed Attempts to Bring the Emmett Till Tragedy to Television Forced Him to Get Creative." *Smithsonian Magazine*. April 1, 2019, https://www.smithsonianmag.com/arts-culture/early-run-censors-led-rod-serling-twilight-zone-180971837/

Mansky, Jackie. "Seventy-Five Years Ago, the Television Musical Made Its Debut: 'Rent: Live' Meet 'The Boys from Boise.'" *Smithsonian Magazine*. January 25, 2019, https://www.smithsonianmag.com/arts-culture/television-musical-actually-debuted-75-years-ago-180971342/

Marechal, AJ. "Greenblatt Discusses 'Sound of Music,' 'Revolution' in journo-chat." *Variety*. November 20, 2012, https://variety.com/2012/tv/news/greenblatt-discusses-sound-of-music-revolution-in-journo-chat-9023/

Masius, John, writer. *Ferris Bueller*. Season 1, episode 1, "Pilot." Directed by Jonathan Lynn, featuring Charlie Schlatter, Richard Riehle, Jennifer Aniston, Ami Dolenz, and Brandon Douglas. Aired August 23, 1990, on NBC, TV.

Mayer, Timothy, writer. *NET Playhouse*. Season 4, episode 17, "Jesus, a Passion Play for Americans." Directed by Timothy Mayer, featuring Laura Esterman, Stephan Mo Hanan, and Asha Puthii. Aired May 26, 1970, on NET.

McCourt, Dee. "Facts and Figures: Mamma Mia! Stage Show." *Judy Cramer*. https://www.judycraymer.com/press-centre/facts-and-figures.php

McGreevey, Michael, writer. *Fame*. Season 3, episode 8, "Break Dance." Directed by Michael Peters, featuring Debbie Allen, Gene Anthony Ray, and Carlo Imperato. Aired December 10, 1983, in First-run syndication, TV.

McKenna, Aline Brosh, writer. *Crazy Ex-Girlfriend*. Season 1, episode 13, "Josh and I Go to Los Angeles!" Directed by Michael Patrick Jann, featuring Rachel Bloom, Vincent Rodriguez III, Donna Lynne Champlin, Gabrielle Ruiz, and Vella Lovell. Aired February 29, 2016, on the CW, Warner Home Video, 2016, DVD.

McKenna, Aline Brosh, and Rachel Bloom, writers. *Crazy Ex-Girlfriend*. Season 4, episode 17, "I'm in Love." Directed by Aline Brosh McKenna, featuring Rachel Bloom, Vincent Rodriguez III, Donna Lynne Champlin, Gabrielle Ruiz, and Vella Lovell. Aired April 5, 2019, on the CW, Warner Home Video, 2019, DVD.

McKenna, Chris, writer. *Community*. Season 2, episode 21, "Paradigms of Human Memory." Directed by Tristram Shapeero, featuring Joel McHale, Donald Glover, Alison Brie, Yvette Nicole Brown, and Chevy Chase. Aired April 21, 2011, on NBC, Mill Creek Entertainment, 2019, DVD.

McNamara, John, and Mike Moore, writers. *The Magicians*. Season 4, episode 10, "All That Hard, Glossy Armor." Directed by Shannon Kohli, featuring Jason Ralph, Stella Maeve, Hale Appleman, and Arjun Gupta. Aired March 27, 2019, on SyFy, Universal Pictures Home Entertainment, 2020, DVD.

McNamara, John, Jay Gard, and Alex Raiman, writers. *The Magicians*. Season 3, episode 9, "All That Josh." Directed by James L. Conway, featuring Jason Ralph, Stella Maeve, Hale Appleman, and Arjun Gupta. Aired March 7, 2018, on SyFy, Universal Pictures Home Entertainment, 2020, DVD.

Mendelsohn, Carol, writer. *Fame*. Season 4, episode 19, "Coco Returns." Directed by Debbie Allen, featuring Debbie Allen, Erica Gimpel, Gene Anthony Ray, and Cynthia Gibb. Aired March 2, 1985, in First-run syndication, TV.

Menotti, Gian Carlo, writer. *NBC Opera Theater*. Season 3, episode 3, "Amahl and the Night Visitors." Directed by Kirk Browning, featuring Chet Allen, Rosemary Kuhlmann, and Andrew McKinley. Aired December 24, 1951, on NBC.

Minnelli, Vincente, dir. *An American in Paris*. 1951; Los Angeles, CA: Warner Home Video, 2000. DVD.

Minow, Newton N. "Television and the Public Interest." Address to the National Association of Broadcasters, Washington, DC. May 9, 1961, https://www.americanrhetoric.com/speeches/newtonminow.htm

Modrovich, Ildy, writer. *Lucifer*. Season 5, episode 10, "Bloody Celestial Karaoke Jam." Directed by Sherwin Shilati, featuring Tom Ellis, Lauren German, D.B. Woodside, and Lesley-Ann Brandt. Aired May 28, 2021, on Netflix, Warner Home Video, 2022, DVD.

Moore Tom, dir. *Geppetto*. 2000; Burbank, CA: Walt Disney Television. TV.

Morais, Annmarie, writer. *American Soul*. Season 1, episode 3, "Lost and Found." Directed by Robert Townsend, featuring Sinqua Wells, Christopher Jefferson, Kelly Price, and Iantha Richardson. Aired February 12, 2019, on BET.

Morgan, Chris. "Remember TV's Rural Purge." *Medium*. May 19, 2017, https://medium.com/@ChrisXMorgan/remember-tvs-rural-purge-b0a115c2a2b2

Morgan, Glen, and James Wong, writers. *21 Jump Street*. Season 3, episode 13, "A.W.O.L." Directed by Michael Robinson, featuring Johnny Depp, Peter DeLuise, Holly Robinson, and Dustin Nguyen. Aired March 19, 1989, on Fox, Visual Entertainment, 2022, DVD.

Morris, Raina, writer. *Schmigadoon!* Season 2, episode 4, "Something Real." Directed by Alice Mathias, featuring Cecily Strong, Keegan-Michael Key, Alan Cumming, Kristin Chenoweth, and Ariana DeBose. Aired April 19, 2023, on AppleTV+, Streaming.

Murphy, Chris. "From Leprechauns to Corn Puddin': All the Musical References in *Schmigadoon*! *Vanity Fair*. July 19, 2021, https://www.vanityfair.com/hollywood/2021/07/from-leprechauns-to-corn-puddin-all-the-musical-references-in-schmigadoon

Murphy, Ryan, Brad Falchuk, and Ian Brennan, writers. *Glee*. Season 1, episode 1, "Pilot." Directed by Ryan Murphy, featuring Matthew Morrison, Lea Michele, Cory Monteith, Jane Lynch, and Chris Colfer. Aired May 19, 2009, on Fox, Sony Pictures Home Entertainment, 2018, DVD.

Murphy, Ryan, writer. *Glee*. Season 1, episode 9, "Wheels." Directed by Paris Barclay, featuring Matthew Morrison, Lea Michele, Cory Monteith, Jane Lynch, and Chris Colfer. Aired November 11, 2009, on Fox, Sony Pictures Home Entertainment, 2018, DVD.

Murphy, Ryan, writer. *Glee*. Season 1, episode 12, "Mattress." Directed by Elodie Keene, featuring Matthew Morrison, Lea Michele, Cory Monteith, Jane Lynch, and Chris Colfer. Aired December 2, 2009, on Fox, Sony Pictures Home Entertainment, 2018, DVD.

Murphy, Ryan, writer. *Glee*. Season 2, episode 12, "Silly Love Songs." Directed by Tate Donovan, featuring Matthew Morrison, Lea Michele, Cory Monteith, Jane Lynch, and Chris Colfer. Aired February 8, 2011, on Fox, Sony Pictures Home Entertainment, 2018, DVD.

Murphy, Ryan, writer. *Glee*. Season 3, episode 11, "Michael." Directed by Alfonso Gomez-Rejon, featuring Matthew Morrison, Lea Michele, Cory Monteith, Jane Lynch, and Chris Colfer. Aired January 31, 2012, on Fox, Sony Pictures Home Entertainment, 2018, DVD.

Murphy, Ryan, Brad Falchuk, and Ian Brennan, writers. *Glee*. Season 5, episode 12, "100." Directed by Paris Barclay, featuring Matthew Morrison, Lea Michele, Jane Lynch, and Chris Colfer. Aired March 10, 2014, on Fox, Sony Pictures Home Entertainment, 2018, DVD.

Murphy, Ryan, Brad Falchuk, and Ian Brennan, writers. *Glee*. Season 6, episode 13, "Dreams Come True." Directed by Bradley Buecker, featuring Matthew Morrison, Lea Michele, Jane Lynch, and Chris Colfer. Aired March 20, 2015, on Fox, Sony Pictures Home Entertainment, 2018, DVD.

Nauffts, Geoffrey, writer. *Nashville*. Season 5, episode 9, "If Tomorrow Never Comes." Directed by Callie Khouri, featuring Connie Britton, Hayden Panettiere, Clare Bowen, and Eric Close. Aired February 23, 2017, on CMT, Walt Disney Studios Home Entertainment, 2017, DVD.

"NBC Aligning Brands with A-list Talent—Online." *Advertising Age*. October 9, 2008, https://adage.com/article/madisonvine-news/nbc-aligning-brands-a-list-talent-online/131605/

Nelson Ralph, dir. *Cinderella*. 1957; Los Angeles, CA: Image Entertainment, 2004. DVD.

Newman, Kristin, writer. *Galavant*. Season 1, episode 8, "It's All in the Executions." Directed by Chris Koch, featuring Joshua Sasse, Karen David, Luke Youngblood, Mallory Jansen, and Timothy Omundsen. Aired January 25, 2015, on ABC, Disney Home Video, 2017, DVD.

Ning, Jason, writer. *Lucifer*. Season 1, episode 6, "Favorite Son." Directed by David Paymer, featuring Tom Ellis, Lauren German, D.B. Woodside, and Lesley-Ann Brandt. Aired February 29, 2016, on Fox, Warner Home Video, 2022, DVD.

O'Connell, Mikey. "TV Ratings: NBC's 'Sound of Music Live' Nears 22 Million Viewers with DVR." *The Hollywood Reporter*. December 23, 2013, https://www.hollywoodreporter.com/tv/tv-news/tv-ratings-nbcs-sound-music-667543/

O'Connor, John J. "TV Review; Barry Manilow Stars in 'Copacabana' on CBS." *The New York Times*. December 3, 1985, https://www.nytimes.com/1985/12/03/arts/tv-review-barry-manilow-stars-in-copacabana-on-cbs.html

O'Donnell, Tim, writer. *Uncle Buck*. Season 1, episode 1, "Pilot." Directed by John Tracy, featuring Kevin Meaney, Dah-ve Chodan, Audrey Meadows, and Lacey Chabert. Aired September 10, 1990, on CBS.

O'Steen, Sam, dir. *Queen of the Stardust Ballroom*. 1975; New York: Tomorrow Entertainment, TV.

Osborn, Ron, and Jeff Reno, writers. *Moonlighting*. Season 3, episode 7, "Atomic Shakespeare." Directed by Will MacKenzie, featuring Cybill Shepherd, Bruce Willis, Curtis Armstrong, and Allyce Beasley. Aired November 25, 1986, on ABC, Lionsgate, 2007, DVD.

Parker, Alan, dir. *Fame*. 1980; Burbank, CA: Warner Home Video, 2003.

Parker, Ryan. "Barbara Bush's Letter to Marge Simpson Revealed by Series Showrunner." *The Hollywood Reporter*. April 18, 2018, https://www.hollywoodreporter.com/tv/tv-news/barbara-bushs-letter-marge-simpson-revealed-by-series-showrunner-1103722/

Patel, Sono, writer. *Crazy Ex-Girlfriend*. Season 1, episode 14, "Josh Is Going to Hawaii!" Directed by Erin Ehrlich, featuring Rachel Bloom, Vincent Rodriguez III, Donna Lynne Champlin, Gabrielle Ruiz, and Vella Lovell. Aired March 7, 2016, on the CW, Warner Home Video, 2016, DVD.

Paul, Cinco, and Ken Daurio, writers. *Schmigadoon!* Season 1, episode 1, "Schmigadoon!" Directed by Barry Sonnenfeld, featuring Cecily Strong, Keegan-Michael Key, Alan Cumming, Kristin Chenoweth, and Ariana DeBose. Aired July 16, 2021, on AppleTV+, Streaming.

Paul, Cinco, Ken Daurio, and Kate Gersten, writers. *Schmigadoon!* Season 1, episode 4, "Suddenly." Directed by Barry Sonnenfeld, featuring Cecily Strong, Keegan-Michael Key, Alan Cumming, Kristin Chenoweth, and Ariana DeBose. Aired July 30, 2021, on AppleTV+, Streaming.

Paul, Cinco, and Ken Daurio, writers. *Schmigadoon!* Season 1, episode 6, "How We Change." Directed by Barry Sonnenfeld, featuring Cecily Strong, Keegan-Michael Key,

Alan Cumming, Kristin Chenoweth, and Ariana DeBose. Aired August 13, 2021, on AppleTV+, Streaming.

Paul, Cinco, writer. *Schmigadoon!* Season 2, episode 6, "Over and Done." Directed by Robert Luketic, featuring Cecily Strong, Keegan-Michael Key, Alan Cumming, Kristin Chenoweth, and Ariana DeBose. Aired May 3, 2023, on AppleTV+, Streaming.

Peña, Ilana, writer. *Crazy Ex-Girlfriend.* Season 4, episode 5, "I'm So Happy for You." Directed by Erin Ehrlich, featuring Rachel Bloom, Vincent Rodriguez III, Donna Lynne Champlin, Gabrielle Ruiz, and Vella Lovell. Aired November 8, 2018, on the CW, Warner Home Video, 2019, DVD.

Perez, Davy, writer. *Supernatural.* Season 15, episode 4, "Atomic Monsters." Directed by Jensen Ackles, featuring Jensen Ackles, Jared Padalecki, and Misha Collins. Aired November 7, 2019, on the CW, Warner Home Video, 2020, DVD.

Perine, Parke, writer. *Fame.* Season 1, episode 9, "But Seriously, Folks." Directed by Alan J. Levi, featuring Debbie Allen, Erica Gimpel, Gene Anthony Ray, and Cynthia Gibb. Aired March 4, 1982, on NBC, Fox/MGM Television, 2010, DVD.

Petrie, Daniel, dir. *The Stingiest Man in Town.* 1954; Pleasantville, NY: Video Artists International, 2011. DVD.

Petty, Dustin. "Glee: Best of Intentions, Problematic Messages." *Medium.* April 17, 2018, https://medium.com/@pettydus/glee-best-of-intentions-problematic-messages-52b15ddca221

Pinkner, Jeff, Wyman, J.H., and Akiva Goldsman, writers. *Fringe.* Season 2, episode 20, "Brown Betty." Directed by Seith Mann, featuring John Noble, Joshua Jackson, and Anna Torv. Aired April 29, 2010, on Fox, Warner Home Video, 2010, DVD.

Plimpton, Martha, writer. *7th Heaven.* Season 9, episode 15, "Red Socks." Directed by Michael Preece, featuring Stephen Collins, Catherine Hicks, Beverley Mitchell, and David Gallagher. Aired February 14, 2005, on the WB, Paramount Home Entertainment, 2017, DVD.

Popli, Nik. "What the Corporation for Public Broadcasting Shutting Down Means for PBS and NPR." *Time.* August 1, 2025, https://time.com/7307069/corporation-for-public-broadcasting-pbs-npr/

Price, Will, dir. *Rock Rock Rock!* 1956; Wayne, PA: Alpha Video, 2022. DVD.

Prince, Jonathan, and Josh Goldstein, writers. *American Dreams.* Season 1, episode 1, "Pilot." Directed by David Semel, featuring Brittany Snow, Will Estes, Jonathan Adams, and Arlen Escarpeta. Aired September 29, 2002, on NBC.

Quinn, Katrina Jesick. "The 1950s: Decade of Economic Prosperity, Rock 'n' Roll, and a Red Scare." *Butler Eagle.* January 14, 2025, https://www.butlereagle.com/20250114/the-1950s-decade-of-economic-prosperity-rocknroll-and-a-red-scare/

Rafelson, Robert, writer. *The Monkees.* Season 1, episode 32, "Monkees on Tour." Directed by Robert Rafelson, featuring Davy Jones, Mickey Dolenz, Mike Nesmith, and Peter Tork. Aired January 24, 1967, on NBC, Rhino Entertainment Company, 2003, DVD.

Rafferty, Chris, writer. *Lucifer.* Season 5, episode 8, "Spoiler Alert." Directed by Kevin Alejandro, featuring Tom Ellis, Lauren German, D.B. Woodside, and Lesley-Ann Brandt. Aired August 21, 2020, on Netflix, Warner Home Video, 2022, DVD.

Rafferty, Chris, and Mike Costa, writers. *Lucifer.* Season 3, episode 7, "Off the Record." Directed by Eduardo Sánchez, featuring Tom Ellis, Lauren German, D.B. Woodside, and Lesley-Ann Brandt. Aired November 13, 2017, on Fox, Warner Home Video, 2022, DVD.

Reilly, Kaitlin. "Hollywood Is Ryan Murphy's Response to Years of the Industry's Homophobia." *Refinery 29*. May 1, 2020, https://www.refinery29.com/en-us/2020/05/9756058/ryan-murphy-hollywood-homophobia-story

Reims, Josh, writer. *American Dreams*. Season 2, episode 4, "Crossing the Line." Directed by Craig Zisk, featuring Brittany Snow, Will Estes, Jonathan Adams, and Arlen Escarpeta. Aired October 19, 2003, on NBC.

Reitherman, Wolfgang, dir. *Robin Hood*. 1973; Los Angeles, CA: Walt Disney Home Video, 2000. DVD.

Renaud, Chris, dir. *The Lorax*. 2012; Los Angeles, CA: Universal Home Entertainment, 2012. DVD.

Rhimes, Shonda, writer. *Grey's Anatomy*. Season 7, episode 18, "Song Beneath the Song." Directed by Tony Phelan, featuring Ellen Pompeo, Sandra Oh, Sara Ramirez, and Jesse Williams. Aired March 31, 2011, on ABC, Buena Vista Home Entertainment, 2011, DVD.

Rocco, Marc, dir. *Dream a Little Dream*. 1989; Los Angeles, CA: Lionsgate Pictures Entertainment, 2003. DVD.

Rosenthal, Karine, writer. *Bones*. Season 5, episode 19, "The Rocker in the Rinse Cycle." Directed by Jeff Woolnough, featuring David Boreanaz, Emily Deschanel, and Tamara Taylor. Aired April 29, 2010, on Fox, 20th Century Fox, 2010, DVD.

Rosin, Lindsay, writer. *Zoey's Extraordinary Playlist*. Season 2, episode 8, "Zoey's Extraordinary Birthday." Directed by Shasta Spahn, featuring Jane Levy, Skylar Astin, Alex Newell, and Mary Steenburgen. Aired April 4, 2021, on NBC, TV.

Rowles, Dustin "The Internet Is Toxic. Zach Braff and Donald Faison's Live Rendition of 'Guy Love' Is Not." *Pajiba*. June 3, 2014, https://www.pajiba.com/videos/the-internet-is-toxic-zach-braff-and-donald-faisons-live-rendition-of-guy-love-is-not.php

Royston, Peter. "Kiss Me, Kate: The Love Connection." *Center Stage Magazine*. Winter/Spring 2002, https://www.portwashington.com/moveweb/Guidewrite/kissmekate.html

Ryan, Maureen. "Perfect Pitch? Not Quite, but There's Much to Enjoy as 'Glee' Returns." *Chicago Tribune*. November 10, 2009, https://web.archive.org/web/20091114080253/http://featuresblogs.chicagotribune.com/entertainment_tv/2009/11/glee-fox-music.html

Ryan, Maureen. "'Smash' Exclusive First Look: Is This the Show That Will Save NBC?" *Huffington Post*. November 21, 2011, https://web.archive.org/web/20120126070044/http://www.aoltv.com/2011/11/21/smash-nbc-exclusive-first-look-katharine-mcphee/

Saettler, Paul. *The Evolution of American Educational Technology*. Charlotte, NC: Information Age Publishing, 2004.

Safran, Josh, writer. *Smash*. Season 2, episode 1, "On Broadway." Directed by Michael Morris, featuring Debra Messing, Jack Davenport, and Anjelica Huston. Aired February 5, 2013, on NBC, Universal Pictures Home Entertainment, 2013, DVD.

Sammond, Nicholas. *Birth of an Industry: Blackface Minstrelsy and the Rise of American Animation*. Durham, NC: Duke University Press, 2015.

Sanders, Sam, Anjuli Sastry Krbechek, Liam McBain, and Jordana Hochman. "There Was Nothing Like 'Soul Train' on TV: There's Never Been Anything Like It Since." *NPR*. September 28, 2021, https://www.npr.org/2021/09/14/1037118049/soul-train-hanif-abdurraqib

Schneider, Michael. "'Fox Rocks' Week misses Catchy Spelling Opportunity." *Variety*. April 7, 2010, https://variety.com/2010/tv/news/fox-rocks-week-misses-catchy-spelling-opportunity-16335/

Schonfeld Longstreet, Renee, writer. *Fame*. Season 6, episode 11, "Go Softly into Morning." Directed by Win Phelps, featuring Debbie Allen, Gene Anthony Ray, and Carlo Imperato. Aired January 5, 1987, in First-run syndication, TV.

Schwartz, Mike, writer. *Scrubs*. Season 3, episode 19, "My Choosiest Choice of All." Directed by Adam Bernstein, featuring Zach Braff, Donald Faison, Judy Reyes, and Sarah Chalke. Aired April 20, 2004, on NBC, Buena Vista Home Entertainment, 2006, DVD.

Sears, Steven L., and Chris Manheim, writers. *Xena: Warrior Princess*. Season 3, episode 12, "The Bitter Suite." Directed by Oley Sassone, featuring Lucy Lawless, Renee O'Connor, and Ted Raimi. Aired February 14, 1998, in First-run syndication, Universal Home Video, 2024, DVD.

Shepard, Richard, dir. *Zoey's Extraordinary Christmas*. 2021; San Jose, CA: Roku Channel. Streaming.

Shorr, Robin, writer. *Galavant*. Season 2, episode 7, "Love and Death." Directed by Paul Murphy, featuring Joshua Sasse, Karen David, Luke Youngblood, Mallory Jansen, and Timothy Omundsen. Aired January 24, 2016, on ABC, Disney Home Video, 2017, DVD.

Sibihwana, Maxine. "'You're All Minorities. You're in the Glee Club': Neoliberalism, and the Disappearing Black People in the Ryan Murphy Cinematic Universe." *Medium*. April 25, 2025, https://medium.com/@maxinesibihwana/youre-all-minorities-you-re-in-the-glee-club-4301d932383f

Siege, Julie, writer. *Supernatural*. Season 4, episode 18, "The Monster at the End of This Book." Directed by Mike Rohl, featuring Jensen Ackles, Jared Padalecki, and Misha Collins. Aired April 2, 2009, on the CW, Warner Home Video, 2009, DVD.

Silverman, Alison, writer. *Schmigadoon!* Season 1, episode 5, "Tribulation." Directed by Barry Sonnenfeld, featuring Cecily Strong, Keegan-Michael Key, Alan Cumming, Kristin Chenoweth, and Ariana DeBose. Aired August 6, 2021, on AppleTV+, Streaming.

Sloman, Tony. "Obituary: Emile Ardolino." *The Independent*. December 4, 1993, https://www.independent.co.uk/news/people/obituary-emile-ardolino-1465147.html

Smail, Gretchen. "*American Soul* Has More of Don Cornelius' Legacy to Explore." *Bustle*. July 15, 2020, https://www.bustle.com/entertainment/american-soul-season-3-renewed-canceled

Smith, Rowena. "The Beggar's Opera Review—the Original Jukebox Musical Reimagined." *The Guardian*. August 17, 2018, https://www.theguardian.com/music/2018/aug/17/the-beggars-opera-review-kings-theatre-edinburgh-international-festival

Smith, Sid, dir. *The Dangerous Christmas of Red Riding Hood*. 1965; New York: Eritas Productions. TV.

Specter, Rachel, and Audrey Wauchope, writers. *Crazy Ex-Girlfriend*. Season 1, episode 16, "Josh's Sister Is Getting Married!" Directed by Alex Hardcastle, featuring Rachel Bloom, Vincent Rodriguez III, Donna Lynne Champlin, Gabrielle Ruiz, and Vella Lovell. Aired March 28, 2016, on the CW, Warner Home Video, 2016, DVD.

Stafford, Nikki. *Bite Me! The Unofficial Guide to Buffy the Vampire Slayer*. Toronto: ECW Press, 2007.

Stagedoor Editors. "The Longest-Running West End Shows: Here Are the 5 Longest-Running Musicals in London History." *Stagedoor*. October 11, 2024, https://stagedoor.com/theatre-guide/stagedoor-editors/the-longest-running-west-end-shows?ia=1820

Stanger, Rama Laurie, writer. *American Dreams*. Season 1, episode 7, "Cold Snap." Directed by Michael W. Watkins, featuring Brittany Snow, Will Estes, Jonathan Adams, and Arlen Escarpeta. Aired November 10, 2002, on NBC.

Stanley, Alessandro. "Singing in the Casino? That's a Gamble." *New York Times*. October 18, 2007, https://www.nytimes.com/2007/10/18/arts/television/18stan.html

Staples, Brent. "Just a Toaster with Pictures." *The New York Times*. February 8, 1987, https://www.nytimes.com/1987/02/08/books/just-a-toaster-with-pictures.html

Starr, Ben, writer. *The Brady Bunch*. Season 3, episode 16, "Dough Re Mi." Directed by Allen Baron, featuring Robert Reed, Florence Henderson, Barry Williams, and Christopher Knight. Aired January 14, 1972, on ABC, Paramount, 2007, DVD.

Straw, Tom, writer. *Parker Lewis Can't Lose*. Season 1, episode 14, "Rent-a-Kube." Directed by Andy Tennant, featuring Corin Nemec, Billy Jayne, and Troy Slaten. Aired December 16, 1990, on Fox, Shout! Factory, 2009, DVD.

Straw, Tom, writer. *Parker Lewis Can't Lose*. Season 1, episode 18, "The Human Grace." Directed by Max Tash, featuring Corin Nemec, Billy Jayne, and Troy Slaten. Aired February 17, 1991, on Fox, Shout! Factory, 2009, DVD.

Straw, Tom, writer. *Parker Lewis Can't Lose*. Season 1, episode 26, "Parker Lewis Can't Win." Directed by Bryan Spicer, featuring Corin Nemec, Billy Jayne, and Troy Slaten. Aired May 19, 1991, on Fox, Fox/MGM Television, 2010, DVD.

Sydell, Laura. "'Buffy' Creator Proves Doogie Can Sing." *NPR*. July 18, 2008, http://www.npr.org/templates/story/story.php?storyId=92678153

Tabori, George, writer. *NET Playhouse*. Season 1, episode 21, "The World of Kurt Weill." Directed by David M. Davis, featuring Lotte Lenya and George Voskovec. Aired February 24, 1967, on NET.

Tagelaar, Liz, writer. *American Dreams*. Season 3, episode 15, "California Dreamin'." Directed by Jim Chory, featuring Brittany Snow, Will Estes, Jonathan Adams, and Arlen Escarpeta. Aired March 16, 2005, on NBC.

Tarses, Matt, and Tim Hobert, writers. *Scrubs*. Season 2, episode 13, "My Philosophy." Directed by Chris Koch, featuring Zach Braff, Donald Faison, Judy Reyes, and Sarah Chalke. Aired January 16, 2003, on NBC, Buena Vista Home Entertainment, 2005, DVD.

Taylor, Millie, and Dominic Symonds. *Studying Musical Theatre: Theory and Practice*. London: Bloomsbury, 2017.

Thompson, Robbie, writer. *Supernatural*. Season 10, episode 5, "Fan Fiction." Directed by Phil Sgriccia, featuring Jensen Ackles, Jared Padalecki, and Misha Collins. Aired November 11, 2014, on the CW, Warner Home Video, 2015, DVD.

Thompson, Wanna. "TLC's 'No Scrubs' Is Still on Top 20 Years Later: The Trio's Hit Single Continues to Resonate with Young Women Across the Globe." *Vibe*. February 2, 2019, https://www.vibe.com/features/editorial/tlc-no-scrubs-anniversary-633169/

Thurber, James, John Crilley, and Fred Sadoff, writers. *The Motorola Television Hour*. Season 1, episode 5, "The Thirteen Clocks." Directed by Don Richardson, featuring Basil Rathbone, John Raitt, and Roberta Peters. Aired December 29, 1953, on ABC.

Ustinov, Peter, writer. *NET Playhouse*. Season 1, episode 24, "Satire." Directed by Francis Coleman, featuring Peter Ustinov, Dudley Moore, Anthony Hopkins, and Bernard Keeffe. Aired February 17, 1967, on NET.

Vance Jr., Norman, writer. *American Soul*. Season 2, episode 5, "Say You Love Me." Directed by Crystle Roberson Dorsey, featuring Sinqua Wells, Christopher Jefferson, Kelly Price, and Iantha Richardson. Aired June 24, 2020, on BET.

Waters, John, dir. *Hairspray*. 1988; Los Angeles, CA: New Line Home Entertainment, 2002. DVD.

Waters, John. "Ladies and Gentleman . . . the Nicest Kids in Town! Keeping the Memory of The Buddy Deane Show Alive." *Baltimore Magazine*. April 1995, https://www.baltimoremagazine.com/section/artsentertainment/john-waters-on-keeping-the-memory-of-the-buddy-deane-show-alive/

Weigand, David. "'Smash' Review: NBC Series Lives up the Hype." *San Francisco Chronicle*. March 27, 2012.

Weinberg, Eric, writer. *Scrubs*. Season 2, episode 2, "My Nightingale." Directed by Craig Zisk, featuring Zach Braff, Donald Faison, Judy Reyes, and Sarah Chalke. Aired October 3, 2002, on NBC, Buena Vista Home Entertainment, 2005, DVD.

Weinberg, Eric, writer. *Scrubs*. Season 3, episode 3, "My White Whale." Directed by Michael Spiller, featuring Zach Braff, Donald Faison, Judy Reyes, and Sarah Chalke. Aired October 23, 2003, on NBC, Buena Vista Home Entertainment, 2006, DVD.

Weinberg, Scott. "High School Musical: Remix." *DVD Talk*. December 5, 2006, https://www.dvdtalk.com/reviews/25544/high-school-musical-remix/

Weinger, Scott, writer. *Galavant*. Season 2, episode 6, "About Last Knight." Directed by Paul Murphy, featuring Joshua Sasse, Karen David, Luke Youngblood, Mallory Jansen, and Timothy Omundsen. Aired January 17, 2016, on ABC, Disney Home Video, 2017, DVD.

Werts, Diane. "Review: CBS' 'Viva Laughlin' a Train Wreck." *Newsday*. October 18, 2007, https://web.archive.org/web/20071020034800/http://www.newsday.com/entertainment/tv/ny-ettell5415699oct18,0,5351094.story

Whedon, Joss, writer. *Buffy the Vampire Slayer*. Season 1, episode 12, "Prophesy Girl." Directed by Joss Whedon, featuring Sarah Michelle Gellar, Alyson Hannigan, Nicholas Brendan, Anthony Stewart Head, and David Boreanaz. Aired June 2, 1997, on the WB, 20th Century Fox, 2005, DVD.

Whedon, Joss, writer. *Buffy the Vampire Slayer*. Season 2, episode 1, "When She Was Bad." Directed by Joss Whedon, featuring Sarah Michelle Gellar, Alyson Hannigan, Nicholas Brendan, and Anthony Stewart Head. Aired September 15, 1997, on the WB, 20th Century Fox Home Entertainment, 2005, DVD.

Whedon, Joss, writer. *Buffy the Vampire Slayer*. Season 2, episode 22, "Becoming (Part 2)." Directed by Joss Whedon, featuring Sarah Michelle Gellar, Alyson Hannigan, Nicholas

Brendan, Anthony Stewart Head, and David Boreanaz. Aired May 19, 1998, on the WB, 20th Century Fox, 2005, DVD.

Whedon, Joss, writer. *Buffy the Vampire Slayer*. Season 5, episode 22, "The Gift." Directed by Joss Whedon, featuring Sarah Michelle Gellar, Alyson Hannigan, Nicholas Brendan, Anthony Stewart Head, and James Marsters. Aired May 22, 2001, on the WB, 20th Century Fox, 2005, DVD.

Whedon, Joss, writer. *Buffy the Vampire Slayer*. Season 6, episode 7, "Once More, With Feeling." Directed by Joss Whedon, featuring Sarah Michelle Gellar, Alyson Hannigan, Nicholas Brendan, and James Marsters. Aired November 6, 2001, on UPN, 20th Century Fox Home Entertainment, 2005, DVD.

Whedon, Joss, dir. *Dr. Horrible's Sing-Along Blog*. 2008; New York: New Video Group, 2009. DVD.

White, Abbey. "Lea Michele Responds to Racism, On-Set Bullying Accusations Ahead of 'Funny Girl' Debut." *The Hollywood Reporter*. September 1, 2022, www.hollywoodreporter.com/lifestyle/arts/lea-michele-racism-bullying-allegations-funny-girl-1235210209/

Wiener, Rick, and Kenny Schwartz, writers. *Galavant*. Season 2, episode 9, "Battle of the Three Armies." Directed by John Fortenberry, featuring Joshua Sasse, Karen David, Luke Youngblood, Mallory Jansen, and Timothy Omundsen. Aired January 31, 2016, on ABC, Disney Home Video, 2017, DVD.

Wiener, Rick, and Kenny Schwartz, writers. *Galavant*. Season 2, episode 10, "The One True King (to Unite Them All)." Directed by John Fortenberry, featuring Joshua Sasse, Karen David, Luke Youngblood, Mallory Jansen, and Timothy Omundsen. Aired January 31, 2016, on ABC, Disney Home Video, 2017, DVD.

Wilcox, Rhonda. *Why Buffy Matters: The Art of* Buffy the Vampire Slayer. London: IB Tauris, 2005.

Williams, A. Zell, writer. *American Soul*. Season 1, episode 4, "Just Us." Directed by Robert Townsend, featuring Sinqua Wells, Christopher Jefferson, Kelly Price, and Iantha Richardson. Aired February 19, 2019, on BET.

Williams, Austin. "Will Smith's 'Just the Two of Us,' and the Protection That Comes with His Love." *Vibe*. March 31, 2022, https://www.vibe.com/features/opinion/will-smith-just-the-two-of-us-yellow-diamonds-lyric-break-down-1234654616/

Williams, Tessa Leigh, writer. *Riverdale*. Season 3, episode 16, "Chapter Fifty-One: Big Fun." Directed by Maggie Kiley, featuring KJ Apa, Lili Reinhart, Camila Mendes, and Cole Sprouse. Aired March 20, 2019, on the CW, Warner Home Entertainment, 2023, DVD.

Williams, Tessa Leigh, writer. *Riverdale*. Season 4, episode 17, "Chapter Seventy-Four: Wicked Little Town." Directed by Antonio Negret, featuring KJ Apa, Lili Reinhart, Camila Mendes, and Cole Sprouse. Aired April 15, 2020, on the CW, Warner Home Entertainment, 2023, DVD.

Willman, Chris. "T Bone Burnett on Quitting Wife Callie Khouri's 'Nashville': It Was a 'Drag-Out Fight.'" *The Hollywood Reporter*. October 30, 2013, https://www.hollywoodreporter.com/news/general-news/t-bone-burnett-quitting-wife-651400/

Wilson, Robert, writer. *Great Performances*. Season 13, episode 14, "Einstein on the Beach: The Changing Image of Opera." Directed by Mark Obenhaus, featuring Lucinda Childs, Philip Glass, and Will Lyman. Aired January 31, 1986, on PBS.

Winsberg, Austin, writer. *Zoey's Extraordinary Playlist*. Season 1, episode 1, "Zoey's Extraordinary Power." Directed by Richard Shepard, featuring Jane Levy, Skylar Astin, Alex Newell, and Mary Steenburgen. Aired January 7, 2020, on NBC, TV.

Winsberg, Austin, writer. *Zoey's Extraordinary Playlist*. Season 1, episode 2, "Zoey's Extraordinary Best Friend." Directed by Adam Davidson, featuring Jane Levy, Skylar Astin, Alex Newell, and Mary Steenburgen. Aired February 23, 2020, on NBC, TV.

Winsberg, Austin, writer. *Zoey's Extraordinary Playlist*. Season 1, episode 12, "Zoey's Extraordinary Dad." Directed by John Turteltaub and Adam Davidson, featuring Jane Levy, Skylar Astin, Alex Newell, and Mary Steenburgen. Aired May 3, 2020, on NBC, TV.

Winsberg, Austin, writer. *Zoey's Extraordinary Playlist*. Season 2, episode 13, "Zoey's Extraordinary Goodbye." Directed by John Terlesky, featuring Jane Levy, Skylar Astin, Alex Newell, and Mary Steenburgen. Aired May 16, 2021, on NBC, TV.

Winters, David, dir. *Dr. Jekyll and Mr. Hyde*. 1973; New York: NBC Studios. TV.

INDEX

ABOUT THE AUTHOR

Erin Giannini, PhD, is an independent scholar. She served as an editor and contributor at PopMatters and has written numerous articles about topics from corporate culture in genre television to production-level shifts and their effects on TV texts. She is also the author of *Supernatural: A History of Television's Unearthly Road Trip*, *The Good Place* [TV Milestones], *Meta Television: A History of US Popular Television's Self-Awareness*, and *Community: Going Back to School with Television's Best Sitcom*, as well as co-editor of the book series B-TV: Television Under the Critical Radar for Bloomsbury.